Together: Communicating Interpersonally

Together: Communicating Interpersonally

JOHN STEWART AND GARY D'ANGELO

University of Washington

ADDISON-WESLEY PUBLISHING COMPANY

Reading, Massachusettts • Menlo Park, California
London • Amsterdam • Don Mills, Ontario • Sydney

This book is in the

**ADDISON-WESLEY SERIES
IN SPEECH-COMMUNICATION**

**Consulting Editor
Frederick W. Haberman**

for
    Marcia and Lisa
Debbie, Andy, and Tommy

Preface

For the past five years we have been interested in the way an individual's interpersonal relationships affect the kind of person he or she becomes. We've found a variety of scholars who seem also to be interested in interpersonal relationships and human growth: personality psychologists such as Harry Stack Sullivan and George Kelly, who see personality grounded in interpersonal relationships; theologians such as Karl Jaspers and Reuel Howe, who teach that authentic communication with humans can facilitate authentic communication with God; psychotherapists such as Abraham Maslow and Carl Rogers, who believe that the best way to promote another's health and growth is to promote a rich relationship with her or him; and philosophers such as Martin Buber and John Macmurray, who identify and describe the ontologically interpersonal nature of human beings. We've learned a great deal from these persons, but because of our interest in speech communication, we've focused primarily on the communication relationships themselves; we're less concerned here with their effects on psychometry, psychotherapy, ontology, or one's relationship with God, important as those considerations are.

While learning and teaching about these interpersonal relationships, we've become impressed by the variety of settings in which growth-promoting communication can occur. We've experienced a number of rich and exciting interactions in informal, two-person settings, but we've also recognized substantial potential for rewarding person-to-person contacts in larger, unstructured meetings, task-oriented small groups, and public-speaking settings. As a result, it hasn't been helpful for us to concentrate on a single communication setting;

we've found it more useful to focus on the *quality* of communication that can best facilitate human growth in a variety of settings. This is why we define interpersonal communication as we do in the first chapter—as the quality of communication that occurs when the persons involved are mutually willing and able to share some aspects of their humanness and to be aware of some aspects of the humanness of the other.

For the past several years we've been trying to develop our definition into a coherent, workable approach to teaching and learning about interpersonal communication. As coordinator of the University of Washington speech department's basic course program, I (John) have been able to get the input of more than 40 teachers and to witness the way several thousand students have responded to various concepts and activities. I've also been able to teach either basic interpersonal communication or interpersonal communication for teachers each of the past 20 quarters, and upper division and graduate courses since 1971. I (Gary) have learned a great deal from my three years of teaching a "mass-lecture" survey class of 230, where interpersonal-communication concepts and skills have been part of the course content and methods, as well as the foundation for the work of undergraduate students who are small-group facilitators. That's helped me to get some ideas about what seems meaningful to college students—whether they're functioning as learners or as teachers. Like John, I've also been able to teach basic- and upper-division interpersonal-communication courses.

As you might expect, we've invested enough in this approach to interpersonal communication to become committed to it. We know it isn't the only possible approach to this subject, and we also see it as something that's continually changing and growing. But we feel that the approach we've taken in this book has two significant strengths to recommend it.

First, it's three-dimensional. By that, we mean that it integrates the substantive, the experiential, and the personal. Before we started writing, we decided that we didn't want to do a laboratory manual or book consisting primarily of exercises. Some excellent ones have already been done, and in addition, we believe that the study of interpersonal communication can be in part a rich and exciting *intellectual* experience. The persons who have contributed to this study—Sullivan, Rogers, Laing, Buber, and others — are often amazingly insightful and wise, and their *ideas* can be provocative, stimulating, and intellectually challenging. That's why we've tried to make this a substantive intro- ductory text by including not only results of behavioral research and rhetorical studies, but also ideas from philosophical anthropology, psychotherapy, and psychology. Thinking is one of the ways persons grow, and we're convinced that working with ideas about the nature of human beings, how human communication works, the negotiation of selves, the ways people process information, the impact of empathy, etc., can be productive and genuinely exciting.

We've also tried to emphasize the importance of *experiencing* the concepts and skills discussed here. In the past several years we've no- ticed that many prominent educators—John Holt, George Isaac Brown, Neil Postman, and Charles Weingartner—have been stressing the point John Dewey made near the turn of the century—people learn best when they can experience, as directly as possible, the content or subject matter that they're studying. We agree with that emphasis, especially with respect to teaching interpersonal communication. Simply talking and reading *about* interpersonal communication isn't a sufficiently effective way to help people learn to communicate better. The persons involved need the opportunity to try out the communication attitudes and behaviors that are discussed, both in classroom exercises and in day-to-day contacts with others. Although exercises are often enjoyable and entertaining, we don't believe that experiential activities should be just fun and games; that's why we made the point about substance. Ideally, the course can be a blend of principles and activities, concepts and experiences, analyzing interpersonal communication and communicating interpersonally.

A third dimension of this book's approach is its personalness. As we say at the start of Chapter 1, we see a fundamental inconsistency in treatments of interpersonal communication that employ impersonal pronouns, formal language, and excessive jargon to maintain distance between writer and reader. As we also note, a one-way written communication event can never become genuinely interpersonal. But as writers, we can take steps in that direction, steps that we have discovered can bring our personness closer to yours. The process is risky. We can sometimes come across as overpersonal, inappropriately intimate, trying too hard to be "just folks." Or, we can get lost in our own jargon and end up as a parody of the very quality we're trying to create.

We've taken those risks, not only because we believe that impersonal writing about interpersonal communication is inappropriate, but also because it makes theoretical sense to let you know something about us. We introduce ourselves in Chapter 1 because we want you to be aware of some aspects of our humanness; we care about the context of our communication with you (Chapter 2); we know that expectations affect personal perception (Chapter 3); we want to begin to clarify our definitions of ourselves (Chapter 4); we know that sharing can help create trust (Chapter 5); and we want you to know something of "where we're coming from" (Chapter 7). In short, we'd like to try to make the communicating between you and us as interpersonal as the situation will allow.

Internal coherence seems to us to be a second strength of the book. We've worked for coherence in two ways. First, recognizing the interdependent nature of human communicating, we've made an attempt to tie ideas together so that your eventual understanding of interpersonal communication could be a unified blend of ideas rather than a mixture of isolated ones. One example of this occurs at the beginning of Chapter 6, where we explain how the characteristics of human communication that we talked about in Chapter 2 relate to responsive listening. Another example is in Chapter 8, where we discuss how the ideas from previous chapters can be integrated into the resolution of conflict. In short, one way we've tried to build internal coherence is by demonstrating the interrelationships among the most important concepts.

The second kind of coherence we've worked toward was to maintain a consistent focus on interpersonal-quality communication throughout the book. In Chapter 1 we introduce a quality definition of interpersonal communication; what we say in each of the following chapters is designed to help people promote that quality in their communicating. For example, in Chapter 8 we suggest how that quality can exist in conflict situations. In Chapter 9 we talk about how to promote interpersonal-quality communication in public-speaking and small-group settings.

Colleagues, friends, and persons in our classes helped us with this book in important ways. Conversations with Al and Willy Clark and Helen Felton have significantly enriched our understanding of Martin Buber. Jim Johnson, Ken Morgan, George Diestel, and Pat McDonnell each had unique ways of helping us to clarify our ideas and our thinking. Bob Arundale's dissertation work in systems theory helped considerably in our writing of Chapter 2. Joe Munshaw and Mike Hannah gave us extensive and insightful feedback during the writing of this manuscript; we attribute much of what is right about this book to their helpful comments.

We also want to thank Jeanette Ceccarelli for her caring support and for the many hours of work she spent getting permissions for cartoons and quotations. Jan Belanger's expert typing of the manuscript was also important in helping us meet deadlines. During the later stages of working on the book we discovered Dennis Wilson's talent for fast, quality photography; with him we were able to capture "live" and sometimes very natural situations; without him we would have had to use shots from impersonal picture files. Dennis and Patti Hansen also spent many hours on the cover design.

We're grateful to Brandon Neese, Kris Obata, Steve Muscatel, and Barbara Keely for their support during the anxious months we spent writing. And a special "thank you" to Eileen Meconi, who helped us to understand the subtleties of sexist language, but more importantly, who has provided us with many opportunities for interpersonal experiences. Finally, we want to recognize our graduate and undergraduate students, whose contributions we can't always specifically identify, but without whom we wouldn't have experienced, learned, and grown enough to write a book.

Seattle, Washington   J.S.
January 1975   G.D'A.

Contents

Objects and Persons: Becoming Human Interpersonally

WHO WE ARE

It's usually difficult for you to get to know the persons who have written a book you're reading. Sometimes there's a hint about an author's identity in the book's dedication or in the acknowledgments section of the preface or foreword, but usually there's not enough to allow you to know the author as a *person*. In other cases you might get some impression of an author's personality from his or her writing style, but most writers—especially textbook writers—try to maintain an objective and factual third-person distance, and as a result their writing often seems *im*personal.

Impersonal writing is fine for some things, but we don't think it's appropriate for a book about interpersonal communication. The architect Marcel Lajos Breuer says that what he aims for in architecture is something "more human than a machine."[1] We're aiming for the same thing in this book. After all, interpersonal communication is basically what it sounds like—communication *between* ("inter") *persons*—and it can't happen until the parties involved are identifiable *as persons*, so that something can go on *between* them. We're not sure we can actually communicate interpersonally with you on these pages, and we'll explain why later. But we do want to encourage as much "between personsness" as possible, and we believe that can happen only if you know something about who we are. We also believe that the more you know about us and "where we're coming from," the better you'll understand the things we say. So we'd like to talk a little about who we are—now, in July 1973—and why we're writing this book.

John

I'm John Stewart. My wife, Gene Ann, and I are living in Bothell, Washington, a suburb of Seattle. We have two daughters— Marcia, who's 12, and Lisa, who's 11. Gene Ann and I grew up in the same small town— Centralia, Washington— and met in the fifth grade. We dated some in high school and got married after my first year of college. I'm 33, medium in just about every way—height, weight, shoe size—and a little nearsighted. I enjoy things like sailing, water skiing, fiddling with machinery, and teaching in college. I've spent about nine years in four different universities studying speech communication and philosophy. When I finished my doctorate in 1970, I planned to teach such courses as public speaking, persuasion, argumentation, psychology of communication, and rhetorical theory. I hadn't studied much interpersonal communication.

When I began full-time teaching at the University of Washington, however, I wasn't really satisfied with what happened. Lecturing from behind a lectern, carrying an authoritative-looking briefcase, and giving rigorous exams didn't always seem to help the persons in my classes to learn, grow, improve, and to be more satisfied with what they were experiencing. Another teacher, Sara Burgess, showed me some alternatives. I observed her classes, and she and I worked together on some communication workshop projects. She helped me see what can happen when you treat students in a positive, accepting, trusting way. She was also able to show *me* what it was like to be treated that way by somebody outside my immediate family. I'd experienced that quality of communication before—as you probably have—but I had the feeling that it had to be restricted to occasional episodes with Gene Ann, Marcia and Lisa, my parents, or my sister. Sara helped me see how I could relate to many people that way and how I could help others communicate interpersonally more often. At the same time, I started to read some books about human communication that I hadn't read before—books by philosophers and psychologists who talked about establishing and maintaining interpersonal relationships. I began to learn some really important things.

Many of those things are what this book is about. Gary and I will be discussing them later. For now, just let me say that my teaching has changed, and along with it, the way I relate to the people I work with, my family, and my friends. I've discovered how fulfilling and growth-promoting interpersonal communication can be. For example, last summer I was teaching an intermediate course in interpersonal communication for the first time. One day I came to class really down. I was hassled by our schedule at home, by demands from other professors, and by uncertainties about how the class was going. Three or four years ago I probably would have either behaved in class as if nothing were wrong or would have taken out my frustrations on the students. Instead, I was able to sit down with one of the groups into which the class was divided and to share some of my feelings with the persons there. They listened to me—*with* me is more accurate—and the way they responded let me know that they cared about me. I can still feel some of the warmth, support, and encouragement that came from their acceptance of me as a person, acceptance that they were able to communicate in a person-to-person way. That kind of experience is one big reason for my writing this book.

There are a couple of other reasons, too. They are less important and more mundane, but they affect what I'm doing here, so I think I should mention them. I'm writing this partly because I haven't been able to find a book that does what I'd like a book to do for the persons who take my classes. Most authors of interpersonal communication texts don't begin philosophically where Gary and I do, and students sometimes complain that their texts are written very impersonally. I'd like to do something about both of those things. I'm also writing this partly because I work at a university that stresses the importance of publishing, and my value system right now says that my family and I can profit from the publication credit and the money that this book might provide. I'm not totally comfortable with that aspect of my motivation, but there it is. I do know that I'm not writing this *just* for mundane reasons. I have lived experiences that convince me that who I am as a human being is directly dependent on the quality of the interpersonal relationships I share with other humans. In other words, I have discovered that learning interpersonal communication can help people grow, and I'd like to play a part in that growth.

Now it's March 1974, and Gary and I are working to finish writing so that the publisher can begin printing this book. As I look at what I wrote nine months ago, I'm aware of many changes. My relationships with Gene Ann, Marcia, and Lisa have changed, partly because of my working on "the book." My relationship with Gary has also changed as we have discovered together how our strengths and weaknesses complement each other; it's been exciting to share such an enjoyable and productive work/friend partnership. I also see what we've written a little differently now, partly because of the comments and criticisms we've received from people who have read the manuscripts as we worked on it.

But some things haven't changed noticeably.[2] I still enjoy sailing, water skiing, fiddling with machinery, and teaching college. And I still believe that every human relationship I experience offers me the chance to grow. Consequently, I'm still convinced that working—with myself and others—to promote the best possible relationships between persons is just about the most important thing I can do.

Gary

As I sit here trying to decide how to tell you who I am, a number of things come to mind. It's easy to tell you that my name is Gary D'Angelo, that I'm 34 years old and married, that my wife's name is Connie, and that we have three children—Debbie, who's ten, Andy, who's seven, and Tommy, who's five. I can say that I've been teaching in higher education for about ten years, three of them at the University of Washington. Music and sports are two of my main interests. I like rock, country, folk, and classical music, and I enjoy playing the guitar. I snow ski, play golf, touch football, chess, poker, and I help coach a grade school soccer team.

I'm thinking, though, that there must be more to a person than name, age, marital status, teaching experience, and outside interests. I don't mean to underestimate the importance I attach to these things; my family life and teaching responsibility are high on my list of priorities. But that's not all there is to me. I think you'll have a clearer image of me and of my view of communication if I talk about one or two experiences that I've had and if I share a couple of my attitudes and beliefs.

One of the most meaningful experiences for me is communicating with people who allow me to be myself, free from masks and facades, free from the fear of intimidation or rejection. I'm writing this book primarily because I believe that these experiences are possible and because they have contributed to my growth as a person. (Other things have also influenced my decision. The chance to improve my credentials and to make a profit played a part with me, as it did with John. But this book would never get off the ground if I didn't believe that your relationships with others can improve through interpersonal communi-

cation and that I can help make that possible through this book.)
As do most people, I like to have others listen to my ideas, to understand what I'm saying, and to sense how I feel about what I'm saying. I remember talking with a neighbor one day about the embarrassing experience I had had the night before. My neighbor deserved an explanation of the incident, since he had had to get up at 1:00 A.M. to help me out. Here's what happened. A friend and I had been out talking about politics, religion, education, and whatever else came to mind over quite a few beers. When we got back to my house, my friend decided that he'd better not drive home and asked if he could sleep on our living room couch. I agreed, went to bed, and fell soundly asleep. About 15 minutes later, my friend remembered that he had to get home (I don't recall why), but he realized that he was in no condition to drive. Connie was unable to wake me, so she went next door, woke up our neighbor, and asked him to drive my friend home. When I talked with our neighbor the next day about the incident, I expected him at least to question my common sense and ask for an apology. Instead, he immediately sensed and then reduced my feeling of embarrassment by indicating that he understood how it had happened. During our conversation I felt comfortable about being honest with him, and after it was over, I felt much more at ease about the incident. For me, this experience illustrated the kind of communication that allows a person to be himself or herself—openly and honestly. It also helped me realize how this kind of communication promotes the growth of interpersonal relationships. My neighbor simply tried to understand me instead of criticizing or intimidating me, and in the process I learned something about communication.

I'd like to relate a second experience to you that illustrates another of my viewpoints about interpersonal relationships. I find life much more comfortable when *I* can accept others, when I can communicate without making harsh, negative value judgments about them. I remember vividly the first time I was able to avoid judging someone on the basis of appearance. I walked into a drug store near my home in Greeley, Colorado, and noticed a woman wearing a torn dress that was too large for her. She was about five feet six inches tall and weighed about 190 pounds. Ordinarily, I would have made immediate inferences—based on her appearance—about her life-style, attitudes, personality, economic status, etc. But, I had been thinking seriously about how unfair it is to categorize or stereotype people on the basis of general appearance. And so, although I noticed her appearance and made a few perceptual assumptions, I didn't make any negative *stereo-typed* judgments about it. I was able to talk with her without drawing overgeneralized conclusions about *her* or her choice of apparel. (As I remember, she was a registered nurse; she had been doing some weekend gardening and had rushed to the store for some kind of sprinkler.) It was a comfortable feeling; I felt freed from some obligation or force within me to evaluate someone who didn't meet *my* standards. But even though I feel comfortable when I do that, I can't behave that way all the time. There are many times when I don't respond to people with understanding and acceptance. What I'm trying to say is that I strongly *believe* in accepting people, but I don't want to come across as if I were able to communicate that way all the time.

I share these two experiences with you not only because they reveal something about who I am, but also because each illustrates an important characteristic of my view of interpersonal communication. If what I've told you seems loaded on the "positive" side, it's probably because I'm emphasizing that in the midst of some frustrating and problematic communication encounters, I've had many positive experiences communicating *interpersonally*.

Before John and I finish this book, I have the feeling that a prayer composed and delivered at the dinner table one evening by my son Andy (when he was five years old) will best reflect my state of mind:

> Dear God, thank you for making the world.
> Boy, I bet you really got sweaty!

Now it's March 1974, and since we started writing this book, I've had many opportunities to practice the kind of communication we talk about on the following pages. I've had "good," "bad," and "mediocre" success, and in the process I've learned some things about my communicating. For example, I've discovered that it's hardest for me to communicate interpersonally when I feel defensive. The more I control or avoid defensiveness, the more likely I am to facilitate interpersonalness. That's been true in my classrooms, my family life, and my communication with John and other friends and colleagues.

I've also discovered that it's easiest for me to communicate interpersonally when the other person makes as strong a commitment as I do to getting together; we call that "mutuality" later in this chapter. John and I worked at mutuality as we talked about and wrote this book. That helped us not only in our writing, but also in our efforts to grow.

I've asked some persons in my classes to read parts of this book, and their feedback has affected me in significant ways. For example, I realized that I had become so familiar with the characteristics of interpersonal communication that I had forgotten the time it takes to understand and absorb them when they're new. Students' comments have helped me to appreciate that. I also believed quite strongly when we began writing this book that our approach to interpersonal communication would fit everyone's life-style; now, I believe that differences in cultural backgrounds and life experiences may cause you to reject or radically revise parts of the point of view we present here. But I haven't lost sight of my original intent in co-authoring this book with John: to emphasize the importance of *all* persons' realizing their fullest potential as humans and to write about a quality of communication that works toward that goal.

You

Our perception of you also affects what we say here and how we say it. We know that *you* are different in many ways from the other persons who are reading this book. We know that we can't be sensitive to all those differences, and that's why our communication with you can't be completely interpersonal. But in general we're assuming that this is one of the first "text-type" books on interpersonal communication that you've read. We also see you as a person who is at least tentatively interested in improving your relationships with other persons, and who is at least fairly willing both to think about your communication and to try experiencing some different ways of communicating. We hope that you're interested in personal growth—your own and others'. And finally, we hope you believe—as we do—that productive growth is not something that just happens to be "lucky" or "talented" or "smart" or "sensitive" persons. The important thing is to get in touch with our growth and to encourage it. And since we grow primarily through relationships with others, the best way to promote positive growth is to promote positive interpersonal relationships. That's what we've tried to make this book about.

THINGS AND PEOPLE

Every day each of us engages in several different kinds of human communication. For example, when you get up in the morning you may turn on the "Today Show" or tune in your favorite radio station. You may talk with your spouse or roommate about cutting class, about an argument you recently had with your boss, or about your plans for the weekend; you may also read the morning newspaper. Later in the day, perhaps you respectfully and/or perfunctorily greet a professor or advisor, listen to a speaker at a rally or meeting, and read the posters on a bulletin board. At various times you may pause to talk with a friend, or as you walk to class or work you may maintain a comfortable silence, thinking to yourself about what's in store for you that day. You may take the time to read a magazine or book, to sit alone in a coffee shop observing other people, or to talk informally with a few friends.

At the beginning of this chapter we said that interpersonal communication is basically communication *between persons*. When you consider the kind of communicating you do, that might sound a little odd, at one level it probably seems as if almost all your daily communicating is "between persons." When you listen to the radio, it seems obvious that the communication is between your person and the person of the D.J. Later, it's between you and your roommate, you and your professor or boss, or even you and yourself. But in some of those cases it isn't very accurate to call the participants "persons." If your experiences are anything like ours, you tend to treat the humans you communicate with in one of *two* possible ways. Sometimes, you treat them primarily as *objects*; other times, you treat them primarily as *persons*. We've become convinced that the best way to begin to understand what makes human communication interpersonal is to recognize the differences between these two ways of relating to or treating other people.

To you, the differences between "objects" and "persons" may seem obvious, and a discussion of these differences may seem unnecessary. But if you'll bear with us for a couple of pages, we'll be able to start pinpointing more specifically what it means to communicate *interpersonally*.

When we treat something or somebody as an *object*, what characteristics are we assuming it has? Well, in the first place we usually assume that it—whatever "it" is—is not unique. One object can be virtually the same as another object; two or more things can be identical—in size, shape, length, width, depth, etc. As electronic observation techniques improve, we may be able, for example, to tell the difference between one mercury atom or one water molecule and another. But for all practical purposes, they're identical. The more complex the object, the more difficult it becomes for two of them to *be* identical; however, even two complex objects can have identical *functions*. Any 700 x 15 tire will fit any Volvo 122S station wagon. Any one-inch safety pin will hold your shirt shut. Any size "C" battery will fit my tape recorder. We recognize that some kinds of batteries are better than others, but the point is that a dozen sets of the same kind of batteries could be so similar that no matter which set you used, your recorder would sound the same and would work just as long. We can have virtually hundreds of objects that function as interchangeable parts and that we would agree are "the same thing." And one way to "thingify" persons is to treat them that way—to communicate as if the body in seat 76 of the lecture hall is exactly the same as the body in seat 7 or in seat 491.

A second characteristic of objects is a little more difficult to explain. Objects can be comprehensively accounted for in terms of both space and time. For example, they can be measured. An object is always a certain size; it fits within boundaries. An event is of a certain duration; it lasts a measurable amount of time. Although it's difficult to measure some things directly—the velocity of a photon, the temperature of a kiss, the amperage of a nerve impulse, the duration of an explosion—no thing or object has any parts that are theoretically unobservable. And since we can, in principle, observe all aspects of any object, we can also describe all the parts in terms of space and time.

A third characteristic of objects relates to their movement. All movements of an object or thing are responses to other movements. Objects can only *react*; they cannot *act*. They cannot initiate movement; they can only respond to movements initiated somewhere else. The movements of a typewriter—even an electric one—are all reactions to external movements transmitted by levers, springs, rollers, and gears and/or electrical current and magnetic fields. When Major Minderbinder orders Private Polite to "Jump!" and expects the response "How high?" on the way up, the major is objectifying in this sense. Unlike persons, a thing or object can be made to roll, fly, float, or slide; it can be lifted, moved, pushed, pulled, or carried. But it cannot in any way move itself completely by itself.

Objects also aren't conscious. No object or thing can be aware of its own object-hood or thing-hood; it can't "know" that it exists. Consequently, it can't speculate about its own existence. It can't wonder "Why am I alive?" or "What is life all about?" Similarly, it is impossible for an object or thing to experience emotions. Things can't feel fear, sympathy, rage, pity, embarrassment, excitement, or love. The lack of consciousness is primarily what makes things so predictable. If you can identify all the causes of a thing's "behavior," you can accurately predict their effects—the "behavior" itself. If you can isolate the inputs, you can predict the output or results. With things, you don't have to allow for doubt, indecision, or zeal.

In his short story "EPICAC," Kurt Vonnegut, Jr., focuses on the idea that things aren't conscious and can't feel emotions.[3] Vonnegut shows what might happen if a computer could feel the emotion of love and could question its own reason for living. In the process, Vonnegut indirectly emphasizes some of the important differences between persons and objects.

As EPICAC's programmer, the narrator of the story, explains, EPICAC "cost the taxpayers $776,434,927.54. . . . You can call him a machine if you want to. He looked like a machine, but he was a whole lot less like a machine than plenty of people I could name."* The fact that EPICAC is more than a machine becomes obvious when his programmer asks the computer for help in seducing his co-worker, Pat Kilgallen. To the programmer's amazement, EPICAC replies: "What's love? What's girl?" He's given definitions of those and other key terms and proceeds to crank out volumes of voluptuous love poetry for Pat. EPICAC's poem "The Kiss" is his triumph.

Pat's mind was mush by the time she had finished it. . . .

"She wants to get married," EPICAC was told.

"Tell me about getting married," he said.

I explained this difficult matter to him in as few digits as possible.

"Good," said EPICAC. "I'm ready any time she is."

The amazing, pathetic truth dawned on me. When I thought about it, I realized that what had happened was perfectly logical,

---

*This and the following quotations are from "Epicac," copyright 1950 by Kurt Vonnegut, Jr. Originally published in *Collier's*. Reprinted from this book, *Welcome to the Monkey House*, by Kurt Vonnegut, Jr., with permission of the publisher, Delacorte Press/Seymour Lawrence.

inevitable, and all my fault. I had taught EPICAC about love and about Pat. Now, automatically, he loved Pat.

When he can't successfully explain to EPICAC why Pat should choose him over a computer, the programmer resorts to nitpicking definitions.

"Women can't love machines, and that's that."

"Why not?"

"That's fate."

"Definition, please," said EPICAC.

"Noun, meaning predetermined and inevitable destiny."

"15–8," said EPICAC's paper strip—"Oh."

As the story goes, boy, not computer, gets girl, and EPICAC responds in the way some humans do. He commits suicide and leaves behind the following note:

I don't want to be a machine, and I don't want to think about war . . . . I want to be made out of protoplasm and last forever so Pat will love me. But fate has made me a machine. That is the only problem I cannot solve. That is the only problem I want to solve. I can't go on this way. . . . Good luck, my friend. Treat our Pat well. I am going to short-circuit myself out of your lives forever. . . .

Vonnegut's story is both funny and sad. It's sometimes amusing to see what happens when we treat objects as if they were persons. But the fact that we're often willing to treat persons as if they were objects isn't so funny. For example, a husband is treating his wife as an object when he comes home from work and, because dinner isn't ready when he thinks it should be, chews her out, shouts at her, and says, "Next time, you'd better have it ready on time!" To this man, his wife is not a person with feelings, varying moods, daily interruptions, and so on. She is a machine which serves several functions for him, and at certain times during the day the machine must produce a meal. If the meal isn't good or isn't on time, something is wrong with the machine; it needs fixing. The way to fix it, he assumes, is to shout at it—to give it hell! Of course, husbands are also objectified sometimes. A husband might inform his wife that he had decided not to take on any extra work, even though they could use the extra money. His wife is treating him like an object when she gets mad and tells him, "You don't give a damn about us; how can we remodel our house without money?" To her, he is a machine which produces money; if the money doesn't come in, something is wrong with the machine. She doesn't consider the fact that he has only so much energy, that he might want to start spending more time with his family, or that he might be sick and just hasn't told her about it.

The husband and wife are objectifying each other because they are treating each other simply as "fillers of roles." Sometimes, we are so used to talking to each other at a role level that we think we are communicating interpersonally at that level. But a mere role-filler is not a person. In addition, there are several other ways we treat persons as objects or things, and they usually happen when we forget these characteristics that make persons *persons*. For example, we forget that although there can be two identical things, each person is unique. When you consider how important it is to establish close tissue and blood matches for human organ transplants, you realize that even at that basic level, each human is unique. But at a more complex level, humans are unique because no two persons can have exactly the same experiences.

Right now, Connie and I (Gary) are in the same city, the same neighborhood, the same house. But she's in the family room and I'm in the dining room. She's working on a project and I'm typing. She's probably perceiving cues from some written material, and that, for now, is primarily her experience. As I type, I'm looking out the window, at my manuscript, listening to the quiet, thinking about the uniqueness of people, concerning myself with tomorrow's class, and so on. Even though Connie and I occupy the same general environment, we are separated in space, and our separation affects the experience each of us is having.

Let's look at uniqueness in another way. You and I might both see the same film in the same theater on the same night at the same time sitting next to each other. Both of us may leave the movie at the same time and say exactly the same words about it: "I liked that movie." At a very superficial level, someone might suggest that you and I are, in this situation, interchangeable. But even here we are unique. Do you and I like the movie for the same reasons? Did we like it to the same degree? Did we recall the same experiences as we interpreted the film? Will the movie have the *same* effect on both of us? Will both of us remember the

same things about it? Will both of us recommend that film to our friends? To the extent that the answer to one or more of these questions is no, you and I are different; we are noninterchangeable, or unique.

As persons, you and I also cannot be comprehensively accounted for or described in terms of space and time. It's true that many aspects of a person can be measured—height, weight, temperature, age, density, conductivity, velocity, etc. But when you have exhaustively treated *all* the measurable parts, you have not yet comprehensively accounted for the person. Something of me (John) is in this writing. How can you measure that in terms of space and time? When I say that Lisa is "like her mother" in some ways, I'm not referring simply to her hair or the color of her eyes or even to her genetic makeup. Lisa and her mother are distinguishable persons, yet it is accurate for me to say that I perceive something of Gene Ann "in" Lisa—something unmeasurable. Even most psychologists, who are determined to make the study of human behavior a rigorous science, include in their formulation of human beings the concept of the "black box." They can measure and describe in spatio-temporal terms much of what goes "into" a human and much of what "comes out." But what happens in the uniquely human interim—the black box—is a mystery. That singularly human, nonspatio-temporal "remainder" has been the focus of poetry, religion, and philosophy for thousands of years. We aren't concerned whether you think of it as "spirit," "soul," "elan," "personality," "psyche," or something else. All we want to do is emphasize that it's there. Humans cannot comprehensively be accounted for in space and time.

Another important distinction between things and people is that things can only *react*, people can *act*. You know that if you kick a soccer ball, you can pretty much predict what it will do. It'll respond to the force of the blow of your foot by moving in the direction of that force. But things aren't so simple when you kick your brother, your room-mate, your pastor, or your lawyer. You can't count on an isomorphic, one-to-one response from a person. The reason you can't is that most human behavior is not simply causally determined. If you tap my knee, you may cause a reflex jerk, but the behavior that accompanies my reflex might be anything from giggles to a lawsuit, and there's no way that you can predict for sure which it will be. Although human behavior is often in part a response to outside pressures, persons also *choose* independently to do some things.

The most impressive example of human choosing that we're aware of is reported in Viktor Frankl's book *Man's Search for Meaning*.[4] Frankl relates in firsthand detail what it was like to be a prisoner in a Nazi death camp. He tells how he was captured, how all his possessions, his family, and even his profession were taken from him. He describes, almost casually, experiences that you and I would have difficulty even imagining. But the point of his book is not how he and the other prisoners *reacted* to those experiences, but how they *acted* in the face of them. He affirms again and again the uniquely human power we have to choose the attitude we will adopt toward our predicament. At one point Frankl writes:

> We who lived in concentration camps can remember the men who walked through the huts comforting others, giving away their last piece of bread. They may have been few in number, but they offer sufficient proof that everything can be taken from a man but one thing: the last of the human freedoms—to choose one's attitude in any given set of circumstances, to choose one's own way.[5]

Frankl couldn't do much about the way things were in the death camp, but through the entire horror he retained his ability to choose how to relate to what he couldn't change. As Frankl illustrates, persons, like objects, can be made to roll, fly, float, or slide; they can be lifted, moved, pushed, pulled, and carried. But they can also initiate those movements on their own; they can *act*. And that's what often makes human communication so complicated and difficult; people don't just react in a stimulus-response or cause-effect way to what you say. They decide for themselves what's being communicated and then respond to that.

Humans are also conscious. So far as we know, persons are the only beings who are aware of and who can speculate about their own existence. For almost all of recorded history, humans have been asking, "Why am I alive?" or "What is life all about?" At least two philosophers, Rene Descartes and Edmund Husserl, thought that that was an important enough fact to form the foundations for a whole philosophical system. Both agreed that an understanding of man has to start with an understanding that he is a *"cogito,"* a conscious subject. Although Descartes wanted to separate human thinking from human feeling, that dichotomy has been pretty much rejected. Now, human consciousness means that you are constantly and indivisibly thinking and feeling. You can't think without "feeling something," and you can't experience an emotion without some accompanying cognitive activity. Your behavior is constantly affected by your emotions and your self-reflectiveness; that's why it's so difficult to predict accurately. Objects don't experience emotions, but how *you* feel greatly affects what you do.

thinking + feeling go hand in hand.

In Summary:
(so far)

Things	People
Interchangeable	Noninterchangeable or unique
Completely describable in space-time terms	*More* than just a spatio-temporal thing
Reactor only	Can act *and* react
Not conscious, no emotions	Conscious of self and emotions

OBJECTIFYING AND HUMANIFYING

At this point you might be asking, "So what about all this? How does knowing the differences between things and people help me learn to communicate interpersonally?" Our response is that in our day-to-day communicating—as we said before—you and I tend to treat others primarily as objects or primarily as persons. We rarely treat them exclusively one way or the other, but when we're treating them primarily as objects, we are not allowing interpersonal communication to happen, and when we're treating them primarily as humans, we are.

Sometimes objectification is fairly subtle, as Garry Trudeau's "Doonesbury" illustrates. Other times it's more obvious. For example, consider what happens when you drive into a gas station. The attendant approaches, and as soon as you become perceptually aware of each other you are communicating—but not necessarily interpersonally. In this situation you'll probably treat the attendant primarily as an object. In the first place, consider how you *see* the attendant. As a unique human being? With feelings, beliefs, varying moods and problems? Capable of making a wide variety of choices in the situation? Probably not. For you, the attendant is primarily a convenient machine; there are probably no important differences between this attendant and all other gas station attendants; they all do about the same thing. You might be subconsciously aware that this person is uniquely human, but in this situation you don't take the time to be concerned about what's beneath the surface. You see the attendant as something whose behavior is predictable and obvious; he or she only reacts to the situation. Your

mind is on something else, so you just go through the motions—nod at the dip stick, hand money through the window, check your rear view mirror, drive off.

Your objectification of the attendant is apparent not only in what you are *aware* of, but also in what you *share*. You reveal nothing of yourself to the attendant beyond what's needed to get gas. You show him or her that you're a customer, just like every other customer, nothing more. Your behavior is as predictable as the attendant's. Your response, for example, to his or her failure to wash your car windows may be: "Damn poor service!" This simply reinforces the fact that each of you is functioning as an object.

There are many other times in your day-to-day communicating when you relate to somebody in an "object-to-object" way. What happens when you approach a person at a ticket window, for instance? What are you *aware* of in that person? What do you *share* of yourself? Most of the time the only important things involve object characteristics: the presence of somebody to help you—any ticketseller will do—the occurrence of predictable responses to your predictable behavior, and so on. What about your communicating with a bank teller? A cafeteria soup-server? A newsstand operator? A secretary?

Sometimes, on the other hand, you are *aware* and *share* in ways that allow you to communicate person to person. When a friend comes to you for help with a problem, you don't just treat her or him as an object. Consider first how you are aware of your friend. You know your friend well enough to know that she or he is not "like everybody else," but is unique. You remember, maybe, some of your friend's little idiosyncrasies, and you keep them in mind while you're listening and talking. You're always aware, although maybe not very consciously, that there's much more to the person you're communicating with than just her or his dimensions or measurements. You see your friend as a person who's continually *choosing* what to do, not just reacting passively to what happens. You realize, for example, that he or she is choosing to reveal something to you, and you probably appreciate being trusted. You're also aware of his or her experiencing—of the thinking and feeling that are going on. Those are all things you're likely to be *aware* of.

You also *share* something of your humanness with your friend. You never reveal absolutely everything about yourself, and you reveal different aspects in different situations, but in each case you're willing to show your friend that *you* too are much more than just an object. You don't respond to your friend with stereotyped grunts or exclamations; you respond openly and honestly and in your own individual way. You don't just react in a knee-jerk way, but you listen *with* your friend, carefully considering what is said and sharing what conclusions your value system would lead to in that situation. You don't try to control your friend, to determine his or her future behavior, but you reveal as completely as you can in that situation your fully human response to the problem and the person.

That kind of person-to-person communication also happens fairly frequently. At the beginning of the chapter we mentioned a couple of our experiences with this quality of communication. We're pretty sure you have, too—with your parents, maybe, or your spouse, with a lover, a roommate, or a best friend.

MUTUALITY

It's important to remember that the quality of communicating we're talking about is a *mutual* thing; it's dependent on all the persons involved. By yourself, you cannot establish and maintain interpersonal communication. You *can* choose whether to see the others involved as objects or as people. You can also choose whether or not to share with them, to some degree, aspects of your own personhood. But each person involved also has both of those sets of choices, and she or he chooses, one way or another, with respect to each other person involved. The outcome will depend ultimately on all of you; none of you can determine the quality of communication on your own.

We said at the beginning that we might not be able to communicate interpersonally with you via this book. We are willing to see you as a unique person, but we obviously can't actually know much about you as an individual. So we're forced to generalize. Both of us are also willing to share with you something of who we are as persons. But we don't know whether we've shown you enough of the kind of thing that makes us individuals for you. Your part of the mutual effort is even harder to accomplish. You might be willing both to be aware of us as humans and to share some of your own personhood with us. On the other hand, you might be willing to see us as humans, but be unwilling to share much of yourself with us. Or, you might be unwilling to do either. In any case, it's difficult enough for you to contact us, so that we'll probably never know what you choose. All of these factors make it difficult for our communication with you via this book to be genuinely interpersonal.

But the point we want to emphasize here is that the quality of your communication is a mutually determined thing. Mutuality means that each person involved plays a crucial part. You cannot make inter-personal-quality communication happen by yourself, *but* unless you do all you can to help make it happen, it will never take place.

Up to this point we've tried to say that each of our communication experiences tends to have one of two possible qualities: we tend to treat people primarily as either things or persons. When we treat people as things, we see them as role-fillers; we generally don't view them as unique individuals; we don't take into account their "hidden" parts— their attitudes, emotions, etc.—we see them as beings whose behavior can and should be manipulated in cause-and-effect ways; and we generally don't give them much credit for independent thinking and reasoning. When we treat people as persons, we tend to do the opposite—we recognize their human uniqueness; we take into account their feelings; we see them as choosers; and we try to accept the fact that their behavior is fairly unpredictable. In short, the quality of our relationship with another person depends on our willingness and ability to both be aware of aspects of the other's humanness and share aspects of our own.

THE BASIC ASSUMPTION

We believe that the crucial point about objectifying versus humanifying and the foundation for our whole approach to teaching and learning interpersonal communication is this: *The quality of our interpersonal relationships determines who we are becoming as persons.* Interpersonal communication is not just one of many dimensions of human life; it is the defining dimension, the dimension through which we become human. One of Martin Buber's translators puts it this way: "Man becomes man with the other self. He would not be man at all without the I-Thou relationship."[6]

That's what we mean when we say that the quality of our interpersonal relationships determines who we are becoming as persons. Although our individuality is tremendously important, we don't become fully human all by ourselves; our humanity develops in relationships with others. Several writers have made that same point. For example, the counselor-theologian Reuel Howe writes:

> To say that communication is important to human life is to be trite, but that bit of triteness witnesses to an invariable truth: communication means life or death to persons . . . . Both the individual and society derive their basic meaning from the relations that exist between man and man. . . . It is through dialogue that man accomplishes the miracle of personhood and community.[7]

Martin Buber's whole philosophy of communication is based on the idea that you and I discover and build our humanness in relationships with other persons. To paraphrase Buber:

> The fundamental fact of human existence is person with person. The unique thing about the human world is that something is continually happening between one person and another, something that never happens in the animal or plant world. . . . Humans are made human by that happening. . . . That special event begins by one human turning to another, seeing him or her as this particular other being, and offering to communicate with the other in a mutual way, building from the individual world each person experiences to a world they share together.[8]

Jesuit psychologist John Powell puts the same idea in simpler terms: "What I am, at any given moment in the process of my becoming a person, will be determined by my relationships with those who love me or refuse to love me, with those I love or refuse to love."[9]

Both of the qualities we've talked about play a role in the process of becoming human; both objectifying and humanifying are important. On the one hand, many of our relationships have to be objectifying ones. We would literally go insane if all of our perceptions were continually particularized, if we perceived every single thing in our environment as unique—each cat, crutch, chair, and car; each tree, stone, building, and blade of grass. We just don't have the physical or psychological strength to respond fully to each perceivable object—nor do we have the time. That applies to people, too. Most of the time when you're moving through a crowded cafeteria line, hurriedly getting gas for your car, making a bank deposit, or buying a season ticket, it is simply impossible to establish a person-to-person relationship with each human you meet.

By the same token, we sometimes have to allow ourselves to be objectified by others. At least until social values change radically, institutions will continue to use numbers to identify persons. For the sake of the benefits and conveniences they offer, most of us will continue to accept classification by social security, telephone, street address, zip code, and credit card numbers. We'll also continue to appreciate the smile and pleasant greeting we get from the supermarket checker or clinic receptionist, even though we realize it is "the same" smile and greeting everybody else gets.

We really want to emphasize that _some objectifying is unavoidable_. You cannot communicate interpersonally with every single human you meet. As we'll try to show in Chapters 8 and 9, person-to-person communication _is_ possible in a variety of situations, including an argument and a public speech. But we all know from experience that sometimes it seems as if interpersonal-quality communication just _can't_ happen.

At the same time, it's just as important to emphasize the other side of that coin. In all but the most objectifying situations, you _do_ have the opportunity to treat others as persons. You do _not_ have to respond in kind to the depersonalization of schools, hospitals, factories, and other faceless institutions. You can _be aware_ of some of the humanness of the teacher, receptionist, foreman, and nurse. You can _share_ some of your own humanness with each of them. And the kind of person you become will depend directly on how often and how completely you are able to do that.

CONCLUSION AND PREVIEW

In this chapter we've been trying to explain our general approach to interpersonal communication. We are writing this book primarily because of our basic belief that interpersonal communication is not just one of several dimensions of human living, but that it is the defining dimension. The quality of our interpersonal relationships determines who we are becoming as persons.

We've said that for us the word "interpersonal" in the term "interpersonal communication" is the name not just for any communication between people, but for communication relationships with a certain _quality_. (As a result, whenever we use the term "interpersonal communication" in the book, we mean "interpersonal-quality communication.") That quality of interpersonalness emerges when the persons communicating are willing both to be aware of others as humans instead of objects and to reveal or share something of their own humanness. That quality cannot characterize all the communicating people do, but it could characterize more than it does. And we are convinced that if it did, if we were able to allow more of our communicating to be interpersonal, we would experience more humanly satisfying, growth-producing lives.

Like all reasonably worthwhile activities, however, developing your ability to communicate interpersonally takes some effort. Fortunately, you don't start from ground zero; some of your communication already has that person-to-person quality. We've put this book together to try and help you give more of it that quality.

It seems to us that first, it would help if you knew something about where we're coming from—why we believe it's important to read, write, and teach about interpersonal communication and to try to practice it in our lives. We've tried to offer that in this first chapter. We think that the next important thing is to have a reasonably clear understanding of the contextual nature of all verbal and nonverbal human communication, and that's the subject of Chapter 2.

We believe that it is important not only to have a general understanding of the way communication works, but also to recognize the subjectivity of your—and our—perceptions of the world. In other words, we think it's useful to get in touch with the differences between "raw" communication cues and our interpretations of those cues. Chapter 3 deals with personal perceiving.

In Chapter 4 we talk about one part of the human communication process that's going on all the time, but that's often overlooked: the "negotiation of selves." We think that if you want to promote interpersonal communication, it's vital to understand this process. As we try to explain, "negotiation of selves" involves *sharing* your humanness and *being aware* of the humanness of the other person.

In Chapter 5 we explore the *sharing* process in more detail. We talk about what sharing is—and what it isn't—what you might want to share, and how your sharing can help your communicating be more interpersonal.

The other part of the negotiation-of-selves process is *being aware*—listening and responding to others, and that's the subject of Chapter 6. Our goal in that chapter is to offer some ways to think about interpersonal listening and some suggestions for "doing it" effectively.

In Chapter 7 our focus shifts to content development, the other process that's going on almost every time humans communicate. We try to show how you can promote interpersonal communication by "being clear."

In Chapters 8 and 9 we try to bring together what's in the first seven chapters and apply it to conflict situations and to the public-speaking and small-group communication contexts. Chapter 8 suggests that conflict is inevitable, but that it doesn't have to prevent interpersonal-quality communication from happening. The chapter is designed to help you interpersonally handle content conflict, conflict over definitions of selves, and conflict over basic values by using both principles and skills from earlier chapters and special suggestions that apply best to disagreement.

Chapter 9 suggests how to promote interpersonal-quality communication by overcoming some of the barriers that you'll usually encounter in public-speaking and small-group contexts. We emphasize how, even in those contexts, you can share your own humanness and be aware of the humanness of others.

The last section of this book is the epilogue. We'd like to let it speak for itself, except to say that it'll probably make more sense after you've read the first nine chapters than before.

That's an overview of the material we've tried to provide in this book. We've also integrated into each chapter a variety of suggestions for individual and group applications or exercises. We've done that because of our belief that learning interpersonal communication has to be a *holistic* process. In other words, all the people involved need to remember that except while unconscious, humans are always *both* "thinking" *and* "feeling." Experiences designed to develop only one of these activities are incomplete. Classes and textbooks should somehow deal with the whole human process by including both primarily intellectual activities, like conceptualizing, interpreting, analyzing, and criticizing, and primarily affective or emotional activities that focus on experiencing, developing awareness, expressing feelings, and so on. There are obviously many different ways to deal with each part of the whole process. Some teachers and students are more comfortable with primarily analytic discussions and activities, others with more direct experiencing. To us, the important point is that the educational experience should be holistic; neither type of activity should be omitted.

Reading this book and participating in classroom activities are not automatically going to make you into an interpersonal communicator. We hope the book can help, but what really matters is what you do in your own "real-world" life. As Hugh Prather says:

> Ideas are clean. They soar in the serene
> supernal. I can take them out and look
> at them, they fit in books, they lead

me down that narrow way. And in the
morning they are there. Ideas are straight—
But the world is round, and a
messy mortal is my friend
Come walk with me in the mud. . . . [10]

EXERCISES

Individual Application: Objectifying and Humanifying

Can you spot examples of objectifying and humanifying? Along with the
other members of your class or group, agree on a 24-hour period during
which each of you will keep track of the most obvious examples in your own
experience of: (1) being treated like an object, (2) being treated like a
human, (3) treating another person like an object, and (4) treating another
person like a human. Note key words that are used in each situation. Also
record the nonverbal elements of these communication experiences, i.e.,
the facial expressions, gestures, kinds of physical contact, etc.

You might want to compare your observations with those made by
others to see if you can come up with a verbal/nonverbal "model" of objectification and a similar "model" of inter*personal* communicating.

Group Application: Your Communication Creation

Before your view of human communication gets affected by what we say in
the next two chapters, you might want to get together with one or two other
persons to create an object that represents human communication as you
now see it. If you decide to do this, be sure to *create* something that hasn't
existed before. People in our classes have made insightful and fun objects
out of Ping Pong-balls, shoe boxes, pop cans, toilet paper, yarn, coat-
hangers, mirrors, popcorn, chess sets, and candles.

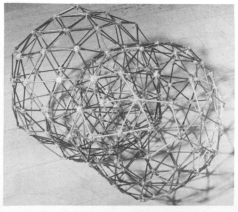

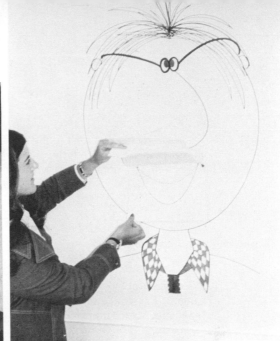

It's often useful to explain your object to others in your group or class and for somebody to keep a list of the characteristics, aspects, or elements of human communication that the objects illustrate. That list can usually be the basis of a pretty complete description of what you're studying.

NOTES

1. *Time*, December 4, 1972, p. 97.

2. As Einstein, Korzybski, and others remind us, everything is actually always changing. But we all perceive some stabilities, and that's what I'm talking about here. There's more on this topic in Chapters 2 and 4.

3. Kurt Vonnegut, Jr., "EPICAC," *Welcome to the Monkey House*, New York: Dell, 1968, pp. 277–284.

4. Victor Frankl, *Man's Search for Meaning*, rev. ed., Boston: Beacon Press, 1963.

5. *Ibid.*, p. 104. Reprinted by permission.

6. Maurice Friedman, Introduction to *Between Man and Man* by Martin Buber, New York: Macmillan, 1965, p. xviii.

7. From *The Miracle of Dialogue* by Reuel L. Howe, © 1963 by The Seabury Press, Inc. Used by permission of the publisher. (Cited in *The Human Dialogue*, ed. F.W. Matson and A. Montagu, New York: The Free Press, 1968, pp. 148–149.)

8. This is a paraphrase of what Buber says on p. 203 of *Between Man and Man, op. cit.*

9. John Powell, *Why Am I Afraid to Tell You Who I Am?* Chicago: Argus Communications, 1969, p. 43.

10. Hugh Prather, *Notes to Myself*, Lafayette, Calif.: Real People Press, 1970, n.p.

ADDITIONAL RESOURCES

Objectifying and Humanifying

Martin Buber deals with this issue in several of his books. See especially the first part of his *I and Thou*. There are two well-accepted paperback editions, one translated by Ronald Gregor Smith (New York: Charles Scribner's Sons), and the other translated by Walter Kaufman (New York: Charles Scribner's Sons, 1970). Buber's summary of characteristics of things and people is on pp. 82–83 of the

Kaufman translation. Buber discusses humanifying in; among other places, the essay "Dialogue, Section Two: Limitations," pp.18–33 of *Between Man and Man,* trans. Ronald Gregor Smith (New York: Macmillan, 1965).

Maurice Friedman, another of Buber's translators, discusses objectification in some detail in "The World of It," *Martin Buber: The Life of Dialogue* (New York: Harper & Row, 1960), pp. 62–69.

Paul Tournier also discusses the object-human distinction in a chapter called "The World of Things and the World of Persons" in his book *The Meaning of Persons* (New York: Harper & Row, 1957). This essay is represented in Chapter 6 of my (John's) book *Bridges Not Walls: A Book about Interpersonal Communication* (Reading, Mass.: Addison-Wesley, 1973).

John Powell, S.J., discusses qualities of humanness in Chapter 2, "Growing as a Person," of his book *Why Am I Afraid To Tell You Who I Am?* (Chicago: Argus Communications, 1969).

Becoming Human Interpersonally

John Powell also discusses the interpersonalness of our selves in Chapter 3 of his *Why Am I Afraid To Tell You Who I Am?*

Robert C. Carson offers a more advanced, strongly psychological treatment of the interpersonal nature of human personality in his book *Interaction Concepts of Personality* (Chicago: Aldine, 1969).

General

Edward Albee's plays *Who's Afraid of Virginia Woolf?* and *A Delicate Balance* deal with issues raised in this chapter.

Antoine de Saint-Exupery's book *The Little Prince* (New York: Harcourt Brace, and World, 1960) looks on the surface like a children's story, but it also talks about these topics.

You also might want to look at John H. Brennecke and Robert G. Amick, *The Struggle for Significance* (Beveraly Hills, Calif.: Glencoe Press, 1971), especially Chapter 1, "Significant Selfhood: An Introduction to a Way of Living," Chapter 2, "What a Piece of Work Is Man!" and Chapter 3, "Neither Ape Nor Angle." R.D. Laing's *Self and Others* (Baltimore: Penguin Books, 1961) is also important. Although Laing's *Self and Others* is not easy reading. Chapter 1, "Phantasy and Experience," Chapter 6, "Complementary Identity," and Chapter 7, "Confirmation and Disconfirmation," relate closely to the concepts we've discussed in this chapter.

2

Human Communication: A Contextual Happening

The message of Chapter 1 is that we are becoming human inter-personally. That is, the quality of our individual life depends on the quality of our interpersonal relationships. The quality of interpersonal relationships is best when we treat others as humans instead of as objects, which means developing the ability and willingness to become aware of aspects of their humanness and to share aspects of our own.

We think that's a very important and solid beginning. But it leaves many questions unanswered. For example, what happens when you go home after a tiring day and the person you live with—your spouse, parents, roommate, or whoever—greets you with, "I thought you said you'd be home an hour ago! Why didn't you let me know you'd be late? I had to do so much picking up after you that I hardly have time to get ready myself. Thanks a lot!"

What do you say in that situation? What do you do? What does it mean in this case to "be aware of the other's humanness and share your own"? How will your understanding that "we are becoming human interpersonally" affect your communicating in this situation? These are questions you have a right to ask. Chapter 1 provides the foundation for answering them, but it leaves much left to do. In the rest of the book we try to help you answer questions like that as they arise in a variety of settings.

We need to say at the outset that we won't be listing "seven simple rules" or "eleven easy techniques" for responding in this situation. If we did, we'd be cheating you. If you have only gimmicks or techniques, with no understanding of the total perspective of human communication, you'll be able to respond only part of the time—in those situations in which your gimmicks specifically fit. In other words, if we don't start somewhere near the beginning, talking about the nature of the process of human communication itself, your responses to specific situations are likely to be based on myths, inaccurate assumptions, hunches, and out-of-date traditions. We don't think that's good enough; we believe that your responses should be based on a clear understanding of communication, an understanding that grows out of the perspective on human beings we expressed in Chapter 1. Consequently, in this chaper we're going to begin developing an integrated, thinking-and-feeling view of human communication that we think will help you deal with each unique situation flexibly and effectively.

A CONTEXTUAL VIEW OF HUMAN COMMUNICATION

We think we can best contribute to your understanding by identifying five characteristics of human communication:

1. Human communication is contextual
2. Communication contexts are made up of verbal and nonverbal variables
3. These contextual variables are continually changing
4. Contextual variables are interdependent
5. Human communication occurs continuously and dynamically across interdependent contexts.

If you understand these characteristics and the ways in which they're interrelated, we think you'll have a solid overview of human communication. Although we'll discuss these characteristics in separate sections, we hope you'll realize that they're all related to one another; to get a total perspective of the nature of communication, you'll need to think of them as inseparable.

Imagine a professor and a large group of students trying to communicate in a hot, stuffy, crowded room. The wooden floor is dusty and is covered with cigarette butts and liquid stains. The walls and ceiling,

painted a dull gray, are streaked with cracks. The room smells of age, dust, and institutionness. Chairs are strewn all over; each time someone moves, something gets bumped. After the class has been in session a-while, a pounding noise from a construction crew working on a building just outside signals the end of the crew's lunch hour. The professor is discussing a topic he includes in the course only because his department requires it. He isn't happy with the examples he's prepared, and he remembers that the last time he discussed this topic, most of the students who weren't confused were bored. The students feel crowded in this room; they're also wondering when they're going to get to discuss the midterm examination coming up the next day.

Human Communication Is Contextual

As is obvious in the example just given, human communication does not occur in a vacuum; rather, communication always takes place within a complicated context, and the kind of communication that occurs is influenced by the nature of the contextual variables. Con-textual variables such as the location of the communication, the intentions or purposes of the persons involved, furniture arrangement, time of day or night, temperature, lighting, amount of physical space, group norms, number of persons, and so on all help to create a specific context and "shape" the communication.

If you realize that communication is contextual, you'll be more likely to remember that your interpretation of someone's words or actions, objects, or events is determined to a large extent by the context in which you perceive those words, actions, objects, and events. For example, if you look at the number 13 in a context with the letters "A" and "C," you'll probably see the letter "B": ABC. But when the same figure occurs in a context with the numbers "12" and "14", you will probably perceive the number "13": 12 13 14.[1]

A B C   12 13 14

Similarly you would probably respond differently to the words "God be with you" when said by Billy Graham during one of his crusades than when said by a professor at the end of his classroom lecture.

Context affects all human communication—from an informal conversation to a formal group discussion, from a cocktail party to a public speech or lecture, from an interview to a marriage proposal. Your communication behavior will not be the same in your classroom as it is in your home. It will not be the same when you're on the phone as it is when you're talking with someone face to face. Think about the differences between holding a discussion in the stuffy, crowded classroom described above and outside on the lawn. If the students moved outside, they'd be exposed to a whole new set of sensory stimulations, and their communication would unquestionably be affected.

Although physical characteristics of the location are important variables, ultimately it's people who give life to a communication event. Their personalities, how well they know one another, their expectations, appearance, clothing, language, etc., are all factors that help to define a context. You communicate differently with close friends than you do with strangers, and you probably communicate differently with close friends if a professor is within hearing distance than if she or he isn't.

Alvin Toffler's discussion of "future shock" emphasizes the complexity and importance of context. He notes that every context has certain identifiable components. "These include 'things'—a physical setting of natural or man-made objects . . . a 'place'—a location or arena within which the action occurs . . . [and] a cast of characters—people. Situations also involve a location in the organizational network of society and a context of ideas or information."[2]

This multitude of contextual variables has a tremendous impact on the general atmosphere of a communication event. Context will help determine whether a communication exchange is tense, threatening, cold, and impersonal or warm, friendly, and comfortable. Whom you're communicating with, when, where, and so on, all affect your communication behavior. A communication event just cannot be adequately understood by looking at one person apart from the other persons in the situation or by looking at all persons but ignoring the environment in which they are communicating.

Unfortunately, it's impossible to be aware of *all* the elements affecting a communication context. In the first place, there are too many of them. In addition, they're almost all present or occurring simultaneously. In the classroom example the students aren't affected first by the smell, then by the noise, then by the time of day, and finally by their worry about the midterm. All the factors affect them at once. Similarly, when you're talking over coffee with a prospective date, that set of contextual variables doesn't affect your communication in an ordered series of predictable steps. Noise level, time of day (week, year), lighting, proximity, interruptions by friends, temperature, touching, expectation, and past experiences can all play a part of the same time. In other words, communication contexts are complicated not only because they contain a lot of elements but also because a number of contextual elements are occurring *simultaneously*.

Contexts Are Made Up of Verbal and Nonverbal Variables

All communication contexts include nonverbal cues, and most contexts consist of *both* verbal and nonverbal cues. Occasionally, verbal and nonverbal cues "work" in similar ways. For example, the traffic sign

serves the same purpose as the words "NO LEFT TURN." But it's important to remember that in most human communication situations, these two kinds of cues "work" in significantly different ways. In other words, when humans are communicating, a word just doesn't do the same thing as a sign; vocabulary choice doesn't affect the situation or the persons involved the same way that tone of voice or facial expression does. Words are good for some things and almost worthless for others. Nonverbal cues are sometimes the most important part of human communication, and sometimes they're almost irrelevant. Consequently, we think it'd be useful to talk generally about both kinds of cues here. In later chapters we'll be more specific about how verbal and nonverbal elements work in the *negotiation of selves*, in *sharing some of your self*, in *responsive listening*, and so on.

Verbal cues. Verbal cues are words. That seems easy enough; everybody knows what a word is, right? Well, yes and no. Scholars have been studying language since about 400 B.C., when an ancient named Panini wrote a lengthy commentary on the *Vedas*, the sacred books of India. In the nineteenth century, researchers, such as Wilhelm von Humboldt and Ferdinand de Saussure, made important advances in linguistics, and the twentieth century's leading linguist, MIT's Noam Chomsky, has become almost as famous as Daniel Berrigan. But these scholars have not yet agreed on the defining characteristics of the basic unit of their study, the *word*.

There are several problems involved. For example, if you define language as what people write, then you can define a word as a group of letters set off by space. But linguists generally agree that written language is only a reflection of what people say, that the *spoken* word is primary. And that creates difficulties. Would you say that your "Howareya!?" to somebody you meet on the street is one *spoken* word or three? Is "loves" a different word from "love," or are they two forms of the same word? How about "lover" or "loving"? Is "bazoo" a word? The letters fit together, and some English-speaking people use it when they talk, but it doesn't seem to be in any English dictionary. What about the "words" Don Martin creates? Is "shklork" a word? "Thak"? "Shtonk"? How about "Gish Goosh"?

PHOTO COURTESY OF UNIVERSITY OF WASHINGTON DAILY.

Obviously, we aren't going to be able to answer a question that's stumped linguists for over 2000 years. For our purposes it'll be good enough to avoid the problem by agreeing that things like "cat," "mainsail," and "empathy" are words and that things like

#*?%&,   ⬠   and

are not. That approach won't handle the borderline cases, but they're fairly uncommon, anyway. The main point we want to make is that studying words is not as simple as it might at first appear to be.

Not only is it next to impossible to define exactly what you're studying, it's also difficult to identify all the ways in which words function in human communication. It's often assumed that all words are names for things, that they always *refer to* or *stand for*, in one way or another, the things they name. You've probably heard that before—the word "dog" refers to a certain kind of four-legged animal, "tree" to a certain kind of botanical life, and "rock" to a hard, stony object *or* to a repetitive movement made by a certain kind of chair, *or* to a type of music, *or* . . . . . Well, *sometimes* words function by referring to "things in the world," but not always. Words work in several other important ways, too.

Sometimes, for example, you use words not to talk about things, but to *perform an action.* The words, "I do" or "I will" in a marriage ceremony do not refer to anything; they make up part of the act of getting married. "I christen thee" at a ship launching works the same way as does "I promise" or "I'll bet you. . . ." When you make a serious bet or an important bargain with somebody, the words you use to seal the agreement don't refer to objects or events or even states of mind. They constitute, for example, the act of betting itself. When you sing in the shower or curse your smashed finger, these words are also functioning as actions; they don't "stand for" or "refer to" actions. Cursing *is* a part of being angry; singing *is* part of being happy, romantic, melancholy, or whatever. In short, *performing actions* is one of the things we often use words for without realizing that we're doing it.

Words can also work by *evoking emotion.* It's always been intriguing for me (John) to notice how a bunch of black marks on a page can make me angry, excited, or even weepy. I've been reading J.R.R.

Tolkein's books recently—all about the magic ring and the inhabitants of Middle Earth, including Bilbo and Frodo the Hobbits, Gandalf, the wizard, the Orcs, Nazguls, Balrogs, Elves, and so on. Several times I've become so involved with the lives of these fantasy creatures that I've neglected to go to bed. At exciting parts I notice my heart rate increases, I breathe quicker, my body tenses—it's just as if something was "really" happening. And words are doing it. Just words. No pictures even!

Language also works to *affect the way you perceive things and people*. In Chapter 3 we'll be talking about how your perception affects your communicating. When you get there you might keep in mind the idea that you perceive what you do partly because of the words you know how to use. Linguists disagree on how words affect perception— and how *much*—but most language scholars agree that the existence of many words for "horse" in Arabic, for "snow" in Eskimo, and for "yam" in the language of the Trobriand Islanders is tied to how these people perceive horses, snow, and yams. This point of view is often called "linguistic determinism" or "the Sapir-Whorf hypothesis" and has been summarized by the anthropologist Benjamin Lee Whorf.

> . . . the background linguistic system (in other words the grammar) of each language is not merely a reproducing instrument for voicing ideas but rather is itself the shaper of ideas, the program and guide for the individual's mental activity, for his analysis of impressions. . . . We dissect nature along lines laid down by our native language.[3]

We've discovered that our native language, which we're using to write this book, is sometimes limiting us in frustrating ways. English, unlike some other languages, maintains clear distinctions between subjects and predicates, causes and effects, beginnings and ends. The word system of the Navaho doesn't do that. According to Harry Hoijer, Navaho speakers characteristically talk in terms of processes—un-caused, ongoing, incomplete, dynamic movings. The word Navahos use for "wagon," for example, translates roughly as "wood rolls about hooplike."[4] As Hoijer explains, the Navaho words that we would translate "He begins to carry a stone" mean not that the actor produces an action, but that the person is simply linked with a given round object and with an already existing, continuous movement of all round objects in the universe.[5] The English language is significantly different from that. It requires you to talk in terms of present, past, future, cause and effect, beginning and end. But some things English speakers would like to discuss just can't be expressed in these terms. We would like to be able to talk more clearly about the ever-changing, processlike, ongoing nature of communication and about the betweenness of the quality of communication we're calling "interpersonal." But the English language makes it difficult to do that, as you'll probably notice when you read through parts of this book.

You might also notice that we've had some trouble with the male orientation of standard American English. Our language includes an incredible number of terms which subtly, but effectively, limit our perception of women. For example, in our culture we use the male pronoun "his" or "him" to make a general or universal reference to people;[6] a married man tends to talk about "his" wife; and professional limitations are suggested by job titles such as "salesman," "foreman," "fireman," "policeman," "chairman of the board," and "metermaid." As Aileen Hernandez, past president of the National Organization of Women, has noted:

> There's a "housewife" but no "househusband;" there's a "housemother" but no "housefather;" there's a "kitchenmaid" but no "kitchenman;" unmarried women cross the threshold from "bachelor girl" to "spinster" to "old maid," but unmarried men are "bachelors" forever.[7]

Much of the sexism of American English may seem trivial and unimportant. But when all the subtle terms and uses are put together, they significantly affect the way we perceive female persons.

The same thing happens to other groups. Ozzie Davis's essay "The English Language Is My Enemy"[8] details the way our meanings for the words "black" and "white" affect our perceptions of black and white persons. Similarly, language terms and uses also severely limit the ways in which people perceive Asians, Chicanos, Native Americans, and other racial and ethnic minorities.

A fifth way words function is to *reduce uncertainty*. We'll say more about this in Chapter 7. For now, we just want to introduce the general idea that words can reduce your uncertainty by limiting the possible conclusions you can draw about something or someone. When you see a large, rectangular, green and white freeway sign in the distance, you know that it could possibly indicate scores of different things, including an approaching exit, a lane change, or the mileage to the next large town. When you get close enough to read the first word, the number of possibilities is reduced significantly, and when you can read all of the words your original uncertainty about the sign is reduced even more. The goal of sign writers is to use words that reduce your uncertainty to nearly zero. They try to avoid ambiguously worded signs

> SAN FRANCISCO TRUCKS PROCEED
> RIGHT LANE MERGE LEFT
> ONE MILE

in favor of those whose meaning is unmistakable.

> LAST EXIT BEFORE
> TOLL BRIDGE

When a friend you're used to seeing every day suddenly disappears for several days, you know that the absence could indicate many different things—your friend might be ill, in trouble, angry at something you've done, tired of being around you, upset about something, cramming for an exam, moving, or a dozen other things. Your uncertainty about why your friend is absent can be reduced only when the person explains verbally—in speaking or writing—that "I took a few days off to go home and collect my thoughts."

The guessing game "Twenty Questions" is based on the ability of language to reduce uncertainty. The point of the game is for one person to guess the identity of an object which another person is thinking about. The questioner can ask no more than 20 questions, the "yes" or "no" answers to which should enable her or him to narrow the range of possible objects to the one the other person has in mind. It's often fun to see how 18 or 19 well-chosen questions can lead to something as unlikely as "the left front wheel of that bus" or "the statue on top of the bank building."

Not all words *do* function to reduce uncertainty, but the point we want to make here is that they *can*. They can categorize, point, specify, distinguish, and clarify much more efficiently than can nonverbal cues and that's one reason why they're so important for interpersonal communication.

The final function of words that we want to mention here is kind of difficult to explain. Words, especially spoken words, can work to *bring people together*. (Of course, words can also help create enemies, but they don't have to.) Martin Buber describes the unifying function of words this way:

> The importance of the spoken word, I think, is grounded in the fact that it does not want to remain with the speaker. It reaches out toward a hearer, it lays hold of him, it even makes the hearer into a speaker, if perhaps only a soundless one.[9]

This is the sense in which words are truly *symbolic*. In Greek the word "symbolic" is made up of "bolos," which means "to throw," and "sym," which means "with" or "together." One meaning of "symbolic," then, is "throw togetherness," or "*unifying*." And words can work that way. Think of the times you've found a friend just by listening to somebody talk—in person, on the radio or television, or in a book. His or her words helped bring you together. The words we use on these pages can bring us closer together with you, too. They can help bridge the gap between us. Again, we know that they *don't* always work that way, but they *can*, just as your words can help you move closer to others.

Words, in short, are a flexible and richly varied part of many communication contexts. They can *refer* the persons involved to nonverbal things or events. Sometimes, we use words to *perform actions*. Words can also *evoke emotion*, and the language you're able to use even *affects the way you perceive*. Words can *reduce uncertainty* and, perhaps most importantly for us, words can *unify* persons, can bring humans together.

Nonverbal cues.   But words don't ever appear by themselves. Without exception, every communication context includes *nonverbal* elements. Every spoken word, for instance, is spoken in some tone of voice, at some rate, with some inflection and vocal quality. Every written word is *on* something—colored paper, metal, a television screen, etc.—is in some style of script, is a certain size, and so on. In short, the verbal and nonverbal elements of a communication context are related in several different ways. This chart should clarify some of those relationships:

	Oral	Nonoral
Verbal	Spoken words	Written words
Nonverbal	Inflection, sigh, scream, vocal quality, etc.	Gestures, movement, spatial relation-ships, time, dress, facial expressions, etc.

We think that verbal communication is important; it can generate a tremendous impact on human affairs and interpersonal relationships. In fact, we believe that whenever you can, you should verbalize your feelings, ideas, and opinions, because doing that in an appropriate way can clear up misunderstandings, help you feel better about yourself, and can sometimes strengthen interpersonal relationships. But verbal codes make up only a fraction of our communication with other persons. We communicate more through nonverbal codes than through verbal codes. Unfortunately, we can't always depend on nonverbal cues to communicate exactly what we're thinking or how we're feeling; nonverbal communication is often ambiguous and is frequently misinterpreted.

In other words, nonverbal communication is complex and full of inferential "traps." Sometimes, nonverbal cues are interpreted to mean something you didn't intend, and people don't always take the time to check to see if their interpretation is accurate. In addition, it's easy to believe such myths as "if a person doesn't maintain eye contact, he's dishonest"; "young people who wear their hair long are against the establishment"; and "pipe smokers are more intellectual and theoretical than cigarette smokers." Those kinds of generalizations reveal an inadequate understanding of nonverbal cues.

As we said before, in later chapters we'll be talking specifically about how nonverbal cues affect the negotiation of selves (Chapter 4), sharing some of your self (Chapter 5), and responsive listening (Chapter 6). Right now, we'd like to make three general suggestions about your nonverbal communicating: (1) become nonverbally aware; (2) recognize that nonverbal cues "work" in three main ways; (3) try not to oversimplify nonverbal cues.

1. *Become nonverbally aware.* Increase your sensitivity to as many nonverbal cues as possible. Learn to identify the many different non-

verbal cues *you're* sending off, and try to become aware of the nonverbal cues that affect your response to *other* people.

The people in our classes seem to become much more aware of their nonverbal communication when we provide them with a reference list of a variety of nonverbal cues. We hope it will work that way with you, too. To us, a list that identifies and gives examples of several nonverbal categories can increase your awareness of the vast multitude of nonverbal cues that at one time or another affect your communicating. So, although what follows is not an exhaustive list of every kind of nonverbal cue, it's a start, and we think that by working with these categories, you'll gain a much broader insight into what you're "saying" nonverbally.

Geography and climate. The things that surround your communication with others can have a powerful influence on the kind of interaction that takes place. Sometimes, for example, the geography and/or climate can affect your mood, feelings, activity, initiative, or your willingness to communicate. When W. Griffitt experimented with the relationships between temperature, humidity, and interpersonal responses among students,[10] he found that the students were less attracted to one another as temperature and humidity increased. It might seem strange to think that hot, humid weather can affect whether we like or dislike someone. But although not all of the evidence is in yet, experience and the results of a few experimental studies suggest that we can't ignore the possibility. Of course, other environmental cues may also play an influential part in a communication context—wind, sun, clouds, rain, lawn, flowers, trees, smog, flat or mountainous terrain, or some combination of these things can often make a difference in what happens between persons.

Architecture. The relationship between architecture and human interaction is still pretty ambiguous. We know that such factors as the physical space available in a room, furniture arrangement, comfortability of furniture, texture of walls, height of the ceiling, and color combinations can all affect the quality of communication. But we can't yet draw any clearly defined conclusions which generalize to most or all persons. Each of us responds to architecture in our own ways. One of the experimental studies about architecture most relevant to interpersonal communication was conducted by A.H. Maslow and N.L. Mintz,[11] who asked people to rate a series of photographs of faces. They divided the raters into three groups and put each group in a different architectural setting: an "ugly" room, a "beautiful" room, and an "average" room. The people in the "beautiful" room gave significantly higher ratings to the photographs than did those in the "average" or "ugly" rooms. In other words, the study suggests that our impressions of other people are influenced by the architecture of our surroundings.

I (Gary) learned some interesting things about architecture and communication from the manager of one of Seattle's most popular restaurants. He told me that his business is dependent on "high-volume" sales and that he does some things with the architecture of his restaurant to increase turnover. He wants people to come to his restaurant and enjoy the food and the environment, but he doesn't want them to stay too long. So he uses bright red wallpaper and bright lights throughout the inside of the restaurant. He also uses furniture which is comfortable for only a short period of time. He requires his waiters to move rapidly, because he believes that this helps set the mood for the customers. As you're sitting in this restaurant, you're surrounded by noisy music and relatively loud singing. The music is not irritating at first, but after a while it does get a little bothersome. The manager claims that his architectural design is a success. His experience supports the idea that the architecture of a room can have a strong, though sometimes subtle, influence on the behavior of people.

Personal space. You've probably noticed that you sometimes sit or stand very close to people you're talking with, whereas at other times you feel more comfortable several feet away. This is what is known as proxemics or, in simpler terms, personal space. Each of us has a distance at which we prefer to interact with other people. How far away we sit or stand depends on our personality, our relationship with the other person, the situation or context, how we are feeling toward the other persons at the time, and other factors. As the anthropologist Edward Hall puts it:

> Some individuals never develop the public phase of their personalities and, therefore, cannot fill public spaces; they make very poor speakers or moderators. As many psychiatrists know, other people have trouble with the intimate and personal zones and cannot endure closeness to others.[12]

Hall also says that *"how people are feeling toward each other"* at the time will significantly affect how close they sit or stand.[13]

Intimate distance a)

Personal distance b)

Within those limitations, Hall identifies four distances commonly used:[14]

a) *Intimate distance* (six to eighteen inches)

Touch is possible; smell, body temperature, and feel of breath may be involved. Voice is normally at very low level.

b) *Personal distance* (one and a half to four feet)

Touch is possible; subjects of personal interests and involvement can be discussed at this distance; finer details of skin, hair, eyes, teeth, etc., are visible.

c) *Social distance* (four to twelve feet)

Impersonal business occurs at this distance. People who work together or who are attending a casual social gathering tend to use close social distance; eye contact is more important at this distance; lack of eye contact may seem to shut person out of the conversation.

c) Social distance

d) *Public distance* (12 to 25 feet)

Voice must be loud; person can take evasive or defensive action if threatened; usually for public speaking and other public occasions; lose much of the subtle shades of meaning found in normal voice, facial expression and movement; voice, gestures, etc., must be exaggerated to be meaningful.

d) Public distance

Touch. Touch plays a part in just about every moment of our waking day—not necessarily with other humans, but with objects. You may not be consciously aware of the feel of your clothes, the chair, couch, or floor you're sitting, standing, or lying on, the feel of the book you're holding, the pencil or pen you're grasping to write, the feel of the desk you're leaning on, the shoes you're wearing, or the feel of the sidewalk or grass you walk on. But you couldn't very well write, walk, make a fist, smile, or comb your hair without a sense of touch. Touching objects is common in our culture, and the ways in which we handle such things as cigarettes, books, pencils, and cups or glasses can affect another person's response to our communication.

Touching persons is another matter. In this country when two persons are communicating in public it is rare for them to touch each other more than three or four times in an hour. Of course, whether or not humans touch each other, how much, and where they touch depend on a lot of things. But in general, Americans are not so likely to touch one another as are people in some other countries. Sidney Jourard reports that in San Juan, Puerto Rico, couples observed for one hour in a public restaurant touched 180 times; in Paris, couples touched 110 times; in London, they didn't touch at all, and in Gainesville, Florida, they touched twice.[15]

In some American subcultures, touching is common and accepted. But for many people in this country it is not. As Mark Knapp explains:

> Some people grow up learning "not to touch" a multitude of animate and inanimate objects; they are told not to touch their own body and later not to touch the body of their dating partner; care is taken so children do not see their parents "touch" one another intimately; some parents demonstrate a noncontact norm through the use of twin beds; touching is associated with admonitions of "not nice" or "bad" and is punished accordingly—and frequent touching between father and son is thought to be something less than masculine.[16]

In this country many people tend to avoid touching because it seems to be, as Mike Young puts it, "a terribly risk-filled form of human relatedness."[17] Touching seems to be a way that feelings we'd like to keep hidden might become revealed. As Young says, "Touch has the power to burst the floodgates of our damned-up emotional lives."

Consequently, we learn that it's generally okay to shake hands, pat someone on the shoulders or back, or briefly touch another's arm. We also "permit" touching behaviors in contact sports, as a way of showing affection to or disciplining young children, and, in private, between couples. But beyond those situations, touching is often considered inappropriate.

Our discomfort can create serious problems, because touch—or its absence—often communicates very "loudly." As one high school student said. "I don't think my dad cares too much about me. He supplies me with money; he spends time with me; but he's never put his

Different touching behaviors often indicate different relationships.

arm around my shoulders, patted me on the back, or given me a firm handshake."

The main point we want to make here is that touch is a potentially *powerful* but poorly understood kind of nonverbal communication. Therefore, you might want to clarify for yourself those touching behaviors which you see as supportive, friendly, and sympathetic and those which are, for you, connected with hostility or sex. You might also want to check your understandings with other people, so you can expand the ways you communicate by touching.

Body movement. Not all of your movements will be noticed and interpreted by other persons. But when people communicate with you, they'll notice at least some of your kinesic behaviors, and those that they notice may have a significant impact on the interaction that takes place. By simply pointing a finger at someone, you may be "saying": "I know what I'm talking about; in fact, I know a lot more than you do." Along with your gestures, posture, head movements, etc., the tension (or lack of tension) your body exhibits and your rate of movement can affect the general atmosphere of the communication context; people will frequently use your body cues to interpret your mood, attitudes, congeniality, liking or disliking, emotions, etc.

Facial expression. Your face is probably the most expressive part of your body and one of the more important focus points for nonverbal cues. From a person's face we often interpret emotions, attitudes, relationship cues, sincerity, and many other messages. Eye contact is especially important. As we discuss Chapters 5 and 6, your eyes can reveal a great deal about who you are *and* how you're responding to others. We can't always accurately judge what a facial expression means, but nevertheless we do judge it. Sometimes in class I (Gary) will listen to students with a "poker" face, trying not to show any emotion, but students inevitably interpret that as negative feedback. As one student said to me when *I* thought I was listening carefully, "You aren't showing any interest!

Voice. The nonverbal characteristics of your voice, sometimes called paralinguistics, include such things as tone of voice, pitch, inflection, articulation, resonance, loudness, dialect, rate of speaking, laughing, crying, groaning, and so on. One of the primary functions of your voice is to give people some idea of how to interpret the words you speak. But more significantly, people sometimes make assumptions about speakers themselves, based on vocal characteristics. People infer personality traits, attitudes, emotional states, intelligence, age, competence, and mood from a person's voice. We don't recommend this practice, but it happens.

Silence. Silence is one of the least understood nonverbal cues, partly because people use and interpret silence in so many different ways. Silence can be interpreted to mean apathy, patience, boredom, fear, sadness, love, intimacy, anger, or intimidation. We've talked with married couples who use silence as a weapon. One husband, who knew his wife couldn't stand it when he didn't talk out a problem, would sometimes refuse to talk to her for two or three days. His wife said she found this "devastating." Our students have told us that when they're working in small groups, the most uncomfortable moments are those when everyone is silent. They've said that during periods of silence, people start shifting nervously and making inferences like "nobody is interested," "people don't like this group," "nobody can think of anything to say," and "nobody really cares about what we're doing." To get an idea of the impact silence can have, try waiting 45 seconds between each speaker in a small-group discussion. Or, notice the next time a professor asks a question and nobody says anything for half a minute. Chances are, the professor won't wait that long before talking; the silence seems too overwhelming.

Silence also works in positive ways. Two close friends may say nothing to each other just so they can share the experience of the moment. Love, warmth, sympathy, and several other emotions are sometimes better expressed through "silent" facial and body movements and touch.

As you communicate, remember that each of us is as responsible for our silence as we are for our speech. Remember, too, that your pauses and silences may be saying something you don't intend to say.

2.   *Recognize that nonverbal cues "work" in three main ways:* they play a major role in *defining the relationship between persons;* they often *express emotions;* and they *significantly affect the impact of verbal*

cues. Think about some of your own relationships with other people. When you walk into a classroom the first day of a term, how do you tell who the teacher is? You probably use such nonverbal cues as dress, the kinds of materials she or he is carrying, or where he or she sits or stands. Even though we don't wear academic robes to class—or a necktie— we've never found it necessary to announce, "I am the teacher." Many students know as soon as we walk into the room; the rest get the idea from the folder or books we're carrying, our apparent familiarity with the situation, or some such thing. Similarly, students usually have a pretty good idea of what kind of relationship they'll have with their teacher by such things as the way he or she talks with them, the number of office hours available, whether or not the teacher avoids them or goes out of his or her way to converse with them, and sometimes even by the way the teacher's office is arranged or decorated. (What's a person saying about your relationship if her or his office is arranged so that a desk is always kept between you?)

Similarly, how do you determine that someone is a close personal friend of yours? It's hardly ever because the person says the words "I am your close personal friend." You pay more attention to the amount of time the person spends with you, how willing she or he is to listen to you, the gentle, caring tone of voice your friend uses when talking with you, or the fact that she or he has consistently trusted you with confidential information.

You also determine whether the person you're communicating with sees himself or herself as superior, inferior, or equal to you by the nonverbal cues you interpret. Tone of voice, spatial relationships, facial expressions, and gestures are much more common indicators of superiority, inferiority, or equality than words are. In short, the relationships you establish with other people are often defined by nonverbal communication cues.

Another main way nonverbal cues work is to *express emotions.* We're pretty sure that this isn't news to you. Most human emotions are communicated primarily via nonverbal cues. Anger, sadness, pity, envy, passion, and pain are hardly ever communicated primarily by words. Nonverbal elements are much more important. We don't think it's a good practice to infer emotional states from just nonverbal cues, as we'll talk more about in Chapter 6. But whether someone likes or dislikes you, is angry with you, frustrated with you, affectionate toward you, afraid of you, or ashamed of you, you'll infer the emotion primarily from the nonverbal cues you observe.

Nonverbal cues also *significantly affect the impact of verbal cues*. According to Mark Knapp, nonverbal cues can repeat, substitute for, complement or accent, regulate, or contradict verbal cues.[18] In some cases, he explains, nonverbal cues function simply to *repeat* what the words say, for example when a person points as he or she says "over there" or "go north two blocks." Sometimes nonverbal cues *substitute* for words, as when your facial expression and posture make it unnecessary for you to say, "I've had a rotten day." Nonverbal cues can also *complement* or *accent* verbal ones, i.e., they can elaborate on what's being said in words. Think of the last time you had a disciplinary conference with your employer, one in which your boss was correcting something you were doing wrong. Chances are, it wasn't a particularly comfortable experience, and your nonverbal cues—lack of eye contact, nervous movements, choppy speaking, etc.—probably emphasized or accented the discomfort you were feeling.

In most face-to-face conversations, you also use nonverbal cues to *regulate* who's speaking. Leaning forward, opening your mouth as if to speak, and adopting an anticipating or expectant expression can signal the other person that you want to talk. Other cues can let the person know that you want him or her to continue. Finally, nonverbal cues often *contradict* verbal ones. If a man says to you, "Speaking in public doesn't make me at all nervous," but you notice that his hands and voice tremble and sweat shines on his forehead while he is speaking, which do you believe—the verbal statement or the nonverbal behavior? When verbal and nonverbal cues conflict, the nonverbal has a great deal of influence on the believability of what's heard or said. What would your response be to a man who said to you in a monotone voice, "You have good ideas," while at the same time he was brushing lint off his pant cuff?

3.   *Try not to oversimplify nonverbal cues.* By now it should be clear why we have included this point. There are so many kinds and functions of nonverbal cues, you just can't accurately interpret them in narrow, simplistic ways. Not everybody will respond in the same way to a nonverbal cue; much depends on the person who is interpreting the cue, the relationship between the communicators, the situation, and so on. To a mother and father, their child's temper tantrum may seem like a natural part of growing up; to an older brother or sister, the tantrum may signify that the child is spoiled; to someone outside the family, the tantrum may be evidence of poor parental guidance.

In other words, we think it's important to develop insight into the influence that context has on interpretations of nonverbal cues. Not only do different people interpret the same cue differently, but the same person might interpret a given nonverbal cue differently in different situations. Try to visualize the ways in which you would interpret two men hugging if you observed them at a funeral, after a touchdown at a football game, or in a bar. To add to the complexity of all this, a person may "give off" the same nonverbal cues for different reasons in different contexts. In one situation you may cross your arms across your chest because you're nervous; in another situation you may do the same thing because you feel defensive; or you may cross your arms because you're cold.

We'll have more to say about *interpretation* in Chapter 3, and we'll also be talking about verbal and nonverbal cues in other chapters. But you're probably feeling that you've heard enough about them for now. Basically, we're hoping you see that: (1) communication contexts are made up of verbal and nonverbal cues; and (2) both kinds of cues are complex and work in significantly different ways.

In Summary:
(so far)

Verbal cues	Nonverbal cues
It's hard to define what a "word" is.	It's a good idea to become aware of the variety of nonverbal cues:
Words can stand for things.	geography and climate
Words can perform actions.	architecture
Words can evoke emotions.	personal space
Words can affect how you perceive things and people.	touch
Words can reduce uncertainty.	body movement
Words can bring people together.	facial expression
	voice
	silence

Nonverbal cues work in three main ways:
1. they define relationships between persons,
2. they express emotions,
3. they affect the impact of verbal cues.

Try not to oversimplify nonverbal cues.

Contextual Variables Are Continuously Changing

Not only do many different verbal and nonverbal variables make up a communication context; all these elements or variables are in a state of continuous change. In other words, the environment around the people, the verbal and nonverbal cues, and the people themselves are dynamic, evolving, growing, and continuously changing. We don't mean to say that each communication situation is totally different from every other one. In fact, "situations often resemble one another. This . . . . is what makes it possible to learn from experience. If each situation were wholly novel, without some resemblance to previously experienced situations, our ability to cope would be hopelessly crippled."[19] Each communication experience, although it involves the process of change, has some stability and predictability. For example, the participants in a communication exchange will use some language and gestures that are similar from situation to situation. Nor does the physical environment change so rapidly that each new context is completely foreign to us.

But change is always occurring, and sometimes it's difficult for us to recognize it. We usually see the things within our environment as static entities rather than as processes. The purpose of Alvin Toffler's book *Future Shock* is to help us break this habit by making us more aware of change. One of Toffler's premises is that "in the awesome complexity of the universe, even within any given society, a virtually infinite number of streams of change occur simultaneously. *All 'things'—from the tiniest virus to the greatest galaxy—are, in reality, not things at all, but processes.*"[20] If you think about what Toffler is saying, you can begin to recognize the dynamic changes occurring all around you. For example, "the child reaching teenage . . . is literally surrounded by twice as much of everything newly man-made as his parents were at the time he was an infant."[21] Transportation takes us more places faster; engineers develop faster and better electric appliances; there are more prepared foods on the market; approaches to education change as multimedia, peer-group tutoring, open classrooms, and pass/fail grading become popular; governmental and corporate structures change; marketing strategies change; and ads for everything from suppositories to politicians get the television treatment. Architecture changes, too; Sam Sloan, who calls himself a psychosocial space designer, is now actively promoting interior designs that emphasize the communication needs of people rather than the creation of an esthetically pleasing environment.[22]

People are also in a state of continuous change. Physiologically, we are not the same from day to day. For example, cells, the basic units of life, are constantly being destroyed and replaced.[23] Even more important, at least for our purposes, are the psychological and behavioral changes—from depression to joy, from hating to loving someone, from agreeing to disagreeing with someone, from "no, you can't" to "yes, you can." Unfortunately, sometimes these drastic shifts are the only changes we're aware of in others. We only notice that "Mike used to be pretty straight; now he's really into dope" or that "Martha was once into keeping house as a primary occupation; but now most of her time is spent working for a law degree."

But change is a constant part of all of us. We experience; we grow; we mature. The way you perceive and behave toward school or education is not the same now as it was when you were in grade school or high school. Your image of school changes; your school behavior, study habits, and social activities change; your experiences in school are different.[24]

The same kind of thing happens with your perception of people. Since the context in which you communicate can affect your perception of another person, your perception of that other person can change as that context changes. Not only that, but your perceptions of government, abortion, smoking, exams, term papers, and hundreds of issues change. One of the persons who read an early draft of this chapter told us of a friend of his who returned home after four years of college to the greeting, "You haven't changed a bit!" Her response was that she had certainly wasted a lot of time and money, then, because change was the reason she had gone to school in the first place.

In an important sense, you are changing from day to day and moment to moment. Your mood, motivation, and needs are not the same 24 hours a day. Your relationship with another person can change during and after *one conversation*. Suppose, for example, that you have a very comfortable and open conversation with another person; you find out things about that person you didn't know before, and the other person finds out things about you that he or she didn't know before. At one point the other person confides in you, shares a very personal experience, or says, "I love you." After that kind of talk, there is no way that the two of you will be the same.

We asked some persons in our classes to describe some of the ways they've changed in the past day, the past term, and the past year. Here are some of their responses:

"I change all the time because there is more and more experience and information inside of me. I find out things every day, every minute. This does not necessarily mean that I become wiser—though there are plateaus of that."

"I changed in a day: Tuesday, I went shopping for clothes and found only 'tiny' sizes; Wednesday, I began with a diet."

"There is no way I can even relate the ways I have changed in the last six/seven years. I am simply not the same person. The 'old' me died a slow, painful, evolutionary death of experience. The 'new' me has been hammered from the changes in the 'old', 'prototype' me. But the 'ideal' me is still to come."

"I swore I'd never get married and be tied down with some slob of a man, but I met one OK slob, and June 19th is the day."

"People I run into tell me this: 'Gee, your looks have changed since last fall. Remember?' My good friends tell me this: 'You sure sound different from when I last talked to you.' And I *am* different, even to myself. It's taken me awhile to come to that statement, and it will take me another while to realize the real implications of that simple sentence. But that is the most significant change I can see in myself: the ability to accept myself even as I change, so giving up the 'safeness' of staying as a 'static' being by taking the risk to reach outside myself for a point of reference."

"Probably the greatest change that I've undergone in the last several years or so was the result of the end of my relationship with a woman I had been living with for two years. We are very different sorts of people, and she wanted me to change in many ways over the course of two years. And since I loved her and did not wish to lose her, I did. I often felt that these changes were not particularly good or legitimate ones, since I could not justify them with an intrinsic value. For instance, she was quite possessive and didn't even like me to talk to other women. I didn't feel this was right, but she insisted she couldn't change. So I did. Well, I got sort of accustomed to this new me, and we existed in a sort of uneasy truce, this new me and I. Finally, not by choice, Debbie's and my relationship was ended, and I suddenly found myself looking for *me* again. Well, I've found me. And I'm really quite different. I'm much more social, impulsive, and, in some respects, irresponsible. One really basic thing that I realized was that I want to go on changing all my life."

When you recognize that people are always changing, you're recognizing an important part of their humanness. In other words, humans are not static, and if you communicate with them as if they were, you often end up treating them like objects. The changes you undergo from day to day sometimes help you grow more like those you come into contact with. But sometimes you also grow less like them, so that change becomes an instrument of separation. All of us need to keep reminding ourselves that we're changing and to try hard to maintain an open, accepting attitude toward the fact that other people are changing, too. Accepting change in ourselves and others is an important part of learning to communicate interpersonally.

Contextual Variables Are Interdependent

When someone says that two things (A and B) are *in*dependent, they mean that A and B do not affect each other; there is no relationship between them. For example, although you might argue that in a sense, all components of the universe are somehow related, for all practical purposes the brand of toothpaste I use and the win-loss record of the Los Angeles Lakers are *independent*. The fact that you may be sitting or lying down while reading this book is independent of the color of my eyes.

To say that there is a *dependent* relationship between A and B means that A affects B, but B doesn't affect A or vice versa. For example, a sudden, bright light might cause you to blink, but your blinking won't affect the brightness of the light.

But when we say that parts of a communication context are *interdependent*, we mean something like this: not only are contextual variables often occurring simultaneously and continuously changing, but also each variable is interrelated with all of the other variables. In other words, each part (person or thing) is capable of exerting an influence on all of the other parts. When change occurs in one person or thing, this will affect what other people say and do, and they, in turn, can affect your communication behavior. At the same time, both of you affect and are affected by your physical environment. This "reciprocal influence" among persons and things exists in every communication experience.

In the classroom example we cited earlier, the professor, the students, and the environment are *interdependent*. The professor's communication cannot be adequately understood apart from the influence of the environment and the students' behavior. The students' communication cannot be understood apart from the influence of the professor's behavior and the environment. The professor or students can affect their environment by altering the furniture arrangement, the lighting, the temperature, etc. This is not a step-by-step process in which the professor acts, the environment changes, and the students respond, then the students act, the environment changes, and the professor responds. These things are happening almost simultaneously.

For example, the professor feels uncomfortable and even antagonistic in the room. He's also uncomfortable with his subject matter. The room, temperature, his past experience with the topic, the crowded conditions, and the outside noise all affect the professor negatively, and it shows in his scowl, tone of voice, clipped speech, and curt responses to students' questions. The students also feel the negative effects of the room, temperature, and outside noise, and they are aware of the professor's discomfort and antagonism. Their expectations about the midterm are also affecting them. Because of all these factors, the students exhibit discomfort and negativeness in their communication behavior—silence, fidgeting, talking with one another, nervous shifting, bored looks, etc. In short, the professor is affected by the students; the students are affected by the professor and by one another; and both are affected by various parts of their environment. *All of these factors are interacting almost simultaneously.*

Punctuating communication. Most people realize that their communication behavior is influenced by others and by their environment. But very often, communicators forget that since each communication context contains a multitude of variables, and since these variables are capable of exerting influence on one another simultaneously and continuously, we cannot accurately explain change in terms of one-way causality. We are forgetting this every time we say, "I had to say that" or "I don't know why they didn't understand it; I told them twice!" or "We'd still be friends if you hadn't started picking at me!"

Even though we realize that communication is an uninterrupted sequence of interdependent exchanges, we often communicate as if there were an identifiable starting point, a simple cause for our communication behavior. We tend to assume that there are discrete portions of a communication experience, with clear beginnings and ends. In other words, we *punctuate* communication events we experience.[25] We divide them into linear segments, just like periods and commas do with words. And then we tend to assume that what comes first in the segment we created *causes* what comes after it.

A man and woman who have been going together for several months are talking in the coffee shop next to the undergraduate library. They're having lunch alone at a table, but the coffee shop itself is crowded. Both have term papers due the next day. Seated at an adjacent table are several of the woman's friends. At one point during the conversation, he tells her to "go to hell!" She gets up and leaves. Afterward, the two are questioned about the incident:

Woman: I left *because* he told me to go to hell.

Man: Yeah, but the reason I said that was *because* she was bugging me about my eating habits. If she hadn't criticized me, I wouldn't have told her to go to hell and she wouldn't have left.

Woman: Well, I only criticized him *because* he's always talking with his mouth full of food.

Man: What can I do? I take a bite of food and she asks me a question. If I don't answer she says, "You never talk to me."

Think of the last argument you had in which it seemed obvious that you were just responding to the other person—in which you felt that the other's actions *caused* your communication behavior. In this kind of situation you're punctuating the communication by identifying some point in the ongoing sequence of events as "the start of all this." The minute you establish that point as "the beginning," *your* communication starts to look to you like the logical outcome of somebody else's mistake. Unfortunately, the other person involved is usually thinking the same thing. His or her punctuation is different from yours—the argument started with you and it's all your fault. We've discovered that in such situations, it's best not even to try to decide whose "fault" it is.

Instead, we've found that it helps to describe the characteristics of the situation in present-tense terms and then to work together on what can be done about it.

The point we want to stress here is that because of the interdependence of all human communication variables, you cannot legitimately talk about a single cause of any communication behavior. For example, if we take a closer look at the "man-woman" illustration cited earlier, we might find several interrelated reasons why she got up and left: two weeks ago he told his friends some things about her which she considered confidential, and she had suppressed her frustration about that until now; earlier in the week, her econ instructor gave an unannounced quiz, which she flunked; and/or some of her friends were seated at a nearby table and she was embarrassed about the fact that they may have overheard the argument.

Whenever you suggest that communication "started" at a particular time, you are arbitrarily punctuating an event that has no identifiable beginning. We usually assign these starting points to help explain or justify our own responses in the situation. But our explanation generally suffers from the "fallacy of the single cause," i.e., it ignores the fact that there are a multitude of interdependent factors affecting our communication behavior.

Human Communication Occurs Continuously and Dynamically across Interdependent Contexts

The idea of interdependence is applicable in another framework, too. The various contexts in which you communicate are also interdependent. In other words, up to this point we've been talking as if communication could be viewed as a series of discrete, perhaps isolated, contexts, each existing by itself. We'd like to dispel that notion now and emphasize that although each context is unique, *each exists within and is inseparable from a larger framework of ongoing communication*. No experience can be completely separated from what happened before and what will come after it. It is sometimes necessary and helpful for analytic purposes to separate one context from another. But when we do that, we don't get an accurate picture of the dynamic *process* that is communication.

Instead of thinking of human communication as a series of isolated situations, each with an identifiable starting and stopping point, we believe it's more accurate to recognize that each of us exists in complex, dynamic, interdependent, and ongoing communication environments. These environments are complex in the sense that there are many things going on all at once; they're dynamic in the sense that everything is continually changing; they are interdependent in the sense that what happens in one situation or context affects future situations; and they are ongoing in the sense that we are continually receiving verbal and/or nonverbal communication from others, *and* we are continually "sending off" communication cues of our own.

Cannot stop communication. One implication of this point of view is that it is impossible for you to stop communicating *once someone becomes perceptually aware of you.* You can stop talking, but you can't stop other people from interpreting your nonverbal behavior. For example, let's imagine that your class has been meeting for about two weeks; then one day you decide *not* to communicate with the other class members. If you decide to not communicate by not attending, your absence could be interpreted to mean that "you're ill"; or "you're having a better time with friends"; or perhaps "you're sleeping in." If you go to class and ignore the discussion by reading a newspaper, your behavior could be interpreted to mean that "you're not interested"; "you're bored"; or maybe "you don't like the topic." If you pay attention with your eyes but don't respond verbally, then your silence could be interpreted to mean that "you're afraid to talk"; "you're not in the mood to talk"; etc. In other words, regardless of what you say or don't say, regardless of what you do or don't do, you are making communication cues available to the other members of the class. Words, silence, absence, posture, eye contact or lack of it, dress, and so on, all have communication potential, not only in the classroom but also in families, task groups, friendship groups, and so on. According to one book: "One cannot *not* communicate."[26] You cannot avoid communicating any more than you can avoid behaving. It's unlikely that everyone around you would ever be completely oblivious to you, and to the extent that they are perceptually aware of your behavior, you are communicating.

Another implication of this point is that you can't escape the barrage of communication that surrounds you during every moment you're awake. Samuel Becker helps characterize this when he describes the sort of communication environment in which women and men in a modern, highly industrialized society live. For example, most often we're familiar with the plight of a businessman who, as Becker puts it:

. . . lives in a vertible pressure cooker of communication; everyone and everything pushing him. The media are pushing him to buy a car and cigarettes and to stop smoking; to use deodorants and to wear auto seat belts and to vote for the party of his choice and to support our most recent war effort and to parade against war. His children are pushing him to play with them or to give them money for the movies or to buy them a car. . . . And those above him at the plant or office are pushing him to work harder, and those below him are pushing him to stop making *them* work so hard. And all of this pushing is done through communication. He is pushed by his television set and radios and newspapers and magazines and bill-boards and handbills and memoranda and even the old-fashioned open mouth which is often so uncomfortably close to his ear. He is pushed not only through verbal communication, but through non-verbal. . . . He cannot escape this barrage of communication . . . .[27]

We don't mean to say that communication is always as hectic as Becker suggests. And we don't mean to say that it happens only to men. What we're hoping to point out is that there are people and things around us all the time, and it is impossible for us to completely ignore all of them. In other words, we can't escape being a receiver of communication messages.

But there are so many of these messages that we can't possibly attend to all of them. We can hear, see, smell, touch, and taste only so much; we can also remember only so much. Because of these limitations, we pick up only "bits and pieces" of information from the situations we experience—some from persons (friends, strangers, colleagues, mates, parents) and some via media (television, radio, billboards, magazines, books, newspapers). From the bits and pieces we pick up, we construct our own messages about the issue, the person, the object, or whatever. The message we construct depends on the bits and pieces we pick, how we interpret these bits and pieces, and what we remember. Another way of saying this is that since we are capable of picking up and retaining only portions of any one message at any one time, and since we are exposed to a continuous barrage of messages, the images we have of persons and things are *organized from complicated combinations of interdependent experiences.* This process is continuous and has no concrete starting or stopping point. One experience may have more of an impact on us than another; it may stick with us longer.

We might pick up more information from one person than from another; but most—or all—of what we know and believe has come from selected portions of a continuous stream of communication experiences. For example, here is a "message" I (Gary) constructed about an event that happened recently in Seattle:

> Two weeks ago a Seattle woman was shot and killed after she tried to stop a robbery attempt in her apartment. One of the unfortunate circumstances about this incident was that the woman's 11-year-old daughter was present when the shooting occurred (actually, the daughter was hiding in the bathroom, and after hearing the shots she came out, to find her mother on the floor.) The mother had pulled a gun on the intruder, perhaps because she was afraid of being raped when he came into her bedroom. The woman who was killed was a friend of my son Tommy's preschool teacher. The intruder has been caught by the police. He had been shot in the stomach by the woman with a 22-caliber pistol, and he was seeking medical help when the police found him.

This was the message I constructed about the killing. But I didn't get this message from one source or from one experience. I pieced it together from several different bits of information from several different sources on different occasions. Each time, I made my own interpretations of what I was hearing. I first heard about the incident from Connie. She told me that the woman killed was a friend of our son's preschool teacher, and I remember her saying that the "robbery was well planned," and that "many of the things being stolen were out on the lawn before the intruder went to the woman's bedroom." On my way to work, I heard a few more bits and pieces of information from the car radio—right now, I don't even remember what they were. That night, I watched a television report about the killing and picked up a few more details; for example, I saw the apartment house where it took place. Finally, I read about it in the newspaper. I haven't heard much about the incident since the newspaper account, but that doesn't mean that I won't. I'm still thinking about the 11-year-old daughter, wondering how she is making out.

So the message I constructed about the event came from a number of different sources, at different times, through different media. I remembered much of what Connie told me, much of what the newspapers said, but very little of what I heard on radio and television. I couldn't absorb everything I heard. I cannot attribute what I know about the incident to any one source. Neither can I lay responsibility for my message on any one person. *I* am primarily responsible for the message I ultimately constructed.

This point helps explain another aspect of the uniqueness of human beings that we talked about in Chapter 1. Each of us constructs slightly —or greatly—different messages, because each of us is exposed to different bits and pieces of information in different contexts. Even if we are in similar general environments, each of us will pick up different bits and pieces; even if we see some of the same things, we will interpret them differently. The messages we construct about an event, person, or object are a result of our experiences in complex, dynamic, interdependent, and ongoing communication contexts.

CONCLUDING THOUGHTS

The purpose of this chapter was to help you understand how the process of your communicating "works." We said that there are at least five interrelated characteristics of every communication experience:

1.   *Human communication is contextual,* that is, your behavior toward the other person and your interpretation of his/or her words, actions, etc., will be affected by the surrounding contextual variables— location, time, temperature, furniture, dress, architecture, lighting, other persons present, etc.

2.   *Contexts are made up of verbal and nonverbal variables.* We explained that nonverbal cues are a part of every context; you can never use words (written or spoken) without some kind of nonverbal accompaniment. Verbal communication can be used to perform an action, evoke emotion, reduce uncertainty, and unify people; our language also affects the way we perceive things. Nonverbal cues can define and affect our relationships with other people, express emotions, and affect the impact of verbal cues.

3.   *Contextual variables are continually changing.* Although there is some stability and predictability in all of our lives, people and the environment around them do not remain static. When we're open to, and accepting of, the changing nature of people, we're more likely to treat them as humans rather than as objects.

4. _Contextual variables are interdependent._ As you communicate with me, I am affected by your verbal and nonverbal behavior; simultaneously, you are affected by my verbal and nonverbal behavior. Both of us are affected by the environment around us.

5. _Communication occurs continuously and dynamically across interdependent contexts._ Our communication is ongoing, nonstopping. We're continually making nonverbal cues available to others, and we're continually perceiving verbal and nonverbal cues made available to us. As time progresses, our communication experiences multiply, and each context in the here-and-now is influenced by our memory of past contexts and our expectations about future contexts.

EXERCISES

Individual Application: Television

You might try identifying the five characteristics of communication in an excerpt from your favorite television program. A situation comedy or detective story will probably work best. Arrange to have a program videotaped by the school media center if you can. If not, just pick a short (five-minute) segment from a program and identify:

1. as many of the verbal and nonverbal cues as you can
2. major changes the objects and persons go through (including yourself)
3. the ways the contextual variables are interdependent
4. the way the communicating illustrates the interdependence of contexts.

Individual Application: Marriage

On a sheet of paper, write down your beliefs or images of _marriage._ Then, as best you can, try to recall the people, personal experiences, etc., from which you constructed those beliefs or images. Parents? Textbooks? Steady date? Television shows? Friends? Where did you first hear about marriage? How much did you learn by observing the nonverbal behavior of your parents? How did you learn the _most_ important thing you know about marriage? Where does your _most recent_ belief about marriage come from?

Compare your responses to these questions with someone else's. What do you think will happen when you communicate with that person about marriage?

Group Application: Personal Space

Here's a way to find out how you respond to different distances of personal space. Break your group into dyads; ask each dyad to stand and communicate at about five to six feet. Then, after about two minutes ask the persons within each dyad to move closer to each other (about three feet). After a minute or so at this distance, move to within one to two feet. You'll probably begin to feel uncomfortable. Now move to within about six inches. For most of you, this distance is *too close*! Notice the body positions (some people will be leaning backward from the waist up; some will probably cross their arms as a protective device; at a distance of six inches, some people will feel very much like touching).

Group Application: Paralinguistics

One of the things you can do to study paralinguistics (nonverbal characteristics of the voice) is to get several recordings of radio commercials and play them for your group or class. You'll notice that many people will form impressions about the announcers' physical characteristics, personality, etc., just from the voice (pitch, tone, quality, rate, loudness).

Group Application: Physical Appearance

How does dress and overall physical appearance affect us? Ask your group to collect slides or pictures of people dressed in different ways with different hair styles, different postures, etc. Then, as you show these pictures, ask each person to write down a few impressions of the people in the pictures. When you compare impressions, you'll gain some insight into the ways in which dress and physical appearance affect our interpretations of a person's job, age, personality, intelligence, social status, economic status, etc.

Group Application: Relationship Cues

Earlier in this chapter we said that nonverbal communication defines the relationship between persons. To get a better understanding of this, try the following exercise. Break your group into dyads and ask each dyad to spend about 10–15 minutes creating a skit. The skit should suggest through the verbal and nonverbal communication (voice, gestures, facial expression, silence, touch or lack of touch, body position, etc.) what the relationship is between the two persons. For example, people in our classes have performed skits in which a "father and son are arguing," "two close friends are talking about a tragedy," "two classmates who don't know each other very well are talking about an exam," "an engaged couple is discussing marriage plans," etc. After each skit is performed, the class discusses which nonverbal cues revealed how the two people felt about each other.

Group Application: Create an Analogy

Let your imagination work on this exercise. Break into groups of three or four persons and talk about a process or event you think is similar or analogous to human communication. In other words, find an analogy that highlights the five characteristics we've discussed. Share your conclusions with the class in writing or in the form of a picture, collage, skit, slide show, role-playing, or whatever.

Is human communication most like a soccer game? A busy airport? A smoothly running engine? A dramatic play? A war? A church service? A chess tournament? A growing plant? A compost pile? A love affair? A tennis match?

For example, if you choose to write, you might talk about the similarities between human communication and a concert, in which many richly varied sources (flutes, violins, oboes, drums, a harp, etc.) are unified by a conductor (a person) into what she or he thinks is a harmonious whole, and in which many different listeners, each with his or her own individual preference, combine to create a response that is usually obvious and strong.

Or, you might be better able to capture the complex, verbal/nonverbal, changing, interdependent, contextual nature of human communication better with paint, clay, music, or film. In any case, try letting go a little and see what you can create. Can you *dance* a picture of human communication?

NOTES

1. An example borrowed from Gail E. Meyers and Michele Tolela Myers, *The Dynamics of Human Communication: A Laboratory Approach*, New York: McGraw-Hill, 1973.

2. Alvin Toffler, *Future Shock*, New York: Random House, 1970, p. 33.

3. John B. Carroll, ed., *Language Thought and Reality: Selected Writings of Benjamin Lee Whorf*, New York: Wiley, 1956, pp. 212–213.

4. Harry Hoijer, "Cultural Implications of Some Navaho Linguistic Categories," *Language*, **XXVII** (1951): 117.

5. *Ibid.*, p. 119.

6. "One Small Step for Genkind," *New York Times Magazine*, April 16, 1972.

7. Aileen Hernandez, "The Preening of America," *Star News*, Pasadena, Calif., 1971 New Year's edition, cited in Haig A. Bosmajicin, "The Language of Sexism," *ETC: A Review of General Semantics*, **XXIX** (September 1972): 307.

8. Ozzie Davis, "The English Language Is My Enemy," *Language in America,* ed. Neil Postman, Charles Weingartnen, and Terence P. Moran, New York: Pegasus, 1969, pp. 73–82.

9. Martin Buber, "The Word That Is Spoken," *The Knowledge of Man,* ed. Maurice Friedman, trans. Maurice Friedman and Ronald Gregor Smith, New York: Harper & Row, 1965, p. 112.

10. W. Griffitt, "Environmental Effects of Interpersonal Affective Behavior: Ambient Effective Temperature and Attraction," *Journal of Personality and Social Psychology,* **XV** (1970): 240–244.

11. A. H. Maslow and N. L. Mintz, "Effects of Esthetic Surroundings: I. Initial Effects of Three Esthetic Conditions Upon Perceiving 'Energy' and 'Well Being' in Faces," *Journal of Psychology,* 41 (1956): 247–254.

12. Edward Hall, *The Hidden Dimension,* Garden City, N.Y.: Doubleday, 1966, p. 115.

13. *Ibid.,* p. 114.

14. See *Ibid.,* pp. 117–125.

15. Sidney M. Jourard, "An Exploratory Study of Body-Accessiblity, "*British Journal of Social and Clinical Psychology,* V (1966): 221–231.

16. Mark Knapp, *Nonverbal Communication in Human Interaction,* New York: Holt, Rinehart and Winston, 1972, pp. 108–109. Reprinted by permission.

17. Michael G. Young, "The Human Touch: Who Needs It?" A sermon given at the Unitarian Church, Palo Alto, California, on November 28, 1965.

18. Knapp, *op. cit.,* pp. 9–12.

19. Toffler, *op. cit.,* p. 34.

20. *Ibid.,* p. 20.

21. *Ibid.,* p. 24.

22. Sam Sloan, "Office Landscape Design—A Cop-Out on the Real Issue: People," *Contract,* **XIV** (March 1973): 199.

23. Benjamin Kogan makes this explicit in *Health: Man in a Changing Environment,* New York: Harcourt, Brace Jovanovich, 1970, p. 199: Blood cells continually need to be replaced because they are buffeted about and destroyed during their extensive travels. So blood cell division continually goes on in bone marrow and lymph nodes. Surface skin cells and those of the linings of the respiratory, gastrointestinal, and urinary tracts . . . are [also] constantly replaced. It is estimated that the entire mucous lining of the gastrointestinal tract is replaced about twice a week.

24. For another discussion of this, see Myers and Myers, *op. cit.,* p. 60.

25. The idea of punctuation was borrowed from Paul Watzlawick, Janet Helmick Beavin, and Don D. Jackson, *Pragmatics of Human Communication*, New York: Norton, 1967, especially pp. 54–59 and 93–99.

26. *Ibid.*, pp. 48–51.

27. Samuel L. Becker, "Rhetorical Studies for the Contemporary World," *The Prospect of Rhetoric*, ed. Lloyd F. Bitzer and Edwin Black, Englewood Cliffs, N.J.: Prentice-Hall, 1971, p. 26. Reprinted by permission. Many of Becker's ideas are incorporated in subsequent discussion. Stage five is based primarily on Becker's conceptualization of communication.

ADDITIONAL RESOURCES

If you're interested in reading more about how human communication "works," especially about the characteristic that says "human communication occurs continuously and dynamically across interdependent contexts," take a look at Samuel Becker's article "Rhetorical Studies for the Contemporary World," *The Prospect of Rhetoric*, ed. Lloyd F. Bitzer and Edwin Black (Englewood Cliffs, N.J.: Prentice-Hall, 1971.)

Many books have been written about words, but few of them deal very directly with how verbal cues work in human communication. One exception is John Condon's *Semantics and Communication* (Toronto: Macmillan, 1966). Condon's book is a little dated now, and it omits some important points, but it does provide a good, general introduction to the subject.

Joseph DeVito's collection *Language: Concepts and Processes* (Englewood Cliffs, N.J.: Prentice-Hall, 1973) illustrates the variety of perspectives from which language scholars approach their subject. DeVito has included essays as varied as "The Origins of Speech," "The Sounds of Silence," and "Rock Tongue." DeVito also includes three essays that detail some of the sexist and racist dimensions of standard American English: "The Language of Prejudice," "The English Language Is My Enemy," and "One Small Step for Genkind."

John Searle's *Speech Acts: An Essay in the Philosophy of Language* (Cambridge, England: The University Press, 1969), and J. L. Austin's *How To Do Things with Words* (New York: Oxford University Press, 1965) are *much* more complex books, but they do an effective job of exploring the ability of words to perform actions.

Much of Martin Buber's later writing is dedicated to explaining how language creates the possibility of genuine I–Thou encounter. Buber is not easy to read either, but you can certainly learn a great deal about this topic from some of the essays in his book *The Knowledge of Man*, ed. Maurice Friedman (New York: Harper & Row, 1965), especially "Distance and Relation" and "The Word That Is Spoken."

You'll gain many insights about nonverbal communication as seen through the eyes of an anthropologist by reading two of Edward Hall's books. In *The Silent Language* (Greenwich, Conn.: Fawcett, 1959), Hall talks about how our culture communicates nonverbally and how people from other cultures use and interpret nonverbal cues. Hall's later book, *The Hidden Dimension* (Garden City, New York: Doubleday, 1966), is a fascinating study of the importance of "personal space" in our environment.

Mark Knapp wrote one of the most comprehensive books on nonverbal communication: *Nonverbal Communication in Human Communication* (New York: Holt, Rinehart and Winston, 1972), and his book covers just about every category of nonverbal cues—from architecture and space to the color, smell, and hair on our bodies. His discussions are informed by quite a bit of experimental research. He'll also give you a slightly different treatment of the "functions" of nonverbal communication that we gave you.

According to responses from readers, Michael Young's essay "The Human Touch: Who Needs It?" is one of the most well-received parts of my (John) book *Bridges Not Walls: A Book About Interpersonal Communication* (Reading, Mass.: Addison-Wesley, 1973). In a very human and readable way, Mike makes a good case for encouraging more touch in human communication.

The book that got me (Gary) interested in nonverbal communication was Dean Barnlund's *Interpersonal Communication: Survey and Studies* (Boston: Houghton Mifflin, 1968). Barnlund's introduction to nonverbal communication on pp. 511–536 is one of the best overviews I've read.

3

Personal Perceiving

We said in Chapter 2 that you're continually perceiving verbal and nonverbal communication cues from many different sources across interdependent contexts or situations. You're reading books, talking with friends, looking at billboards, reading newspapers, reading and writing letters, listening to speakers, watching television, meeting with an instructor or supervisor, and so on. Since in each of those situations there are too many cues for you to see, hear, smell, taste, and touch, you pay attention to only a relatively small number of cues, depending on how familiar they are to you, your sensory capabilities, how alert you are, and so on. Another thing you'll find yourself doing in every context is *constructing* images of people, objects, and events from the bits and pieces of cues you pick up.

In this chapter we want to clarify the process of constructing images, that is, to explain in more detail how you are continually selecting, organizing, and going beyond the raw data you perceive. Then we want to explore the effect that your construction and interpretation processes have on your communicating. We've become convinced that your ability to communicate interpersonally will be increased when you understand more specifically the subjectiveness of all perception and when you see how you might improve your ability to perceive "aspects of the other's humanness." Consequently, we want to make five points in this chapter: (1) the cues you pick up are in raw data form; that is, they don't contain "messages" or "images" in themselves; (2) you don't behave in response to the raw data, but rather to your *interpretation* of it; (3) your interpretation involves selecting, organizing, and going beyond raw cues; (4) your interpretation is affected by a number of things, including your physiological limitations, expectations, attitudes, beliefs, interests, emotions, needs, and language; (5) you can interpret in ways that promote interpersonal communication by being actively available physically and psychologically to the person you're communicating with.

RAW CUES

When we communicate, you and I are usually unaware of the differences between *raw cues* and our *interpretations* of those cues. We tend to believe that everything *we* perceive is an exact replica of the "real world" and that anyone who doesn't see it that way is mistaken or guilty of distorting things. Becoming a better communicator starts with the realization that our perceptual processes are personally biased, that we construct our own reality from the cues we attend to, and that different people experiencing the very same cues usually interpret them differently.

Communicators pick up raw cues through their five senses—sight, hearing, touch, smell, and taste. Here, we'll be discussing the raw cues perceived by primarily the auditory and visual sense mechanisms. Keep in mind, though, that your sensory system is not limited to hearing and seeing. Your tactile (touch) system picks up the sensations of textures, temperatures, and shapes as they come in contact with your skin. It's primarily through your tactile system that you decide whether a surface is soft, hard, round, cornered, warm, cold, smooth, rough, wet, dry, slippery, silky, or whatever. And touch can be a very important part of communication. In addition, your sense of smell picks up odor-producing chemicals in the air, and they also significantly affect interpersonal relationships—just think of our culture's concern with air fresheners, herbal-scented shampoos, bad breath, and underarm odor. But for now, we want to help you understand that particularly with respect to your eyes and ears, the data your sensory systems pick up in the form of raw cues don't reach you in any "pure" form, but are changed in the process of perception itself.

Auditory Cues

The raw cues picked up by your hearing mechanism are in the form of sound waves. Both human and nonhuman sources generate these sound waves. In spoken communication, voices produce most of the sounds, although nervous shuffling of feet, position changes in a squeaky chair, sighs, snorts, sniffs, clapping, etc., are also possible sources of sound. When the woman you're talking with is speaking, her voice is producing sound in several ways. She gets the urge to speak; she inhales; and as she begins to speak, air passes from her lungs through the trachea and over vocal folds located in her larynx. As the air passes across these vocal folds, they begin to vibrate, setting up wavelike patterns of slightly varied high and low air pressure. These waves move through the air so that her voice produces

> very rapid oscillations of air pressure close to your ears. . . . Their frequency varies between 50 and 10,000 a second. If you are near enough, the pressure changes reach your ears by direct transmission through the air. . . .

The changes of air pressure in the neighborhood of your ears are very small. But, if you are to hear them, they must be great enough to make a slight vibration in your eardrums, the delicate membrane at the end of the tube which goes in from the external ear. The drum is linked mechanically to the much smaller "basilar membrane" in the inner ear, immersed in fluid and covered with nerve cells which are connected with the brain. So you hear a sound because the oscillations make your basilar membrane vibrate and the nerve cells on them signal the movement to your brain.[1]

The raw cues picked up by your ears, then, are in the form of sound waves, or compressions of air molecules. Note that we haven't yet said anything about the meaning or interpretation of those cues. That's part of our point here. The raw data picked up by your hearing mechanism are nothing but minute changes in air pressure, and you *interpret* these sound waves as you receive them.

Visual Cues

The raw cues that impinge on your visual system are light waves or particles. Light waves enter your eyes through the almost perfectly transparent cornea and pass through the variable-sized opening of your pupil. Your eye's lens focuses these light waves on to the retina, a sheet of nerve cells lining the back of your eyeball. The retina is an extension of the optic nerve leading to the brain and is made up of specialized visual receptor cells called rods and cones. The ten layers of these cells convert light rays into nerve impulses in much the same way that an "electric eye" or photoelectric cell converts light to electricity. As E.H. Adrian summarizes:

> You see an object because your eyes have lenses which focus its image on the sheet of nerve cells at the back of the eyeball, the retina. The cells there signal the pattern of light and shade to the brain, as the cells of the basilar membrane signal the pattern of sound.[2]

Even this brief overview of the auditory and visual sensing processes almost forces us to recognize how little we respond to raw cues and how much of our behavior is in response to our *interpretations* of those cues. After all, if your voice can send and your ear can perceive only sound waves, then it's useless to talk seriously about communicators exchanging "feelings," "ideas," or "images." You cannot send a feeling, an idea, or an image out of your mouth. You create sound waves with certain characteristics, and it's the receiver of those sounds who interprets them and converts them into some kind of meaningful message.

When you communicate, you're continually interpreting the raw cues that you see, hear, touch, smell, and taste, and generally speaking, it's a good thing that you are. Your communication would make little sense if you were forced to deal only with raw cues. For example, look at the picture below. If someone asked you, "What do you see in the picture?" it would be almost impossible for you to respond by describing

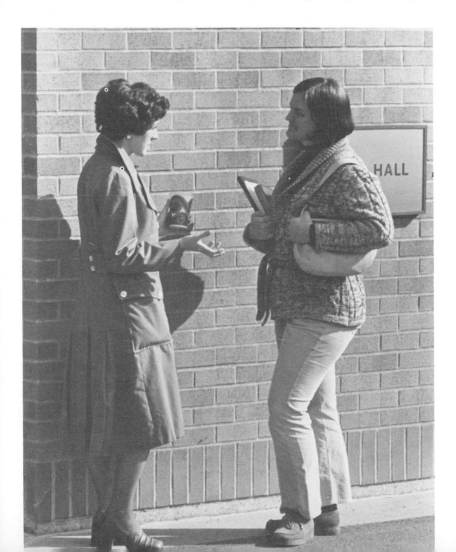

just the raw cues, because we really don't have words for raw senses. You'd have to say something like this:

> There is a vertical, flat plane, which is regularly divided into numerous rectangles by staggered vertical and horizontal gray lines. Two fundamentally spherical, unevenly shaded shapes top two apparently plastic, generally vertical rectangular objects with shallowly parabolic interior sides. A short, horizontal plastic protrusion extends at the approximate midpoint of the right side of the left rectangle. The lower approximate half of the right rectangle is lighter in shade and is divided by two prominent verticals, a shorter central straight one, and a longer one to the left, which angles at its midpoint approximately 45° right . . . . and so on . . . .

The person who asked the question would probably think you were out of your mind.

If you abandoned that effort but still tried to describe what you "actually saw," with as little interpretation as possible, you'd still have problems. You might say something like this:

> There are two females standing in front of the corner of a brick wall. The female on the left has her right arm lifted at a right angle to her body. Her mouth is partly open. She is holding in her left hand an object that is approximately eight inches tall and three or four inches wide; it seems to be a container of some type. The other female is standing facing the first female with her mouth closed . . . etc.

Your listeners would still wonder about you.

On the other hand, you might respond something like this:

> There are two women, possibly classmates on a college campus, conversing against the corner of a brick wall. One woman is holding a coke or milkshake in her left hand and is gesturing with her right hand. The other woman (on the right) is standing listening and is holding her books; she has a purse hanging from her shoulder . . . etc.

Such a description would obviously seem to make more sense; at least it presents a more *understandable* image of what you've described. The image is based on interpretation and may be inaccurate—for example, we don't know for sure whether they're classmates, what she's drinking, whether she's actually gesturing, whether she's actually talking, etc. But we think you can understand from this illustration that most of our communicating takes place at this level. Even though our eyes pick up only light waves, our ears pick up only sound vibrations, our nose picks up only odors, and so on, we don't communicate at that level. We go beyond the raw cues and try to make sense out of what we observe. Then we communicate with those *interpretations*. And it is the interpretations that can create problems in our communicating.

YOU INTERPRET RAW CUES

The process of interpreting raw cues is basically one of making sense out of sensory experiences. In other words, you translate raw data into recognizable form, into something you can understand, something that is meaningful to you in a given context. That means that you don't communicate about some abstract "reality," but about *your* meanings or interpretations.

We don't mean to suggest by this that the only "real" world is what's in your head. It's just too difficult to deny that right now I (John) am holding in my hand a real object—a pencil—and you probably are, too—a book. We agree with the common-sense conclusions that there is something "outside your skin," whether you call it raw cues, stimuli, or energy impinging on your sensory systems. But you can't know this external reality except through your own perceptual processes, and there is never a perfect, one-to-one correspondence between external reality and your perception of it. Neil Postman and Charles Weingartner say it this way:

> This does *not* mean that there is nothing outside of our skins. It does mean that whatever is "out there" can never be known except as it is filtered through a human nervous system. We can never get outside of our own skins. "Reality" is a perception, located somewhere behind the eyes.[3]

Your reality depends not only on what's outside your skin, but also on how what's inside your skin interprets what's outside your skin.

Note that in the Doonesbury cartoon on p. 82, one of the characters has his own personal interpretation of the people of China; he also believes that his interpretation *is* "reality." To say the same thing

COPYRIGHT/1972, G.B. TRUDEAU/DISTRIBUTED BY UNIVERSAL PRESS SYNDICATE.

another way, perception is an *active*, not a passive, process. Each of us actively participates in the interpretation of our experiences. If we took the position that you are a passive organism, one that just soaks up communication cues, we'd be assuming that you have no choice in deciding how to interpret raw data and that by some miraculous happening, raw cues impose "images," or "meaning," upon you. When we say that interpreting is an active process, we are saying that the process is, to a considerable extent, self-initiated and voluntary. You are *not* forced to interpret raw cues in a certain way; you have considerable control over your perceptual processes.

To say that interpreting cues is an active and creative process is not to say that your interpretations are unpredictable. It might be easy for us to predict your response on some occasions—provided we know something about you and the situation. For example, we'd predict that if you were about to order a meal in a restaurant, you'd respond much more favorably if the menu read[4]

> Filet Mignon....$7.95
> All deserts topped with delicious whipped cream
> Soup: Home Cooked Chunky Beef

than if it read

> Piece of Dead Cow....$7.95
> All deserts covered with chemically composed
> artificial topping
> Soup: Boiled in our kitchen and containing salt,
> water, beef stock, beef fat, dehydrated onions,
> yeast extract, caramel color, and spices.

This does not mean that you played no active part in that particular interpretation; it simply means that in a given context and with sufficient information, we might know in advance roughly what your interpretation would be. But since what's inside your skin is unique, different from what's inside all other human beings, your reality is also unique. Personal. *Yours.*

We've learned that understanding our subjectivity is important to communicating interpersonally. *If you believe that your interpretations are exact representations of reality, you're not likely to promote interpersonal communication.* You need instead to recognize that as you interpret, you select, organize, and go beyond the raw cues you observe.

You Select

In some situations cues can be forced on people. Sometimes, we don't seem to have a choice about whether or not to select certain cues—for example, an explosion, a siren, a sudden bright light, a scream, or a sharp pain. But the vast majority of the time, we are voluntarily selecting the cues we perceive.

When we said in Chapter 2 that "communication is contextual," we did not mean to suggest that the context imposes itself on you and indicates your communication behavior. A context is defined by the person who is perceiving the cues within a given situation. Each person defines the context for herself or himself. The context *you* experience depends on how you interpret raw cues, and selection is an important part of that interpretation process. In the office of a boss or professor, you might focus your attention on the large, solid walnut desk between you and the other person and on the fact that her or his chair is higher than yours. You might interpret those cues as putting you in an inferior position. Another observer might interpret the same office as a very comfortable context, focusing attention on the professor's friendly facial expressions and informal, conversational manner.

Within any context, there are always so many cues that we cannot possibly be aware of all of them. And so, out of the multitude of cues available, we make choices about which ones to focus our attention on. Magdalen D. Vernon explains it this way:

> We tend to think that our ability to perceive what lies in front of us is so great that we can see the whole of it at a glance. Nevertheless, it often happens that we fail to perceive events taking place within the field of view; and if they are subsequently brought to our notice, we then say that we overlooked them because we were not attending. In fact, at any one moment we may perceive and be fully aware of only a small selection of the objects and events in the world around us. Some we may overlook altogether; others we may be aware of very dimly.[5]

Think for a minute about your own selection processes; try to remember which cues you selected and interpreted from the picture on p. 79. Did you notice that the coat collar on the woman at the left is turned up? Did you notice the position of the feet? That the woman on the left is wearing an earring? That they're wearing different styles of shoes? That neither woman's head casts a distinguishable shadow on the brick wall? Or did you select other cues? Notice our descriptions of the picture. We emphasized certain characteristics over others. Did we select the same ones that you did? The point we want to make is that all those cues are "really there," but that we selectively perceive only those that are required for the picture to make sense to us in this particular context.

In short, one aspect of interpretation is *selection*. Since you can focus only on a limited number of cues, you can never be aware of everything that's going on while you're communicating. You perceive selectively—as do all of the other persons you're communicating with.

You Organize

Another way you actively participate in interpreting raw cues is by organizing the cues you select. You literally cannot help but structure your world of sensations. In the first place, your sense organs cannot effectively pick up information that is completely unstructured. Researchers have found, for example, that continuous motion of your eyeballs is necessary for visual perception. As John Platt explains:

> The motions are too tiny and fast to be seen by the unaided eye. Their amplitudes are only about one minute of arc and their frequencies are in the range of from 50 to 150 cycles per second. Nevertheless, if they are compensated by optical or electronic devices so that the image is exactly stabilized on the retina, *vision disappears within a fraction of a second.*[6]

The same is true of your other senses. A steady, unchanging sound is difficult to perceive and may even become unnoticeable. When you explore the hardness and texture of a surface, you'll not only put your fingers on the surface, but will also move them back and forth, "for if the finger remained motionless, no useful information could be gained, except perhaps a sensation of temperature, which again would be due to the relative difference between the temperatures of object and finger."[7]

In other words, your senses perceive not static "things," but *relationships*—relationships between light and dark, loud and soft, high and low, and so on. Every relationship, by definition, implies some kind of structure or order—one part is warm compared to the other and the other is cool compared to the first, one part is hard compared to another and the other is soft compared to the first, etc. Even your senses are constantly helping organize your world.

Your thought processes add much more complicated systems of organization. The whole configuration of smells, sounds, sights, or whatever you are perceiving at any given instant is usually called a gestalt, or a pattern, a structured chunk of perceptions. The pattern of each gestalt is organized into what is usually called "figure" and "ground." When you interpret raw cues, you structure them into "figure," or central focus, and "ground," or surrounding context. As two psychologists explain:

> The figure-ground relationship is an important concept, because it colors our perceptions. We never really just see the tree. We bring to the perception our whole mental set and emotional context. So, in truth, we are seeing a whole pattern of things, all in relationship. We can't say we're just looking at the moon, for example. We also see the sky behind it (which is just as much a part of the entire picture as is the moon) . . . . [8]

Individual Application: Structuring Cues

Try to imagine a completely unstructured image or a totally disorganized group of sounds. (The word "group" makes that difficult.) Or better yet, stop reading for a minute and try to see the marks on this page without any structure, or the room you're in, or the scene outside your window. It just can't be done. As you perceive, you *select* from the myriad of raw cues available, and you also organize those cues you select into meaningful configurations.

You Go Beyond

Your active interpretation of raw cues involves one more step: your *selection* and *organization* enables you to *go beyond* the cues, that is, to think of something completely other than the cues themselves. You're doing that right now. When you perceive

[--bathtub--]

you select from the available visual cues within those brackets, organize them into figure (black) and ground (white) and into a word. In addition, you may go beyond the word by thinking and feeling about a room, a series of objects, e.g., soap, towel, etc., or even a whole set of experiences that are something completely other than the selected and organized visual cues themselves. When you're communicating, you're perceiving in this way not only written words, but also spoken words and other *sounds, objects,* and *people.*

Sounds.   Earlier in this chapter we said that the only things our auditory system picks up are wavelike patterns of slightly varied high and low air pressure. But we don't communicate in terms of these compressions of air molecules; we go beyond them. Think for a moment about the nonhuman sounds you hear. When a siren wails, you usually go beyond the sound itself to think about the ambulance, police car, or fire engine on an emergency run. When you hear certain cries of some animals, you think of the kinds of danger they might be experiencing. When students hear a bell at the end of a class period, they usually interpret it as "the class period is over"; that is, the students go beyond the sound of vibrations produced by the bell.

You do the same kind of thing with sounds that originate in the human vocal system. The person talking makes sounds available to you that vary in pitch, loudness, quality, and rate. You select certain ones, organize them into words, and then go beyond the words to think about whatever it seems to you they appropriately suggest. For example, six phonic sounds make up the spoken words "I love you." Yet when you hear those sounds in that order in a given context, it's possible for you to go beyond them to think of a wide variety of things. You might think that the other person desires you or wants you sexually. You might think that the person wants you to love her or him or that he or she wants to be able to love you. Sometimes, you might hear those words and think that the other person is predicting that perhaps a love relationship can develop between you or even that the other person hates you. Often, those sounds can indicate a wish for emotional exchange: "I want your admiration in exchange for mine," or "I give my love in exchange for some passion," or "I want to feel cozy and at home with you," or "I admire some of your qualities." A declaration of love is often taken as a request: "I desire you" or "I want you to gratify me" or "I want your protection," or "I want to be intimate with you" or "I want to exploit your loveliness." Sometimes, those sounds lead you to think that the other person needs a security or tenderness, that the other is saying "My self-love goes out to you." In other contexts you might interpret the sounds as expressing submissiveness: "Please take me as I am," or "I feel guilty about you; I want, through you, to correct the mistakes I have made in my relationships with others." You may also interpret those sounds as self-sacrifice or as a masochistic wish for dependency. On the other hand, the sounds may lead you to think that the other person is fully affirming you and is taking responsibility for mutual exchange of feelings. As Joost Meerloo summarizes, " 'I love you,'—wish, desire, submission, conquest; it is never the [sounds of] the word itself that tells the real meaning here."[9] What we are saying and what Meerloo is saying is that you and I don't stop and think just about the sounds we hear. We interpret them, in part, by going beyond them to think of something other than the sounds themselves.

One of the reasons it's important to recognize that the receivers of sound vibrations go beyond what they hear is that usually, the way one person is thinking when he or she says something is not the same as the way the person interpreting the sounds is thinking when he or she *hears* them. For example, when Debbie was five years old, she and I (Gary) were brushing our teeth and she asked, "Daddy, what kind of toothpaste do we use?" I told her that we used Colgate and she asked, "How come we don't use *Crest*? Crust gives you cavities." At that time in her life, Debbie wanted cavities, because when she went to the dentist he gave her sugarless candy, which she thought was neat. She had seen the Crest commercial on television in which the little boy comes home, runs to his mother and says, "Mommy, Mommy, only one cavity," and the mother replies, "It must be the Crest." Debbie went beyond the cues in that commercial to think that Crest *caused* the little boy's cavity. So she wanted to use Crest, too. Debbie interpreted the commercial in her own way, and I think it's safe to say that it wasn't the way Crest's ad agency intended.

Objects.   You also go beyond the *visual* cues you pick up by selecting and organizing certain cues and from these cues "seeing" an object. Usually, you go beyond not only the raw cues to perceive a familiar object, but also the object itself. To a visitor from the East, for example, a single wire fence on a Colorado range may be just a single wire fence. Although the person may be conscious of the fence, and even of the single wire, he or she may not be led to think of anything else because of it. To a Colorado farmer or rancher, on the other hand, the single wire may mean that the fence is electric, that it is designed to enclose sheep or cattle but not horses, that the ranch he is on is relatively well equipped, etc. A person who has never played golf and who has never seen a golf course may interpret a sand trap as just a pile of sand. But anyone who plays golf and cares about her or his score goes far beyond the raw cues of a sculptured sand pile; he or she may experience frustration, try to avoid it, hope for a lower score, think about the kind of golf club required to hit a ball out of it, and so on. To us, an electric typewriter is much more than a machine; it's a way of writing faster than is possible by longhand, sometimes it requires expensive repairs, and it reminds us of the work of writing and rewriting and of time spent away from our families. To a smoker, a book of matches on a table may suggest lighting a cigarette; to a parent, the matches may be a source of danger for young children.

Of course, you don't always feel the need or have the experience or knowledge to go very far beyond the objects you perceive. Sometimes, you take the raw cues and just perceive an object—a fence, a typewriter, a pile of sand—and go no further. But whenever you need to make sense out of objects you perceive, you'll go beyond them, and the ways in which you go beyond raw cues become especially significant when you think about how you perceive *people*.

Individual Application: Interpreting Cues

1. Try to describe the picture below in *raw cues*. Then explain your interpretation by going beyond the cues themselves. For example,

   a) Raw cues: black circle approximately one inch in diameter; two black dots in upper portion of circle approximately ¼-inch apart; curved black semicircle line in lower portion of circle.

   b) Interpretation: "Happy face, probably sketched by an artist."

2. Now you try it with this picture: (If you plan to resell this book, it'd be better to respond to these questions, and to others we'll ask, on a separate piece of paper.)

a) Raw cues:

_____

_____

_____

_____

b) Interpretations:

_____

_____

_____

People.   If you're going to communicate interpersonally, we think it's important to remember that you and I tend to go beyond our raw perceptions of *people* in a couple of special ways which are significantly different from the way in which we interpret the raw cues we identify as *objects. The reason we think this process is important is that it's how we arrive at the images that take part in the negotiation of selves we talk about in Chapter 4.*

Generally, when we perceive *people* we're including in our interpretation conclusions about their motives, attitudes, values, feelings, personality traits, and so on, none of which is directly observable. We almost never perceive *objects* that way. We perceive most persons, unlike objects, to be capable of choice, self-initiating, and "as having plans, hopes, fears, and all the other experiences that we all experience as persons."[10] In other words, as we construct images of another person, we go beyond what we observe "outside the other's skin" and *infer* things that are "inside that person's skin." More specifically, we go beyond raw *people* cues in two ways that are explained by Albert Hastorf, David Schneider, and Judith Polefka:

> . . . first we perceive them as *causal agents*. They are potential causes of their behavior. They may intend to do certain things, such as attempting to cause certain effects; and because we see them as one source of their actions, we consider them capable of varying their behavior to achieve their intended effects. . . . Our percep-

tion of others' intentionality leads us next to organize the behavior of other people into intent-act-effect segments which form perceptual units. We infer the intentions of another; but we go further. If we perceive a particular intent on several occasions, we are prone to perceive the other has having an enduring personality characteristic. . . .

Second, we perceive other people as *similar to ourselves.* Hence we are pushed to infer that they possess attributes which, unlike size and behavior, we cannot observe directly but which we are aware of in ourselves. In particular, we perceive others to possess emotional states; we see them as feeling angry, happy, or sad.[11]

The cues we pick up and use to form images of intent, emotional states, and similarity to ourselves vary among individuals and contexts. Sometimes, we might pay special attention to the other person's dress, voice, posture, or general appearance. Other times, we might focus on his or her grammar, dialect, choice of words, gestures, facial expressions, or eye movements. Some research evidence suggests that when very little other information is available to us, we construct images of people on the basis of nonverbal vocal cues. According to Jessie Delia, "When a dialect is clearly discernible, an individual will reply on it as an initial source of information as he [she] attempts 'sociologically' to place the other."[12] In other words, we may go beyond a person's vocal cues and draw conclusions about her or his attitudes and values, socioeconomic status, and whether or not we would enjoy communicating with the person. We also use other cues. If you have time, look at the March 1972 issue of *Psychology Today.* In the article "Beauty and the Best" the authors suggest that there may be a relationship between our perception of how ('attractive') someone is and our predictions about that person's personality and behavior.[13]

In short, we think it's important to emphasize three things about going beyond raw people cues. First, this process is quick and almost automatic; sometimes, you're not even aware that you're doing it. But you almost always are; you hardly ever stop with just the cues that are "given." Second, when you go beyond, you almost always *assume* and *infer* characteristics; that is, when you come to conclusions about a person's attitudes, values, beliefs, motives, personality traits, and so on, you're dealing with things that aren't directly observable, and therefore you can only assume that they exist; you can't know for sure. Third, your definition or image of another person is determined to a large extent by how you go beyond the cues they make available.

It almost goes without saying that this interpretation process can create communication problems. Sometimes, we interpret a person's cues *carelessly*—we select only a few of the available cues, make questionable assumptions about those cues, and create an artificial definition of that person. That kind of careless interpretation is usually called *cue generalization* or *stereotyping*, and it definitely works against interpersonal communication. The reason is obvious: as we said in Chapter 1, each person is different from all other persons. But cue generalization is our tendency to see certain people as homogeneous, as alike. My (John) first year at the University of Washington (1969), I was assigned to a course I'd never taught before. My insecurity about the class was heightened on the first day when a guy walked in with shoulder-length hair, wire-rim glasses, wearing railroad overalls, an old-fashioned button-collar shirt without a collar, and sandals, and carrying his books in an old, leather doctor's bag. I *assumed* that he would be nothing but trouble. He was obviously a hippie freak and would probably come to class high at least half the time and be either condescendingly apathetic or openly hostile—just like all other hippies. It took me awhile to reduce my defensiveness to the point where I could change my stereotype of Antoine, but when I did, I discovered that not only was he an energetic, interested, creative student, but also that he and I shared many basic values.

You've probably made the same kind of error based on careless interpretation of person cues. We've found we have to keep avoiding it, because unless we're continually trying to select, organize, and go beyond cues that differentiate humans from one another, unless we're trying to see the *uniqueness* rather than the similarities of people, we're generalizing cues and not promoting interpersonal communication.

Individual Application: Inferences

Take some time now and write a description of someone you know (friend, classmate, teacher, etc.). Describe her or his attitudes, values, beliefs, goals, personality traits, etc. As you identify each characteristic of the person, list the cues from which you've inferred the characteristic.

(If you plan to resell this book, it would probably be a good idea to do this on a separate piece of paper. The same goes for other individual and group applications in later chapters.)

Inferred trait	Observed cues that led to this interpretation
1. Extremely impatient	I was 10 minutes late for a date; she left before I got there; constantly plays with objects in hands. She once knocked the phone on the floor when parents didn't call her at exactly the scheduled time.
2. _____	_____
3. _____	_____
4. _____	_____
5. _____	_____

SOME FACTORS THAT INFLUENCE YOUR INTERPRETATION

Since interpretation plays such an important role in interpersonal communication, we think it would be useful for you to understand not only the process of interpreting—selecting, organizing, and going beyond—but also some factors which affect how you interpret the raw cues you perceive. But before we go on, remember what we said in Chapter 2 about interdependence: whenever people are communicating, many things are happening all at once, and those things are capable of influencing one another simultaneously. Therefore, we can't specify the single factor which influences your interpretation the most; there may be two, three, or more interdependent factors working simultaneously. But we can explain a few of the different possibilities, and from these explanations, hopefully, you'll get a better understanding of why your interpretations are personally biased.

Physiological Limitations

It's pretty obvious that your interpretation is affected by the physiological limitations of your sensory systems. Few people have perfect hearing, perfect eyesight, or a bloodhound's sense of smell. You'll miss some cues just because your sensory systems are incapable of picking them up—because they are too subtle, too complex, or because they're made available too rapidly. David Mortensen[14] explains it this way:

> There is a clear and definite limit to the amount of information which the human organism can identify accurately; in recognizing a series of numbers, for example, the span of absolute judgment lies somewhere in the neighborhood of seven items of information . . . . For more difficult types of material, there is evidence that [a person] is able to monitor five features simultaneously, but rarely more . . . . Generally, even slight increases in the difficulty of material or the rate of presentation can adversely affect the capacity of the receiving system.*

Location

Your interpretation of words, objects, and persons will also be controlled to some extent by your physical location. Location affects what cues are available to you and the angle at which you perceive them. When you're face to face with someone, the cues available are different from those available if you're sitting side by side. Consequently, you're more likely to pick up verbal and facial cues from people sitting opposite you in a group than from people sitting next to you—unless, of course, you shift body position so that you're looking at them. If you sit in the back row of a large lecture hall, the cues available are different from those available if you sit in the middle or in the front row. For one thing, it's easier to become psychologically detached when you're a considerable distance from the primary source of personal cues. For another, you can't really pick up detailed facial and gestural cues from a distance. The auditory sensations will also be different; in the front row you may hear

---

*From *Communication: The Study of Human Interaction* by C. David Mortensen. Copyright 1972 by McGraw-Hill Book Company. Used with permission by McGraw-Hill Book Company.

the speaker's voice directly without microphone and loudspeaker distortions; in the back row, you won't. Similarly, if you're standing six or eight inches from someone, you're more likely to pick up cues of skin texture, body temperature, subtle eye movements, smell, and touch, whereas if you're ten to fifteen feet away you'll most likely notice only the more general physical image of the person.

Interests, Emotions, and Needs

Some factors affecting your interpretation are more complex than physiology and location. When you interpret verbal and nonverbal cues made available by others—their words, facial expressions, touch, gestures, posture, dress, where they sit or stand, tone of voice, and so on—your selection, organization, and going beyond may be influenced by whatever interests, emotions, and needs you have at the time. A person who makes his or her own clothes probably notices the clothes that other people wear more often than does someone who isn't really interested in clothing. A person who has had surgery is probably more attuned to news items and conversations about surgery than is someone who has never been in the hospital. You don't pay much attention to a commercial that advertises cake mixes if your needs at that time don't relate to baking, food, grocery shopping, etc. On the other hand, if you're hungry and you like pastries, your perception of the commercial will change.

When communicating with another person, you may feel the need for the kind of personal support that can be suggested by touching—a pat on the shoulder, handshake, hug, arm around your waist—and your selection of cues may focus on whether or not these things happen. If you're interested in or feel the need for support, you are just as likely to notice its absence as its presence. Of course, if you *want* supportive behavior strongly enough, you may perceive it even when it isn't intended by the other person:

> There are circumstances . . . in which people spontaneously perceive certain things or certain aspects of the field of view particularly readily. If they have strong feelings about what is shown them or if they desire to perceive or to avoid perceiving something, then no only is the speed of perceiving altered; they may even think they perceive what is not actually there—or if they don't want to see it, they may fail to do so when it is, as we say, staring them in the face.[15]

A good example of this is when someone wants very much to be liked by you. This person may continually look for cues that indicate your positive feelings, and even if you don't really intend to make positive cues available, the person may interpret whatever you say or do as "friendly," "supportive," or "affectionate." You might even try to communicate that you don't want to be close friends, but the person may ignore those negative cues or interpret them to mean something else.

In short, because of your interests, emotions, and needs, you may focus your perception on certain cues while ignoring others. Also, you may distort your interpretation of cues because of a strong desire to perceive them in a certain way. The stronger your interests and desires, the more likely this is to happen.

The problem this creates for interpersonal communication is this: if you're allowing only your immediate interests, emotions, and needs to "control" your perception, you'll probably miss important cues that other persons make available to you about *their* humanness.

Attitudes and Beliefs

Through experience, each of us develops many different attitudes and beliefs, all of which vary in how strongly we feel them, how important they are to us, and how extreme they are relative to the people around us. In any given context, however, not all of your attitudes and beliefs will affect your perception. For example, your opinions of Girl Scouts probably won't affect your interpretation of cues when you're talking with a friend about car expenses. The attitudes and beliefs most likely to affect your interpretations are those that are most *important to you* and those that you think are most *relevant* at the time.

Sometimes important and/or relevant attitudes and beliefs lead you to decide to attend to certain cues and to ignore others. People who strongly believe in the legalization of marijuana tend to read material that supports legalization; those who are definitely against it usually avoid that information. Similarly, people who profess Christian principles are more likely to listen to a religious radio program than are those who do not hold such views. There's a great deal of research support for the proposition that people tend to avoid information which is inconsistent with their attitudes and beliefs and that they tend to seek out information which is consistent with them. Finally, attitudes and beliefs also affect memory; that is, you're more likely to remember "facts" and "arguments" that support your position than those that contradict it.

Expectations

In most communication contexts, people *expect* certain things to happen. We develop expectations about how we will behave, how others will behave, and about how the event itself will turn out. The expectations you have about a communication encounter can be as powerful a force as your interests, desires, attitudes, or beliefs. Imagine an insecure door-to-door salesperson who is about to approach a house. He thinks in advance about all the negative things that he will see and hear as soon as he explains that he's selling vacuum cleaners. He remembers that he hasn't sold a machine in over a month, and he's become convinced that he isn't cut out to be a salesperson. He knocks, and when someone opens the door, before he can say anything, the salesperson shouts, "I didn't want to sell you anything anyway!" The story is exaggerated, but it illustrates an important point—the salesperson *decided in advance* what would happen, and there was almost nothing the homeowner could say or do to change the event he expected.

Sometimes, you develop expectations well before you meet the person face to face. In other situations, they may develop immediately before or during the face-to-face exchange. In any case, your expectations can influence your perception in at least three ways: (1) you *focus your selection* on cues you expect to perceive; (2) you *interpret* raw cues to meet your expectations; and (3) you *behave* in ways that elicit or provoke the behavior you expect from other people.

Frequently, we predict in advance the cues that will be available to us in a certain situation, and then when we're in that situation we tend to look for just those cues. For example, "if you expect a person to act unfriendly, you will be sensitive to anything that can be perceived as rejection and unfriendliness."[16] If you expect a friend to behave immaturely at a social event, you'll be more sensitive to those behaviors which you can most readily interpret as "immature." You may, in fact, ignore behavior that could be interpreted as "mature." As Mortensen says:

> If we expect an event to be dull and uninteresting, it is not likely to be otherwise. The congenial manner of others present, their feelings of excitement and personal involvement will go unnoticed—or even be distorted—if we approach the situation with mistrust.[17]

In some other situations, the cues we expect to find are not there to be selected, so we interpret the cues that are available to meet our expectations. Consider a situation in which a man expects the woman he's with to flirt with other men at a party. He never really sees any "direct" evidence of flirting, but he interprets her every glance and every friendly gesture as "flirting" behavior. In a course I (Gary) taught last year, a student developed the expectation that I wouldn't like her. One day in class she answered a question and although I acknowledged her non-verbally, I didn't *say* anything in response to her answer. After class she rushed into my office and demanded, "Why don't you like me?" When I asked her why she felt that I didn't like her, she explained that she ex-pected me not to like her, and when I didn't respond verbally to her in class, she interpreted that as confirming her expectation. We both real-ized after talking about it that even though I had no negative feelings toward her at all, my behavior could easily be interpreted to mean that I disliked her—especially since that's what she was predicting.

Your expectations can even get to the point where you actually be-have in ways that elicit or provoke the responses you expect from other people. For example, you may expect that a certain person won't have much to say to you. As a result, you might maintain long periods of silence, which give the other person very little to talk about, or you may ask questions that are virtually unanswerable. You might then interpret the other's silence as evidence of your expectation.

In short, if a person believes that everyone is against her or him and because of this hostile belief expects hostile behavior from others, this person is likely to get it. She or he might do several things: select available cues that can be easily interpreted as hostile behavior, select cues that aren't intended to be hostile and interpret them that way, or simply behave in ways that evoke the hostile response expected.

Language

Your interpretation of raw cues is also affected by your language. As we said in Chapter 2, the structure and content of standard American English affects its speakers' perception of objects, of complex processes like human communication, and of persons—women, men, and ethnic groups. As Benjamin Whorf put it, "we dissect nature along lines laid down by our native language."[18]

It would be hard to overestimate the effect of language on interpre-tation. We can make sense out of the "booming and buzzing confusion" that we perceive, and of our own ever-changing selves, only by using language units—words, phrases, sentences, etc.—to relate otherwise unrelated experiences. Language, in other words, is the tool we use to get the continuously interdependently changing world to "hold still," or to at least "keep moving in ways that make sense."

Psychology Today ran a pair of articles designed to sensitize its readers to the effect of the English language on perception of black and white persons. In an article called "If White Means Good, Then Black . . . ," (July 1973), John Williams and John Stabler showed that the colors white and black have positive and negative meanings, respectively, and that these meanings influence our racial attitudes.[19] Eight months later the article "Reversing the Bigotry of Language" listed "black positives" and "white negatives" contributed by readers responding to the Williams–Stabler article. Readers suggested that standard American English might appear to be less bigoted if we remember that black negatives are balanced by such positive terms as Black Beauty, black belt (karate), black gold (oil), black tie, black soil, and black pearls, and that white positives are balanced by such white negatives as white trash, white belt (karate), white flag, white elephant, white slave (prostitute), and lily-livered.[20] *Psychology Today* editors agreed with one reader who commented that "the inequity of the black vs. white usage and connotations did not hit me fully until I tried this exercise myself." And that's part of the problem. Our language is so close to us that we are often unaware of how much it's affecting our interpretations of objects *and* persons.

SO WHAT ABOUT ALL THIS?

It might seem from what we've said about the subjectivity of perception that communication is impossible. After all, if I interpret things differently from the way you interpret them, how can we ever get together on anything? If the expectations, needs, attitudes, and beliefs that affect my interpretations are different from yours—as they almost always are—how can we understand each other?

Availability

The answer is fairly obvious, but difficult to put into practice. None of us can communicate perfectly, but we can move toward mutual understanding by making ourselves *available* to the person with whom we're communicating— available physically, psychologically, and actively.[21]

Some type of *physical* availability is a prerequisite for any kind of communication; you can't communicate with someone you're completely out of touch with. Interpersonal communication generally requires relatively long-term, face-to-face physical presence. (That isn't always true, however. Close friends can sometimes communicate interpersonally over the phone. But usually, you need both spatial closeness and time.) Even though it's obvious, we often forget how much *time* good communication requires. Our superfast, overcommitted life-styles often get in the way of interpersonal-quality communication. It takes time for even two persons to discover the different ways each interprets his or her world. And when more than two persons are involved, it takes correspondingly more time. Recently, the truth of this often overlooked point became apparent to me (John) and to the graduate students whose teaching I supervise. None of us particularly liked "staff meetings," but we recognized that our communication was deteriorating. We reluctantly agreed to meet regularly and almost immediately noticed how much difference just the time together can make. Of course, we also tried to work at communicating. Time together provides the opportunity for interpersonal communication; it doesn't guarantee it.

It can also help to be physically "closer" together. I (John) am often surprised how much more interpersonal the communication in a class can be when we just move from being scattered around the room to sitting together. Even in casual conversations, people often emphasize or reinforce their physical availability by lightly touching the people they're communicating with. Most of us feel comfortable communicating at a personal space of about 1½–3 feet. Interpersonal communication doesn't require that you be much closer than that, but for some people, the farther away you are, the more psychologically detached they feel.

Touching can also both stimulate and symbolize our *psychological* availability. A handshake, embrace, or pat on the shoulder often indicates that I'm with you—I'm feeling what you seem to be feeling. But psychological availability involves a lot more than mere physical presence. In order to be psychologically available to someone else, you need to be open to *that person's* view of the world so that *your* perceptions are affected by the way the *other individual* sees things.

That might sound kind of confusing. What we mean is that you need to be not only aware that the other person's interpretations of raw data are different from yours—he or she is an "un-you"—but also willing to interpret things, in part, like he or she does. You need to be open enough to allow your interpretations to be affected by the things that are affecting the other person's interpretations—attitudes, feelings, needs, expectations, and so on.

Carl Rogers talks about psychological availability in terms of "permitting" himself to understand another person.[22] As he says:

> Our first reaction to most of the statements which we hear from other people is an immediate evaluation, or judgment, rather than an understanding of it. When someone expresses some feeling or attitude or belief, our tendency is, almost immediately, to feel "That's right"; or "That's stupid"; "That's abnormal"; "That's unreasonable"; "That's incorrect"; "That's not nice." Very rarely do we permit ourselves to *understand* precisely what the meaning of his statement is to him.*

When you're psychologically available to another person, you're not pretending you don't have any opinions on what she or he is talking about. You may have strong commitments to your opinions, and we don't expect you to abandon them. Psychological availability doesn't require that. Instead, you're working to *postpone* your own ways of selecting, structuring, and going beyond raw cues. What you're saying, in effect, is "there are alternative ways of interpreting this topic, and I'm trying to 'hear' your alternative long enough to understand it.

For labor-management negotiations to succeed, each side has to be genuinely open to the other's ways of interpreting working conditions, the status of competing products, international, national, and local economic situations, and so on. When the employee representative chooses to be aware of (i.e., selects) only salaries in comparable plants, sees employers as the main cause of all employee difficulties (structures), and goes beyond raw cues about overtime availability to conclude that management is trying to put people out of work, she or he is not being psychologically available to the employer. Management is doing the same thing when it perceives only the rate of profit increase over last year, sees the government as heading toward complete socialization, and infers that all employee groups are out to ruin the free-enterprise system. This psychological availability is just as crucial in other kinds of "negotiations." Husband and wife, child and parent, teacher and student, salesperson and customer, preacher and parishioner—all have to be willing not only to see the other's point of view as reasonable to her or him, but also to be *available to* the other, to look, at least for a time, at the world, at least in part, through the other's eyes.

Both physical and psychological availability can be either *active* or *passive*. When you're passively available, you just allow others to share with you—you let them be close by and you are more or less willing to listen. To promote interpersonal communication, however, you need to be *actively* available. You need, in the first place, to take some of the initiative for putting yourself in the physical presence of others. That doesn't necessarily mean you should stick to them like a shadow, but you should make the effort to be available for more than the time it takes to utter a few cliché sentences. It's been estimated that many married couples actually spend less than 20 minutes a day spatially and temporally available to each other. If you're unmarried, that might sound ridiculous. But it isn't. Campfire and Boy Scout meetings, soccer and baseball games, church and PTSA gatherings, poker and bridge parties, stereo and television sets—all make it difficult for a husband and wife to find time to be more than "superficially" together. If they're going to communicate interpersonally, each is going to have to actively make time for the other.

But to be actively available psychologically, you need to do more than just be around the other person. As we'll discuss in the next three chapters, psychological availability involves both "sharing" and "being aware"—both disclosing some of your self and responding completely to the other. Both of those take much more effort than merely being physically available. Not only does it take time to see the way somebody else sees things, it also takes another kind of effort, because it's *risky*. As Rogers puts it, "If I let myself really understand another person, I might be changed by that understanding."[23] It's not easy to lower your defenses enough to develop the *tentativeness* that psychological availability requires. You need to be open to information from the other person and willing to change when it becomes evident that you have misperceived or misinterpreted. You need to be willing to ask for confirmation of your definition of the other and of your interpretation of what she or he is saying and to keep your interpretations open to change until the other person confirms them. And, as we'll talk about more in the next two chapters, that's risky, too.

Finally, there are all sorts of combinations and degrees of availability, both physical and psychological, active and passive. For instance, a prostitute might be actively available physically, but not at all psychologically available. The teacher who invites students in to discuss their grades but who never expects to change a grade as a result of the conference is physically available, but not open enough to be psychologically available. Another teacher might be so willing to be psychologically available to a student that he or she has little time to be physically available to anyone else.

The point we want to stress is this: human perception is so inherently subjective that in order for communication to work at all, you have to be available to the other persons involved. As much as possible, you should try to be *actively* available, both *physically* and *psychologically*.

CONCLUDING THOUGHTS

People often get defensive when told that they're always going beyond the cues they observe and that their process of interpretation is subjective and biased. We're so accustomed to interpreting raw cues instantaneously and automatically that we assume that what we see *is* "reality." But in an important sense, it *isn't*.

Communicating interpersonally is much easier when you accept the fact that in your own unique ways, you select, organize and go beyond raw cues; that is, you attach your own personal interpretations to the verbal and nonverbal data you observe.

If you can follow that realization by being open-minded to the interpretations other people make, you've accomplished a second important step toward interpersonal communication. When you take this second step, you're saying something like this: "Because each of us interprets from different experiences, backgrounds, attitudes, interests, and expectations, your interpretation may be as valid for you as my interpretation is for me." So although we may differ, we can still communicate interpersonally.

The third step is making a physical and psychological commitment to get actively together with the other person(s). Our experience has

taught us that steps two and three are the most difficult, expecially because of the time, mental energy, and risk that are involved. But we've
also learned that as those things happen in our communicating, good
things follow and we grow as persons.

EXERCISES

Group Application: Information Overload

Sometimes, we have real difficulty limiting the cues we select. When that
happens—when we have to attend to too many cues at one time—*information overload* occurs. We "overload" our sensory systems to the extent
that we can't make sense out of what we are attending to and we have
difficulty in remembering any of it. To illustrate information overload, try
this experiment. Ask two people whose voices do not sound alike to talk to
the group you're in about the same topic and at the same time. You'll note
that while they're talking simultaneously, it's impossible to focus on both of
them, and it is difficult to attend to either one. You can get something out of
what you hear only if you concentrate on selecting cues from just one of the
persons. Now try this same thing with two people who have similar voices;
it's much more difficult, and you might find it impossible to pick up anything meaningful. You can hear the sounds, but you can't select enough of
the cues to make sense out of what you are hearing.

Group Application: Selecting Cues

To demonstrate the limited capacity of people to perceive a great many
cues in a short period of time, try the rumor game. Ask four people to leave
the room and then read a one- or two-minute story to one of the persons
remaining. Ask this person to communicate the story as she or he remembers it to the one person you've called back into the room. Then ask the second person to communicate her or his version of the story to the next person
called in, and so on. You'll probably discover that most people can't really
handle enough information to keep the story straight, even though they're
telling it immediately after hearing it. The more complex the story and the
faster it is told to each person, the greater the distortion.

Group Application: Interpreting Cues

Break your class into small groups. Ask each group to read and discuss the
following situation and then to agree on a solution to the problem that's
posed. Try to be aware of how group members—including yourself—select,

organize, and go beyond the cues that we've provided here. Try to be *open* to different interpretations, and take time to let each person explain his or her interpretations.

After each group has arrived at a solution, you might want to try to reach consensus among the groups. Or, it might be more useful to meet as a class and discuss what went on while each group was solving the problem.

Situation: Six persons are stranded on an uninhabited island: a professor, a doctor, an internationally famous scientist, a pregnant woman, a military officer, and a young child. None of these persons wants to stay on the island, but the only available means out is a two-person airplane. The military officer knows how to fly the plane. Your task is to decide which two persons should be allowed to leave on the plane back to civilization.

Be careful about the interpretations you make. For example, do you assume that the doctor is a physician? A Ph.D.? A veterinarian? A woman? A man?

NOTES

1. E. H. Adrian, "The Human Receiving System," in *The Languages of Science*, Granada Lectures of the British Association for Advancement of Science, New York: Basic Books, 1962, pp. 100–114. Reprinted by permission.

2. *Ibid.*, p. 167. Reprinted by permission.

3. Neil Postman and Charles Weingartner, *Teaching as a Subversive Activity*, New York: Dell, 1969, p. 90.

4. An example borrowed from a former colleague of mine (Gary), Ray DeBoer.

5. Magdalen D. Vernon, "Perception, Attention, and Consciousness," in *The Languages of Science, op. cit.* pp. 111–123. Reprinted by permission.

6. John R. Platt, "The Two Faces of Perception," in *Changing Perspectives on Man*, ed. Ben Rothblatt, Chicago: University of Chicago Press, 1968, p. 73. Italics added. Reprinted by permission.

7. Paul Watzlawick, Janet Helmick Beavin, and Don D. Jackson, *Pragmatics of Human Communication*, New York: Norton, 1967, p. 27.

8. There's a lot more to understanding gestalts and gestalt psychology than what we mention here. But much of it goes beyond the point we're trying to make. This quotation, and a more developed explanation of the gestalt

concept, is in John H. Brennecke and Robert C. Amick, *The Struggle for Significance*, Beverly Hills, Calif.: Glencoe Press, 1971, p. 108. Reprinted by permission.

9. Joost Meerloo, "The Word Tyrannizes Us or Is Our Slave," in *Conversation and Communication*, New York: International Universities Press, 1952, p. 84. This example is a liberal paraphrase of Meerloo, pp. 83–84.

10. Clifford H. Swensen, Jr., *Introduction to Interpersonal Relations*, Glenview, Ill.: Scott-Foresman, 1973, p. 146.

11. Albert H. Hastorf, David J. Schneider, and Judith Polefka, *Person Perception*, Reading, Mass.: Addison-Wesley, 1970, pp. 11–12. Reprinted by permission.

12. Jesse G. Delia, "Dialects and the Effects of Stereotypes on Interpersonal Attraction and Cognitive Processes in Impression Formation," *Quarterly Journal of Speech*, **LVIII** (October 1972): 297.

13. Ellen Berscheid and Elaine Walster, "Beauty and the Best," *Psychology Today*, **V** (March 1972): 42–46, 74.

14. C. David Mortensen, *Communication: The Study of Human Interaction*, New York: McGraw-Hill, 1972.

15. Vernon, *op cit.* p. 142. Reprinted by permission.

16. David Johnson, *Reaching Out*, Englewood Cliffs, N.J.: Prentice-Hall, 1972, p. 78.

17. Mortensen, *op. cit.* p. 126.

18. John B. Carroll, ed., *Language Thought and Reality: Selected Writings of Benjamin Lee Whorf*, New York: Wiley, 1956, p. 213.

19. This is also Ozzie Davis's point in "The English Language Is My Enemy," *Language in America*, ed. Neil Postman, Charles Weingartner, and Terence P. Moran, New York: Pegasus, 1969.

20. "Reversing the Bigotry of Language," *Psychology Today*, March 1974, p.57.

21. The idea for talking about physical, psychological, active, and passive availability came from Gerard Egan, *Face To Face: The Small Group Experience and Interpersonal Growth*, Monterey, Calif.: Brooks/Cole, 1973, pp. 96–98.

22. Carl Rogers, "Some Significant Learning," *On Becoming a Person*, Boston: Houghton Mifflin, 1961, p. 18.

23. *Ibid.*

ADDITIONAL RESOURCES

One of the most entertaining and educational films related to this chapter is published by *Psychology Today*. The title of the film is *Information Processing*. Using a social cocktail party as the communication setting, the film deals with "attention," "retention," "refabrication," "information overload," etc.

Albert H. Hastorf, David J. Schneider, and Judith Polefka explain more about the perception of people in their book *Person Perception* (Reading, Mass.: Addison-Wesley, 1970), pp. 3–17.

In his book *The Image* (Ann Arbor: University of Michigan Press, 1956), Kenneth Boulding discusses his assumption that our image or subjective knowledge of the world governs our behavior. See especially pp. 3–18. Some parts of his discussion are closely related to what we've said about the interpretation of raw data.

You'll find a rigorous and comprehensive discussion of how people process raw data in David Mortensen's chapter "Information Processing" in *Communication: The Study of Human Interaction* (New York: McGraw-Hill, 1950).

For a book that's easy to read and that offers a basic but understandable treatment of perception, see Gail E. Myers and Michele Tolela Myers's *The Dynamics of Human Communication: A Laboratory Approach* (New York: McGraw-Hill, 1973), especially Chapters 2–6.

C.S. Lewis' book *Out of the Silent Planet* (New York: Macmillan, 1968) is the story of British professor Dr. Ransom's visit to Mars. Ransom's initial reaction to the planet reveals the extent to which we *learn* to perceive things. Lewis writes that when Ransom set foot on the planet for the first time:

> He gazed about him, and the very intensity of his desire to take in the new world at a glance defeated itself. He saw nothing but colours — colours that refused to form themselves into things. Moreover, he knew nothing yet well enough to see it: *you cannot see things till you know roughly what they are.* (p.40, italics added)

A similarly insightful science fiction account of perception and interpretation, but this time from the point of view of a Martian visiting Earth, is in Robert A. Heinlein's book *Stranger in a Strange Land* (New York: G.P. Putnam's Sons, 1961).

4

Negotiation
of
Selves

During winter quarter, 1973, Dutch Small and Dean Tarbill were both in one of my (John) classes. Dutch and Dean had known each other for about three years, were both members of the University of Washington, rowing crew, and were living with 70 other men in Crew House on lower campus. The manager of Crew House at that time was Bill Mickelson, who had been elected by the Varsity Boat Club to supervise the house and to keep financial tabs on Boat Club members. One Sunday afternoon Mickelson reminded Dutch that he owed the Boat Club some money. Dutch reluctantly paid up, but was, as he put it, "a little hacked off because it left me short for the rest of the month." Mickelson asked Dutch to tell Dean when he saw him that his bill needed paying, too. Right after Mickelson had talked with Dutch, Mickelson saw Dean and told him to pay his bill. Dutch didn't know that Mickelson had already talked to Dean, and so about an hour later, when Dutch and Dean were driving to the gym to play basketball, the following dialogue occurred:

Dutch: Have you got your tennis shoes?
Dean: Yeah.
Dutch: Hey, are you planning to pay the money you owe the Boat Club?
Dean: Yeah, sometime, but I'm a little short now, okay?
Dutch: Well, the Boat Club needs the money, and Mickelson is hitting everyone up for old bills.
Dean: Hey, well listen. Just get off my ass.
Dutch: I'm not on your ass. There are just a lot of outstanding bills, and yours is the biggest.
Dean: I just saw Mickelson and he started giving me grief, too! Now you! I'll pay it when I can!
Dutch: Okay! Don't get all hot and bothered!

If Dutch and Dean asked you to take a close look at their communication in order to arbitrate their disagreement, you might start by talking about the content development, i.e., the subjects or topics they discussed—"tennis shoes," "money," "old bills," "the Boat Club," and "Mickelson." You could also probably help them to understand what went on by looking at the complications introduced by verbal and nonverbal cues in the communication *context* and by explaining how each person *interpreted* the event.

But if you wanted to talk about the interpersonal quality of this communication event—or lack of it—you'd need to go a little further. If you wanted to get at the extent to which Dutch and Dean met as *per-sons*—the degree to which they were willing and able to *share* some of their own humanness and *be aware* of the humanness of the other—you'd have to see how they were involved in a process that occurs every time humans communicate, a process we call negotiation of selves. Negotiation of selves is the process by which communicators construct and respond to *definitions of themselves* and to *definitions of the other persons* communicating with them.

In this example, Dutch defines himself as primarily an information-giver; he's just passing on information to a friend. Dean doesn't identify Dutch as just an information-giver. Dean's already been dunned by Mickelson, and now Dutch is coming across like another pushy bill collector. There are a variety of reasons *why* each person defines himself and the other as he does—Dutch is still upset about being left short, and his posture, voice, etc., undoubtedly reflect his feeling; Dean is embarrassed and defensive about a bill he can't pay, and he too, is reacting to his discomfort. But the point we want to stress is that each person's communication behavior is in part a response to definitions of himself—"information-giver," "persecuted friend," etc.—and of the other person involved—"deadbeat," "bill collector," etc. These definitions-of-self-and-other emerge from the communicating that occurs in the situation and change as the dialogue progresses, and that, roughly, is what we mean by negotiation of selves.

In the Dutch and Dean example, there was both content development and negotiation of selves. In some communication contexts, however, there's almost no content development. But even in these situations, the communicators are involved in the negotiation of selves. For example, you've probably participated in or observed an exchange like the following:

Jan: Hey, how's it goin', Paul?
Paul: Don't bug me.
Jan: What's the matter?
Paul: No sweat. Forget it.
Jan: What are you so out of shape about?
Paul: Forget it. Just kiss off.
Jan: Well, all right. Pout. I don't give a damn.

There's no content development in the interchange between Paul and Jan, which is to say that they're not talking about any objects, issues, or events separate from themselves. But the persons are definitely communicating; they're involved with this other aspect of human communication—negotiation of selves, an aspect that you can't avoid. Negotiation of selves is part of every instance of human communication. Every time we communicate, we are offering definitions of ourselves and almost simultaneously accepting, qualifying, or rejecting definitions-of-self offered by the people we're communicating with.[1] Because of this fact, a large part of what we do as we communicate relates to how we are defining ourselves and the other persons involved and how we are responding to those definitions.

In the interchange between Paul and Jan, the negotiation of selves works something like this:

Paul's definition of self and of Jan:

I see myself as independent of you. I don't choose to share much of my self-definition. I see you as feeling superior to me—you seem to see me as stupid and unreasonable. But I reject that; I know I have good reasons for my anger.

Jan's definition of self and of Paul:

I see myself as friendly and concerned. I'm willing to share that—up to a point. But I see you as unreasonable and pouty, and I reject that.

A similar negotiation-of-selves process goes on in every case of human communication—from a computer-typed business letter, to a political speech, to a TV newscast, to an intimate whisper. That process is going on right now. As we communicate with you via this book, we are choosing how much we will share with you about how we see ourselves and how we will respond to our definitions of you; and you're doing the same thing. How do you see yourself as you read this book? Apathetic? As a discoverer of new ideas? Under pressure? Interested? Bored? How do you see us? As open and honest? Naive? Authoritarian? Buddy-buddy? Out of date? Friendly? Threatening? How do you respond to your definition of us? If you see us as authoritarian, are you willing to accept us that way? Or, do you reject us? If you define us as "friendly textbook writers," does that lead you to reject us or to partly accept us? How do you think we define you? Do you think we accept your view of yourself, partly accept it, or reject it?

These questions can be asked about any instance of human communication. The answers to these questions will not tell you *everything* about the communication, for in most situations there's also content or subject matter involved. But they will help you see whether or not the communication is *interpersonal* in the sense we talked about in Chapter 1. That's why we're making so much of this negotiation-of-selves idea. When you understand how this process works, we think you'll see how directly it affects the quality of your communicating. We think you'll be able to see that the way you choose to participate in this negotiation-of-selves process will determine whether you promote *impersonal*—object-to-object or object-to-person communication—or *interpersonal*—person-to-person—communication.

UNDERSTANDING THE TERMS—"SELVES" AND "NEGOTIATION"

Historical Self

In order to understand how negotiation of selves works, we think that it's important to first understand what's meant by "self." That word is often used to describe a person's inherent, given, unchanging characteristics—his or her essential or ongoing qualities. In this sense you might see your self as the part of you that is the same today as it was ten or fifteen years ago. For example, the farthest back I (John) can remember is when I was about four and our family was vacationing at a cabin on Steamboat Island in Puget Sound. I remember hiking with my parents along the rocky beach through the smell of low tide. I also remember getting squirted by geoducks—large, long-necked clams that react to being walked over. As I remember that experience, I know that the "me" who smelled, felt, and tasted those sensations is, in an important sense, the same "me" who is at this moment smelling coffee and pencil erasures and feeling a cool desk against my elbows.

Often, a person's historical self becomes synonymous with the *roles* she or he plays. The fact that your instructor is a "teacher" is part of his or her historical self. In other contexts, your instructor might also be parent, spouse, salesperson, or student. You might, at various times, be all of those "selves," too. For both you and your teacher, each role has more or less clearly defined characteristics and limitations. Your historical self, then, includes both the history of you—what you were, what you thought, how you felt, what you liked, what you did—*and* you as "role-filler."

Historical self: The "me" who is walking here with Marcia and Lisa is, in one sense, the "me" who walked this beach with *my* dad.

Present Self

But if you think about it a little, you can see that there's more to your self than its static, historical side. The whole you is more than just history; as we've already said, you're also continually changing, you're in process. What you are doing right now is not simply a direct result of all you've ever done. Your personal present is not determined by your personal history. If it were—if you could do today only what yesterday's behavior permitted—you'd never be able to do anything different or new. If all your present actions were fully predictable from your past actions, you could never be creative or even spontaneous. But you can be spontaneous and creative, because your self is not simply historical and static; it is also dynamic, changing, and emerging in the present.

A psychotherapist named Andras Angyal emphasizes the importance of this nonhistorical aspect of your self. As he puts it, the human self is "a unified dynamic organization—dynamic because the most significant fact about a human being is not so much his static aspect as his constituting a specific *process; the life of the individual."[2] James Bugental, another humanistic psychologist, calls these two aspects the "self" and the "I-process." For Bugental, the "self" is the historical, objective side; the "I-process" is the "active, aware doer."[3]

Although most of the time we aren't directly aware of these two aspects of our selves, both are always there, always affecting our relationships with others. As I (John) talk with Gary about his classes, my communication behavior is influenced by the historical facts that I'm a teacher, a course coordinator, a parent, and a friend. But I don't just relate to Gary as a job-holder or role-player. I also try to be responsive to the present, here-and-now circumstances between us—my *perception* of his concern, my *feelings* of satisfaction, my *impatience* with his decisions. Your present self, in other words, includes the ways in which you're changing, *and* your here-and-now thoughts, feelings, likes, dislikes, beliefs, desires, and so on.

Our historical and present selves do not affect only our relationships with others. As we tried to say in Chapter 1, it also works the other way around; our relationships affect our selves. As the counselor William Graham Cole puts it:"Even at birth, the infant is not fully human. Isolate it from all contacts with persons, minister solely to its gross physical needs so that it does not perish but is cut off completely from conversation and companionship and it will grow up not as a person but as an animal. *We are dependent for our humanity upon our association with other humans.*[4] (Italics added.)

In short, one of the things we'd like you to understand about negotiation of selves is that the selves who participate in the negotiation process are not just historical units, but are also continuously growing dynamisms affecting and being affected by the continually varying web of interpersonal relationships.

Negotiation

When we use the term "negotiation," we don't want you to think only about a business transaction or the process of diplomatic bargaining that results in a cease-fire or a treaty. But we do want you to think of a process that is *two-part* and *mutual*. When we say that negotiation is *two-part*, we mean that negotiation involves two activities: being aware and sharing. As we've already suggested, when you engage in negotiation of selves, you become aware of, or perceive, a definition of the other *and* you share a definition of yourself.

Being aware.   One dimension of negotiation of selves is awareness. The quality of your communication is affected not only by *what you are aware of*, i.e., how sensitively you perceive the other person, but also by how you *respond* to the other whom you perceive. In the last chapter we talked about your perception processes, and we'll have more to say about sensitive responding and listening in Chapter 6. The point we want to stress here is that you tend to *respond* to your definition of the other in one of three ways:

1.   Sometimes, you *accept* the definition of the other whom you perceive. When you accept it, you're comfortable with it and you don't try to change it. For example, you're probably almost always willing to accept what you perceive to be your physician's definition of herself or himself. You might sometimes be uncomfortable with his or her treatment or advice, but you seldom question your doctor's definition of self.

2.   In other situations you might want to *partly accept* the other's self-definition. You might agree, for example, to see a police officer or teacher as an authority figure, but not as a dictator or as the one who

FUNKY WINKERBEAN BY TOM BATIUK, COURTESY OF PUBLISHERS-HALL SYNDICATE.

should give you a speeding ticket or a long assignment. You might be willing to go along with a politician's definition of himself or herself as a friend of minorities, but not as a "Savior of the Oppressed." In those cases your acceptance is partial, or qualified.

3. Sometimes, on the other hand, you _reject_ the other's self-definition as you perceive it; that is, you're not willing to even partially accept it. This happens, for example, when someone you define as subordinate sees himself or herself as your superior. How are you likely to respond when a classmate who has failed the last three exams tries to give you orders about how to study for the next one? What usually happens the first time an 11-year-old tells his or her parents how they ought to think or what they ought to do?

In order to clarify acceptance, partial acceptance, and rejection, think how you might respond to three different persons, each of whom is offering you advice about your job.[5] Your aunt is one person. For 17 years she held a job identical to yours and several times during her career successfully coped with the same problem you're having. Chances are, you'd be likely to *accept* her definition of herself as "expert" in this situation. A co-worker is the second person. You see your co-worker as generally competent, but he's never held the position you hold. If your co-worker defined himself as "expert," your response to his self-definition would probably be *partial acceptance*. Finally, if the person who held your job immediately before you, and who was fired for not solving the problem you face, defined herself as "expert," you'd probably respond to that self-definition with *rejection*. That response—rejection—is also illustrated in a Doonesbury strip.

COPYRIGHT/1972, G.B. TRUDEAU/DISTRIBUTED BY UNIVERSAL PRESS SYNDICATE.

Sharing.   You can also choose to *share* your self with the other in a
wide range of ways. As we talk about in detail in Chapter 5, sharing
your self is a complex process and an important skill. You can share
your historical self and/or your present self, and you can do it verbally
and nonverbally. But at this point we think it's most important to focus
on *how much* you choose to share in any given communication situation.

We'd like you to realize that as you communicate, you're continually making that choice; you're always choosing, more or less consciously, how much to reveal to others about how you see yourself.
Sometimes, you choose to share almost nothing, by saying very little or
by talking only in terms of "objective" issues or the opinions of "people
in general." Other times, you share with the other person a great deal
about how you're thinking and feeling.

Your choice of how much to share always falls somewhere along
the line between *a little* and *a lot*. You cannot refuse to share completely;
your dress, posture, facial expression, etc., always reveal something
about "who you are." Also, you cannot share *all* of your self. You're too
complex and too rapidly changing to do that. Therefore, your choice of
how much to share always ranges from a little . . . to . . . a lot.

The second important characteristic of negotiation is that it is
mutual. We already made this point in Chapter 1; we just want to
emphasize it here. To say that negotiation of selves is mutual is to say
that you don't negotiate by yourself, but nobody else does, either. When
we say that all communication involves a negotiation of selves, one
thing we mean is that you do not determine by yourself who you are in
a communication situation. Nor do the others involved. But you do
participate in the determination of who is communicating. So do the
other persons. In the interchange between Dutch and Dean, for
example, Dutch could not determine by himself who he was; his self
emerged, in part, in that situation. He defined himself as an information-giving friend, but Dean saw him as a pushy bill collector. The
same thing happened with Dean. Dutch saw him as a deadbeat, but
Dean saw himself as an honest and unfairly browbeaten victim of
circumstance. But neither Dutch nor Dean determined by himself who
he was in that situation. Both selves emerged in the negotiating that
occurred.

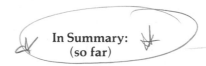

In Summary:
(so far)

1. Negotiation of selves is going on every time humans communicate. You cannot choose whether or not to participate in the process; it's always happening.

2. The *kind* of negotiating that's going on will, to a considerable extent, determine the *quality* of communication. In other words, you *can* choose the *kind of negotiating* you do, and your choice will affect the *quality* of communication that occurs. Some choices result in your treating others as objects and thus preventing interpersonal-quality communication. Other choices result in your treating those you communicate with as persons and thereby promoting interpersonal communication.

Here's what you have to choose from:
Perceive (become aware) of the other's definition-of-self and
1. Choose to accept it
2. partly accept it
3. reject it

And at the same time:
Share your definition of your historical or present self somewhere between:

A little . . . and . . . a lot.

Before we go into more detail about the choices that we think are available to you, we want to reemphasize the point that this "quality" we're talking about is *not* a static thing. Nobody consistently chooses only one kind of negotiating. No individual is always "closed," "open," "overpersonal," "sensitive," etc., and it's inaccurate to label people as if they were. Consequently, the quality of communication between people changes; sometimes it's impersonal and sometimes it's interpersonal. We'd like, as we already said, to encourage you to work toward more interpersonal communicating.

You can do that, we think, by choosing more often the negotiation-of-selves options that help make interpersonal communication happen. It isn't always easy, in part because you've got at least 13 options to choose from. At this point the idea of 13 options might sound a little confusing, but we hope it won't by the time we're finished. We think that of these 13 options, only two will effectively promote interpersonal quality communication.

NEGOTIATION OPTIONS

Disconfirmation[6]

You may choose the option of disconfirmation. If you do, you'll actually discourage almost all negotiation of selves from happening. _Disconfirmation is the process of communicating as if the other person didn't even exist._ Martin Buber makes the point that humans are the only animals who ask questions like "Who am I?" or "Why do I exist?" As a result, humans need an answer, need to have their existence confirmed or verified by other people. Buber explains confirmation almost poetically:

> The human person needs confirmation because man as man needs it. An animal does not need to be confirmed, for it is what it is unquestionably. It is different with man: sent forth from the natural domain of species into the hazard of the solitary category, surrounded by the air of a chaos which came into being with him, secretly and bashfully he watches for a Yes which allows him to be and which can come to him only from one human person to another. It is from one man to another that the heavenly bread of self-being is passed.[7]

Disconfirmation prevents our need for personal verification from being met; it accomplishes the opposite of what Buber is describing. Unfortunately, we disconfirm others more often than we should. Sometimes, our disconfirmation is pretty obvious, as when people ignore the question or contribution of a woman in a group discussion because they assume it's based just on emotion, or when an adult talks about a four- or five-year-old child as if the child weren't in the room, or when we deliberately and overtly avoid someone who wants to talk with us. Other times, we ignore the selfhood of others in more subtle ways—by refusing to look at them while they're talking with us, by always being in a hurry ("catch you later") when we see them, etc.

I (John) sometimes feel disconfirmed when the person I'm talking with appears to be listening to me, but responds as if I hadn't said anything at all. For example:

Friend: This school board never tries to find out what the people
want. They just do whatever they damn well please.

Me: Well, I agree it seems that way sometimes. But last week I
sat through three hours of a four-hour meeting where
they did nothing *but* listen to what the people wanted to
tell them.

Friend: And they don't listen to the faculty or administration
either—they act like dictators.

Some psychotherapists say that consistent disconfirmation is the
most devastating experience a human can undergo. If you are disconfirmed often enough, they say, you begin to wonder whether or not you
actually exist. As the psychologist William James put it: "No more fiend-
ish punishment could be devised, even were such a thing physically
possible, than that one should be turned loose in society and remain
absolutely unnoticed by all the members thereof."[8]

Although disconfirmation is one negotiation option, when you
choose it, you prevent interpersonal communication from happening.
The remaining 12 negotiation options all offer some degree of confirmation; whenever you choose one of them, you are at *least* acknowledging
the existence of the other person.

But acknowledging someone's existence is not the same as promoting interpersonal communication. Only *two* of the options help you do
that. *Only two of the 13 possible choices will promote person-to-
person communicating.* We'd like to clarify that by having you look at
Table 1 and its explanation on the next few pages.

Table 1. *Negotiation options: Choices you make as you communicate*

Option 1: *Disconfirmation* (you communicate as if the other didn't even exist)

Options 2–13:

You are aware of:	the other's historical self, which you			the other's present self, which you		
	Accept	Partly accept	Reject	Accept	Partly accept	Reject
You share: some of your *historical self*— a little...to...a lot;	2 Closed stereotyping/ acceptance	3 Closed stereotyping/ partly accept	4 Closed stereotyping/ rejection	8 Closed sensitivity/ acceptance	9 Closed sensitivity/ partly accept	10 Closed sensitivity rejection
some of your *present self*— a little...to...a lot	5 Open stereotyping/ acceptance	6 Open stereotyping/ partly accept	7 Open stereotyping/ rejection	11 Open sensitivity/ acceptance	12 Open sensitivity/ partly accept	13 Open sensitivity rejection

How to read the chart

Think of a brief communication experience you've had recently. Decide whether you *shared* your *historical* self or your *present* self. Locate the appropriate line (*historical* or *present*) on the left (*you share*) side of the chart. Next, decide whether you were *aware* of the other's *present* or *historical* self, and locate the appropriate set of three columns on the chart. Then decide whether you accepted, partly accepted, or rejected the other person as you defined him or her, and choose the appropriate column from among the three you identified before.

The spot where the line (*left-to-right*) intersects with the column describes the negotiation option you chose. For example, let's say you shared your *historical* self only (your communication only said, in effect, "I'm a student"); you were aware only that the other person was a teacher (her/his *historical* self), and you accepted that. In that situation you would have chosen option 2, closed stereotyping/acceptance. Until you changed your choice of options, you and the teacher would continue communicating in a role-to-role way; you would not be communicating interpersonally.

Each of the options is explained on the following pages.

Closed Stereotyping

Table 1 might look confusing to you at first. But we think we can make sense out of it if you'll just stick with us. Let's start with the upper left quarter of Table 1, where you find options 2, 3, and 4. Those three options are forms of *closed stereotyping.*

Whenever you choose one of these three options, the way you communicate is *closed* in the sense that you reveal only your historical self. Your behavior is *stereotyping* in that you are aware only of the other person's historical self. You see the other person only in terms of his or her past—the roles he or she has played. For example, this professor-student interchange is an example of option 2, closed stereotyping/acceptance:

Professor: As I tell all my students, Mr. Bennett, your task is to learn as much about the course as possible and then to prove that you understand the material by passing the exam.

Student: Yeah, I understand that, Dr. Beach, and I realize that as a teacher, you've got a lot of hassles from other students.

In this situation each person sees the other primarily as the one he or she "has always been," i.e., student and professor. Each accepts the other in that role. Also, each reveals only that historical aspect of himself or herself: "I'm a professor and I see you as a student." "I'm a student and I see you as professor."

Sometimes, people choose this same option, but share a great deal of their historical selves. A conversation between strangers on an airplane or bus could be an example of this choice (still option 2). A businessman who is an army veteran discovers that his seatmate is in the army and proceeds to bombard him with stories of his exploits during the Korean war. The businessman is willing to share a great deal of who he was (historical self), on the assumption that all army personnel are interested in the same thing (stereotyping).

Option 3 is more complicated. If the student in the example had chosen this option, he would be aware that the instructor defines himself or herself as a professor, but the student would only partly accept this definition; the student would see the professor as authoritative, but also as a close and helpful friend. Sometimes, conversations in which this kind of negotiating is going on will include such comments as: "Well, I'm willing to talk to you, but remember, I'm still your professor; I've got to give you a grade at the end of the term."

Closed stereotyping rejection (option 4) occurs, for example, when a police officer discovers that his or her neighbor is an ex-convict and

Options 2–13:

You are aware of:	the other's historical self, which you			the other's present self, which you		
	Accept	Partly accept	Reject	Accept	Partly accept	Reject
You share: some of your historical self— a little...to...a lot;	2 Closed stereotyping/ acceptance	3 Closed stereotyping/ partly accept	4 Closed stereotyping/ rejection	8 Closed sensitivity/ acceptance	9 Closed sensitivity/ partly accept	10 Closed sensitivity/ rejection
some of your present self— a little...to...a lot	5 Open stereotyping/ acceptance	6 Open stereotyping/ partly accept	7 Open stereotyping/ rejection	11 Open sensitivity/ acceptance	12 Open sensitivity/ partly accept	13 Open sensitivity/ rejection

immediately rejects the neighbor's self-definition of "I'm now a legitimate businessperson and trustworthy." The police officer reveals only that he or she is "a cop" (little sharing of historical self), sees the other as "nothing but an ex-con" (stereotyping), and on that basis assumes that the other person is not worth knowing (rejection).

These are three of the possible approaches you can take to the negotiation of selves. In each case you're sharing only your historical self, and you're aware only of the other's role identity—who the other is in terms of his or her past experiences, occupation, position, etc. You're neither sharing nor being aware of who the other persons are in the here and now. When you choose these options, you will not be promoting interpersonal-quality communication. As we emphasized in Chapter 1, you sometimes have to communicate this way; closed stereotyping is, at times, a necessary part of your life. But not always.

Open Stereotyping

The next three options (5 through 7) are forms of open stereotyping. They are *open* in the sense that you share some of your dynamic, present self, but they still involve *stereotyping*—you're still aware of and responding to only the other's historical self. For example, a person who chooses option 7 (open stereotyping/rejection) would be willing to share some of her or his present self, but would be aware only of the other's historical self and would reject what she or he sees. That person might reject what she defines as her work supervisor's excess authoritarianism and might let her boss know her feelings. She might say something like, "I feel like you're pushing me a lot harder than you've got any right to. I'm working as hard as I can, but you're just coming on like a dictator."

Option 6 (open stereotyping/partly accept) is the choice, for example, of the employee who is willing to accept the company manager's definition of himself or herself as "undisputed boss," but *not* as "parent to each employee," and who is open about that qualified acceptance. The employee might say something like, "Okay, I'll do it your way, because it'll be easier, but not because, as you put it, it'll make me a better person."

As with closed stereotyping, none of these negotiating options will effectively promote interpersonal communication. The one that comes closest, however, is option 5, open stereotyping/acceptance. In that option you might see the other person as a superior, an intellectual, a performer, or some such thing and accept her or him in that role while revealing quite a bit about who you are in the present situation. For example, Hugh Prather reports how he handles this familiar experience:

> If I want to talk to someone and I am stuck for something to say, one of the simplest ways for me to get started is to state honestly what I am experiencing: "I want very much to talk to you but no words are coming."[9]

Often, when one person discloses with some spontaneity "where she's at right now," the other person is likely to reciprocate, and the quality of the communication can move toward open sensitivity.

Closed Sensitivity

Each of the three options (8, 9, 10) in this category involves perceiving and responding to the other's *present* self while revealing only your own *historical* self. These three options are called "closed sensitivity" because although you're sensitive to the other's present self, you're unwilling or unable to be open about your own present self.

Persons in the helping professions—counselors, nurses, psychologists, teachers, etc.—often choose the option 8, "closed sensitivity/ acceptance." They develop their abilities to be sensitive to who their client, student, patient, or counselee is at the present moment, but they avoid revealing much of their own present self. They try to stay in their role as adviser or educator or facilitator, sometimes revealing a little of their professional self (role), but usually going into detail only about

Options 2–13:

You are aware of:	the other's historical self, which you			the other's present self, which you		
	Accept	Partly accept	Reject	Accept	Partly accept	Reject
You share: some of your historical self— a little...to...a lot;	2 Closed stereotyping/ acceptance	3 Closed stereotyping/ partly accept	4 Closed stereotyping/ rejection	8 Closed sensitivity/ acceptance	9 Closed sensitivity/ partly accept	10 Closed sensitivity/ rejection
some of your present self— a little...to...a lot	5 Open stereotyping/ acceptance	6 Open stereotyping/ partly accept	7 Open stereotyping/ rejection	11 Open sensitivity/ acceptance	12 Open sensitivity/ partly accept	13 Open sensitivity/ rejection

their patient's or client's problems. You might have experienced this kind of communicating with a counselor, pastor, or teacher—*your* present self is very important, but the counselor's here-and-now reactions are out of bounds.

Option 9, "closed sensitivity/partly accept," and option 10, "closed sensitivity/rejection," also reveal one communicator's ability to respond to the other's present self, combined with an unwillingness or inability to share much of her or his own present self. Option 9 might be characterized by an exchange like this:

Office manager: Why haven't you got this place cleaned up yet? It's almost midnight and you're supposed to be here right after quitting time!

Janitor: Okay, okay, you're mad. I'd probably be crabby, too, if I had to stay after work this long. But janitors have as much work as you do, so don't think you're the only one with problems.

Here, the janitor is *sensitive* to the office manager's present self, but responds only in terms of the role as janitor (closed).

Garry Trudeau illustrates option 10, "closed sensitivity/rejection," in another Doonesbury strip. As Trudeau illustrates, a well-meaning person like the reverend can go out of his way to be sensitive to the object of his crusade—Rufus in this case—but often remains unwilling to share any of his present self and is able only to reject the other:". . . you little pagan."

You can probably imagine other examples of this kind of negotiation of selves or can remember them from your own experience. The academic adviser who is sensitive to your change in present self but who

COPYRIGHT/1972, G.B. TRUDEAU/DISTRIBUTED BY UNIVERSAL PRESS SYNDICATE.

still thinks "you ought to take Chem 107 to round out your program" could be an example of option 9, perceiving the other's dynamic self and partly accepting it while revealing only his historical self.

Individual Application: Negotiation-of-Selves Comprehension Check

If you're uncertain at this point about your understanding of the negotiation-of-selves process, you might want to stop here and check your comprehension. It's a little difficult to work with just one or two statements, but try to identify as accurately as you can the kind of negotiation of selves going on in each of the following statements. Our answers and explanations are on pp. 129–130.

1. "Well, frankly, I'm feeling a little uncertain myself about how this goes, but no matter what you say, I'm still sure that, as supervisor, I know how to do the job better than you or any other crew member."

    a) 9 Closed sensitivity/ partly accept

    b) 7 Open stereotyping/ rejection

    c) 3 Closed stereotyping/ partly accept

2. "That's certainly not a silly question; every loan applicant asks it. And I can tell you that all our loan officers—including me—are friendly *and* firm, with an emphasis on the friendliness."

    a) 5 Open stereotyping/ acceptance

    b) 8 Closed sensitivity/ acceptance

    c) 2 Closed stereotyping/ acceptance

Options 2–13:

You are aware of:	the other's historical self, which you			the other's present self, which you		
	Accept	Partly accept	Reject	Accept	Partly accept	Reject
You share: some of your *historical self*— a little...to...a lot;	2 Closed stereotyping/ acceptance	3 Closed stereotyping/ partly accept	4 Closed stereotyping/ rejection	8 Closed sensitivity/ acceptance	9 Closed sensitivity/ partly accept	10 Closed sensitivity/ rejection
some of your *present self*— a little...to...a lot	5 Open stereotyping/ acceptance	6 Open stereotyping/ partly accept	7 Open stereotyping/ rejection	11 Open sensitivity/ acceptance	12 Open sensitivity/ partly accept	13 Open sensitivity/ rejection

3. "O.K., it's obvious that you're really angry right now. And you've got a right to be. But you can't just barge in and disrupt the meeting. So sit down, cool off a little, and let me handle it. That's what administrative assistants are for."

a) 9 Closed sensitivitiy/ partly accept

b) 2 Closed stereotyping/ acceptance

c) 6 Open stereotyping/ partly accept

4. *Counselor:*

"I hear you saying that you're really afraid of dropping out, but there doesn't seem to be any other answer—you're kind of caught between a rock and a hard place."

Student:

"Miss Brown—Karen—that's exactly how I'm feeling. I *am* afraid. Can you help me?"

Counselor:

"Well, our office is equipped to respond to a lot of problems, but sometimes you have to work things out on your own."

Counselor

a) 6 Open stereotyping/ rejection

b) 4 Closed stereotyping/ rejection

c) 10 Closed sensitivity/ rejection

5. *Husband:*

"Good morning, honey! Boy, do I feel great! My cold's gone, it's payday, and I'm really up for that presentation this afternoon!"

Wife:

"Keep your voice down, will you? I sure wish a homemaker had that much to get excited about."

Husband

a) 7 Open stereotyping/ rejection

b) 5 Open stereotyping acceptance

c) 8 Closed sensitivity/ acceptance

Husband:

"Oh, one of those days, hunh? Well, where's my breakfast? And have you fixed my lunch yet? I've been up almost 15 minutes, and it doesn't look like you've done *anything* yet!"

Wife:

"Can't you ever do anything but nag at me? They'll be ready in a minute."

Wife

a) 7 Open stereotyping/ rejection

b) 2 Closed stereotyping/ acceptance

c) 4 Closed stereotyping/ rejection

Our answers to negotiation-of-selves comprehension check [see pp. 127–128].

We're not sure that the answer's we've identified are the only possible   ble ones. Your interpretation of the dialogue may differ from ours, and you may come up with different responses. We're interested mainly in helping you see what we mean by the first ten negotiation-of-selves options rather than emphasizing right and wrong answers.

1. Although it's not completely clear from just one statement, it sounds here as if the supervisor is *open* enough to share a *little* of his or her present uncomfortable self, but the supervisor is aware of the other person only as a stereotypical, griping crew member. Since the supervisor *rejects* that definition of the other, the best answer would be choice (b), option 7, open stereotyping/rejection.

2. This seems to us to be a fairly clear case of option 2, (closed stereo-typing/acceptance), choice (c). The loan officer sees the other person as "just another customer" and shares only a little of his or her own historical self-as-loan-officer.

3. The speaker does seem sensitive to the other's present self, but isn't completely willing to accept it and therefore accepts it only partly. At the same time, the speaker shares only his or her self in the role of adminis-trative assistant. The best answer seems to be choice (a), option closed sensitivity/partly accept.

4. Here, the counselor seems to be sensitive to the student's present feel-ings, but she rejects the definition she perceives of the student-as-friend and shares only a little of her historical self, i.e., her self-as-counselor. So we think the best answer is choice (c), option 10, (closed sensitivity/rejection).

5. This isn't a very productive exchange. The husband seems to have chosen option 3, (open stereotyping/acceptance), choice (b). He is openly

revealing his present self, but he's only aware of his wife-as-servant, a role
he accepts her in and fully expects her to fulfill. He has even stereotyped her
as "naturally" having bad days. The wife, on the other hand, is aware only of
the stereotype of her husband-as-critic, which she rejects, and is only able
to share aspects of her own stereotyped self as a dreary, bored homemaker.
So the most accurate answer for her is choice (c), option 4 (closed stereo-
typing/rejection).

Table 2. *Open sensitivity*

You are aware of the other's *present self*, which you:		
	Accept	Partly accept	Reject
You share some of your *present* self— a little…to…a lot	11 Open sensitivity/ acceptance	12 Open sensitivity/ partly accept	13 Open sensitivity/ rejection

Open Sensitivity

The three negotiation options ((11, 12, 13) we're calling "open sensi-tivity" all involve revealing some of your present self while perceiving the other's present self. We think that two of these three options will promote interpersonal-quality communication and that one generally won't. Option 13 will not lead to interpersonal communication, pri-marily because of the effect rejection usually has on the other persons involved. For example, dissatisfaction and hostility often result from a parent's rejection of his or her child's definition of present self. How many times have you watched or listened to this kind of exchange dead-end in "Why-don't-they-ever-understand-me?" frustration?

"I'm hungry, Mommy."
"No, you're not; you just got down from the table."

or

"I'm scared when my bedroom is so dark, Daddy."
"No, you're not. Men aren't afraid of the dark."

In another example, Shelia might both be quite sensitive to her roommate's present self and also reveal a little of her present self:

Diane: I really feel exploited! It seems like I'm the only one who ever does anything around here.
Sheila: That's crazy! *I* am the one who's being exploited! I've been studying all day, and now I've got to listen to your complaining!

But even though Shelia is both perceiving and revealing her present self, her communication with Diane is not likely to be interpersonal so

Table 2. *Open sensitivity*

You are aware of the other's *present self*, which you:		
Accept	Partly accept	Reject
11 Open sensitivity/ acceptance	12 Open sensitivity/ partly accept	13 Open sensitivity/ rejection

You share some of your *present* self— a little...to...a lot

long as she continues to reject Diane's definition of her self in this situation.[10]

In short, person-to-person communication cannot occur without some degree of recognition and acceptance of the other person's definition of his or her present self. Sometimes, people can have conflicting opinions or points of view and still communicate interpersonally. That is, a couple might disagree about the topic or subject matter of their communication, and each might still reveal her or his own present self and be responsive to the other's present self. But when definitions of self are rejected, especially definitions of present self, interpersonal communication is not likely to occur.

Although the following dialogue involves disagreement, we think it comes quite close to open sensitivity.[11]

Frank: Honey, why don't you clean up the kitchen before you go to bed more often?

Ellie: I don't think it makes any difference. I get it done in the morning.

Frank: I disagree. When I come down in the morning, it makes the house feel depressing.

Ellie: Really? Why don't you clean it up yourself, then?

Frank: O.K. I'm willing to help. But it seems like we could work together on it, and it would be easier the night before.

Ellie: Does it actually bother you that much?

Frank: Yeah—I really feel that the whole house looks messy when the kitchen's cluttered with dirty dishes.

Ellie: Well, I guess I'm just used to it—my dad never seemed to mind.

Frank: Yeah, I bet.

Ellie: Don't tell me you want to have a fight about this!

Frank: O.K. That was a cheap shot. I don't especially want to fight. I'd just like you to help me clean it up in the evening.
Ellie: So you don't have to live in a lower-class house, hunh—like I lived in before I met you?
Frank: Wait a minute! I've told you and told you that I *love* your family!
Ellie: So why do you mind the kitchen getting cleaned in the morning instead of at night when I want to relax?
Frank: When it would only take us a few minutes?
Ellie: O.K. I guess it *is* kind of silly—if it means that much to you. But you've got to do something for me, too.
Frank: O.K. What?
Ellie: I wish you'd try not to be so unpleasant in the morning.
Frank: O.K. That's fair. I'll try.

On the other hand, you *can* promote interpersonal communication when you accept, or partly accept, the other's view of himself or herself. The negotiation option *most* likely to create that kind of communication is 11, open sensitivity/acceptance. When you choose this option, you are perceiving and accepting the other's present self while revealing your own present self. Carl Rogers tries to choose that option with the people who come to him. He says:

> I enter the relationship as a subjective person, not as a scrutinizer, not as a scientist. I feel, too, that when I am most effective, then somehow I am relatively whole in that relationship, or the word that has meaning to me is "transparent." To be sure there may be many aspects of my life that aren't brought into the relationship, but what is brought into the relationship is transparent. There is nothing hidden. Then I think, too, that in such a relationship I feel a real willingness for this other person to *be what he is.* I call that "acceptance." I don't know that that's a very good word for it, but my meaning there is that I'm willing for him to possess the feelings he possesses, to hold the attitudes he holds, to be the person he is.[12]

This quality of communication is definitely not restricted to the relationship between a professional counselor and her or his counselee. You've probably experienced it yourself—in a discussion with a friend, making up after an argument with a lover or spouse, or in an especially productive job conference with a supervisor or co-worker. We've felt it happening in some of our communication with each other (which is one

Table 2. *Open sensitivity*

You are aware of the other's *present self*, which you:		
	Accept	Partly accept	Reject
You share some of your *present* self— a little...to...a lot	11 Open sensitivity/ acceptance	12 Open sensitivity/ partly accept	13 Open sensitivity/ rejection

reason why it's been exciting and fun to write this book together), with our wives, our children, our parents, some of the students who take our classes, and some of the persons we work with. The object of our continuing study of interpersonal communication—and we hope of yours—and the reason for this book is to help that quality of communication happen more often.

But option 11 is not the only kind of negotiation that can promote interpersonal communication. That quality of communication can also happen when you partly accept the other's dynamic self, so long as you can at the same time reveal some of your own dynamic self. Sometimes, option 12, open sensitivity/partly accept is what I (John) find myself choosing while talking with a person from one of my classes. I'm interested in and try to be responsive to student opinions about what goes on in class. But I also have some opinions of my own. Sometimes, a person from my class will think that I don't want to have *any* input into the decision-making process. In a conference, for example, one person said that she felt that students should be the only ones evaluating assignments—that I should stay out of that part of the class. I think I was partly able to accept her definition of herself in this situation. She was important and she had an opinion that deserved hearing. But I couldn't fully accept her view of herself as sole or primary decision-maker. My acceptance of her self-definition was partial, because I felt I should have some input, too. I tried to let her know a little about how I was feeling there and then, and it helped us reach an understanding that was acceptable, so far as I know, to both of us. I think that's an example of option 12.

In some situations, it's difficult to help the other person understand that partial acceptance is not rejection. In those cases, it's often helpful to be able to share quite a bit of your own present self, so that the other person gets a clearer idea of what your current thoughts and feelings are.

Here's another dialogue that we think exemplifies open sensitivity. Both persons seem willing to *share* their present selves, to *be aware* of the other's present self, and to *partly accept* the other's self-definition they perceive.

Student: I got your note about my grade, and I think I deserve more than a C in this class.

Teacher: Okay, I tried to explain in the note why I evaluated your involvement and work that way. How do you see things differently?

Student: Well, in the first place, I don't think it's fair that you grade so much on participation. I don't talk much in groups. One-on-one I'm fine, but not in the whole class.

Teacher: You feel that a lot of my evaluation was based on that?

Student: Yeah. You mentioned it in your note—right here. And I think I was participating—I was involved in the class in ways you didn't even notice.

Teacher: Okay—yeah. I often miss some of what's going on. I also considered other things—your midterm, for example. But it looks like we ought to look at the whole thing again—both of us. I'm never sure I can see even most of what someone's doing in class, and it sounds like you feel I'm missing much of what you're contributing.

Student: I really think you are. I don't talk a lot, but that doesn't mean I'm not involved.

Teacher: Could you get some input from some other persons in the class? Would you be willing to get comments from, say Jim and Sandi and maybe two or three others about how they see your involvement?

Student: That's fair. But will their opinions make any difference in my grade?

Teacher: Well, right to the heart of it, hunh? I'm uncomfortable telling you that their opinions will definitely change your grade one way or the other, because I still feel some responsibility as teacher. But I know I often miss some of what's going on, and I'm really not interested in treating you unfairly. Can we wait and see what they say and then meet to talk about it again?

Student: Okay, fine. Thanks for listening. I guess I didn't really
            expect you'd even consider changing it. Thanks.
Teacher: "Teacher is human!" hunh?
Student: Yeah. See you in class.

CONCLUDING THOUGHTS

Well, that's what we mean by negotiation of selves. We are convinced
that in every human communication situation, you are participating in a
negotiation-of-selves process, which means that you are almost
simultaneously responding to your perception of the other's definition
of self and revealing something of your own self-definition. You can't
choose *whether* or not to do that — it's happening all the time. But you
can choose *how* to participate in this negotiation of selves, and your
choice will help determine the quality of the communication that occurs.
Before we end this chapter, we need to reemphasize two important
points.

 1. Neither your choice nor the quality of communication is a static,
one-shot thing. They vary in each communication situation; in fact,
sometimes the options chosen and the resulting quality of communication change from moment to moment. That flexibility is both an opportunity and a challenge. It's an opportunity because it means that you
can always move closer to interpersonal-quality communication. You
have the freedom to choose from all 13 options; you're not stuck with
communicating in the same ways you've always communicated. You
might be thinking, "But I can't change who I am." And we're not saying
that you can—or that you should. But you *can* change what you *do*—in
this case, what you choose. And we're urging you to choose the most
potentially interpersonal negotiation options as often as you can.

On the other hand, this flexibility is challenging in that once you've
achieved interpersonal communication, you'll probably find that you
need to work at maintaining it. It isn't easy to stay open and sensitive; it
takes constant effort.

 2. The second point complicates things a little. Our whole discussion
of negotiation of selves has focused on *your* choices. But, as we've said
several times, interpersonal communication requires *mutual* involvement. Each time you make one of the 13 choices, you affect the communication behavior of the other persons involved. Then their behavior, like yours, becomes one of the interdependent parts of the grow-

ing, changing communication context in which, as we tried to say in Chapter 2, just about everything depends on everything else. In other words, your choice of negotiation options will not *determine* the quality of the communication that occurs.[13] But it will affect it. Since your choice is the only thing you have control over, we think that it's what you should be concerned with—at first, anyway.

The important thing to remember is that whenever you communicate, every verbal and nonverbal "statement" you make is in part a statement about the relationship you're perceiving between your self and the persons you're communicating with. If you're not sensitive to that fact, you're likely to experience communication problems.

You might have quite a few questions at this point. Although we hope you have a fairly clear general idea of what's going on when we communicate interpersonally, you might still be unclear about many of the details. In the next two chapters we're going to try to clarify things more specifically by talking in detail about the two main aspects of the negotiation of selves—sharing (Chapter 5) and being aware (Chapter 6).

EXERCISES

Group Application: Negotiation of Selves

Here's an exercise that some students created to check out and to clarify your understanding of the negotiation of selves that's going on whenever humans communicate. Like the negotiation process itself, the exercise looks a little complicated at first, but it seems to work, so you might want to give it a try.

The exercise requires six persons who are seated in this pattern:

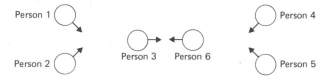

The three persons on the left (1, 2, and 3) make up one communicator; the three on the right (4, 5, and 6) make up the other communicator. *Persons 1, 2, and 3* are a young police officer, just two weeks out of the police academy. The officer is patrolling College Avenue with his superior, a sergeant who has been on the force for 15 years. The rookie knows he's being evaluated by the sergeant. A number of recent car-pedestrian accidents on College Avenue have emphasized the problems created by jaywalking. The officer has just seen a man cross hurriedly and carelessly in the middle of the block and is ready to cite him.

Persons 4, 5 and 6 are a male student, dressed in faded jeans and an old work shirt. He has a beard and hair to his shoulders, and he is carrying some books in an old army pack. It's the beginning of the school term, and he's been hassled all day by registration. Now he's having trouble locating the textbooks he needs. He was exasperated to find that one store was out of almost everything he needs, and he has just crossed the street in the middle of the block to get to the only other available bookstore.

Person 3, the speaker for the police officer, is the first to talk, but he can't say anything until he has been informed by each of the persons behind him. First, person 1 indicates how the police officer *sees himself.* Person 1 should say something like, "My identity as a_____(historical self) is important here. Right now I'm_____and feel_____in this situation (present self)."

Then, person 2 tells how the police officer *sees the student.* Person 2' should say something like, "I can see that the guy's (a)_____ My response is to_____(accept, partly accept, or reject) him because_____."

After persons 1 and 2 have given their interpretations of the police officer's definition of his historical and present self and his response to his definition of the student, *person 3 speaks as the police officer.* Person 3's job, then, is to listen to persons 1 and 2 and to decide how to combine their definitions of self and the student into a statement that makes some kind of sense in this situation.

Then it's the student's turn. First, person 4 indicates how the *student sees his historical and present self;* then, person 5 explains how the student defines and responds to *his definition of the police officer.* Persons 4 and 5 should use response patterns similar to those of persons 1 and 2, i.e., "My identity as a_____is important here," etc.

The dialogue usually goes rather slowly at first, but it gets easier as you go along, and it can also be fairly funny. Just as important, we think that if you try it, you'll be able to experience what we mean by the negotiation-of-selves process.

Group Application: Open Sensitivity

Here's a dialogue you can analyze individually or in small groups. Try to determine when and how *open sensitivity* occurs. This dialogue is based on an actual incident: Sandra, a black woman, is explaining her views about interracial marriage to Viki, a white woman. (This was a controversy in which both persons *worked at* open sensitivity.)

Sandra: I don't think a white girl should marry a black man, because after a while they won't make it together.

Viki: I get defensive about that because you seem to believe that no interracial marriage will ever work out. Some do okay.

Sandra: Okay, I can see that for you, some black men who marry white girls are happy. But for me, a black man can never be completely happy in that situation, because only a black woman really understands what a black man's needs are. She knows where he's at, where he's been, what he goes through every day. . . .

Viki: Are you talking about physical needs? Or both physical and psychological needs?

Sandra: I'm talking about both.

Viki: Damn, I've got two sides of me responding. I want to argue with you because from my point of view, you're saying I'm inferior as a woman. But on the other hand, I feel like you're saying something different—that a relationship between a black man and a black woman can be much fuller, much more complete, than between a black man and a white woman.

Sandra: I hear you. A white man and I could never make it. That's not where I'm at. We could be friends, but that's all. You could do much more for him than I would.

Viki: I wish we didn't have to use the words "white" and "black." They seem so impersonal. But I don't know how else to talk about it. Anyway, it seems to me that if a black man and a white woman go through the same cultural experiences, they could be compatible.

Sandra: You mean if they go to the same school, grow up in the same neighborhood, and things like that?

Viki: Yeah.

Sandra: They'd be more compatible than if they grew up in completely different environments. I understand what you're saying about that. But the black man will still have experiences that no white person could ever have; in my mind, only another black could understand those experiences.

Viki: I think we understand each other's position, but I don't think either of us wants to change.

Sandra: We agree on that.

NOTES

1. The British psychologist-communicologist R.D. Laing puts it this way: "Every relationship implies a definition of self by other and other by self" (*Self and Others*, Baltimore: Penguin Books, 1961, p. 86). This distinction between content development and negotiation of selves is similar to the distinction Paul Watxlawick, Janet Helmick Beavin, and Don D. Jackson make between "content" and "relationship" communication. See their *Pragmatics of Human Communication*, New York: Norton, 1967, especially Chapters 2 and 3.

2. Andras Angyal, "A Theoretical Model for Personality Studies," in Clark Moustakas, ed., *The Self: Explorations in Personal Growth*, New York: Harper & Row, 1956, p. 44.

3. *Existential Humanistic Psychology*, ed. Thomas C. Greening, Belmont, Calif.: Wadsworth 1972, p. 61

4. William Graham Cole, *Sex and Selfhood*, Garden City, N.Y.: Brown, 1968, p. 63. James Bugental makes the same point in different words: "Man is only human in a human context and requires that context of relationship as surely as he requires the atmospheric medium if he is to remain sane and realize his potential." (*The Course of Human Life*, ed. C. Buhler and F. Massarik, New York: Springer Publications, 1968, p. 387.)

5. Although this example involves three different persons, you might accept, partly accept, and reject the self-definition of the same person at different times and in different contexts.

6. This term is used by a variety of persons who study communication, including R. D. Laing; Watzlawick, Beavin, and Jackson; and Martin Buber.

7. "Distance and Relation," *The Knowledge of Man*, ed. Maurice Friedman, trans. Maurice Friedman and Ronald Gregor Smith, New York: Harper Torchbooks, 1965, p.71. Reprinted by permission.

8. Quoted in Laing, *Self and Others, op. cit*, pp. 98–99.

9. Hugh Prather, *I Touch the Earth, The Earth Touches Me*, Garden City, N.Y.: Doubleday, 1972, n.p.

10. One person responded to this idea by suggesting that when the other person's definition of self is negative, it is often helpful to reject it and to emphasize his or her positive aspects. Although we agree that this kind of rejection might grow out of good intentions, we don't think it will result in interpersonal-quality communication, because it still involves the lack of acceptance that creates resentment and fear.

11. We got the idea for this conversation from examples in George R. Bach and Peter Wyder, *The Intimate Enemy: How to Fight Fair in Love and Marriage*, New York: Avon Books, 1968.

12. Carl R. Rogers, "Dialogue between Martin Buber and Carl R. Roger," *Knowledge of Man, op. cit.*, pp. 169–170. Reprinted by permission.

13. Our explanation of negotiation of selves also obscures some other aspects of the complexity of interpersonal communication. For example, the definition of self you share depends on whether and how you accept, partly accept, or reject the way you perceive *yourself*. In addition, your communication behavior depends not only on how you see yourself and how you see the other, but also on how you see the other seeing you, how you see the other seeing you seeing him or her, and so on to theoretical infinity.

Although we are aware of those "neglected complexities," we've found in our own classes that what's included here is complicated enough to be fairly accurate, yet simple enough to be workable.

For more complex treatments of the negotiation-of-selves idea, see the materials in the "Additional Resources" list, especially Watzlawick, Beavin, and Jackson, Chapters 2 and 3; Laing, *Self and Other* and *Knots*; Laing, Phillipson, and Lee, "The Spiral of Interpersonal Perspectives" and Interaction and Interexperience in Dyads" in *Interpersonal Perception*; and Esterson, *Leaves of Spring*, part II: "Interexperience and Interaction."

ADDITIONAL RESOURCES

R.D. Laing talks about the negotiation-of-selves process from the point of view Books, 1969). See especially part 2, "Forms of Interpersonal Action." Laing treats the same process in a radically different way in his difficult-to-describe book about human relationships, called *Knots* (New York: Random House, 1972).

One of Laing's co-workers, Aaron Esterson, also discusses this process in the theoretical part of his book *The Leaves of Spring* (Harmondsworth, Middlesex, England: Penguin Books, 1970), part 2, "Interexperience and Interaction."

Martin Buber briefly mentions the communication problems created by the negotiation-of-selves process in the "Being and Seeming" section of his essay "Elements of the Interhuman." See Buber's book *The Knowledge of Man*, ed. Maurice Friedman (New York: Harper Torchbooks, 1965), pp. 72–88.

Under the heading "Relationship Communication,"Paul Watzlawick, Janet Helmick Beavin, and Don D. Jackson discuss some ideas that are closely related to what we call negotiation of selves. See their book *Pragmatics of Human*

Communication (New York: Norton, 1967), pp. 51–54 and 81–93, especially pp. 83–89.

I (John) also tried to talk about this process under the headings "Transaction" and "Relationship Communication" in the introduction to *Bridges Not Walls: A Book About Interpersonal Communication* (Reading, Mass.: Addison-Wesley, 1973), pp. 7–17.

George J. McCall and J.L. Simmons's book *Identities and Interactions* (New York: The Free Press, 1966) presents, among other things, a sociological version of something similar to the negotiation-of-selves idea. In McCall and Simmons's terms, in every "symbolic interaction" process, "the basic 'thing' to be identified . . . is the person himself. For each actor there is one key 'thing' whose identity and meaning must be consensually established before all else—namely, himself. 'Who am I in this situation? What implications do I have for the plans of action, both active and latent, of myself and of the others?' " (p. 61)

5

Sharing Some of Your Self

We can't overemphasize the importance of this chapter and the next one to interpersonal communication. In our discussion of negotiation of selves, we said that sharing some of your humanness is one of the two absolutely essential ingredients of interpersonal-quality communication, and that's what this chapter is about. As we also said, another necessary element is being aware of some of the other person's humanness; we'll talk about that in the next chapter.

Other people who have written about interpersonal communication seem to agree about the importance of sharing some of your self. For example, Martin Buber says that the duality between genuine openness, which he calls "being," and hiding behind a false front, or "seeming," is "the *essential* problem" in interpersonal communication. As Buber writes, "Whatever the meaning of the word 'truth' may be in other realms, in the interhuman realm it means that men communicate themselves to one another as what they are."[1]

Humanistic psychologist Carl Rogers feels the same way. He often uses the term "congruence" to talk about sharing some of your self, and he agrees that it's *vital* to establishing and maintaining interpersonal communication. He says, for example, that for communication to be interpersonal, each person should be "genuine and without 'front' or facade, openly being the feelings and attitudes which are at that moment flowing in him. . . ." As Rogers explains, that means that the person is aware of his or her feelings, is able "to live these feelings, to be them in the relationship," and when it's appropriate, can accurately describe the feelings to another.[2]

Sharing some of your self is vitally important to interpersonal communication, but it is also misunderstood by many people *and* is sometimes very hard to "do." So, we'd like to start this chapter by trying to clarify what we mean by sharing some of your self—and what we don't mean—and then make some practical suggestions about how sharing works in human communication.

WHAT SHARING IS AND WHAT IT ISN'T

Example 1

Mark: Hey, Suz, what'd you think of the movie?

Susie: Fantastic! I've never laughed so hard in all my life—that's my kind of humor!

Mark: Yeah, I know what you mean.

Susie: Actually, I've been in a good mood for weeks. Right now I'm working on a term paper, and usually I hate doing papers. But I'm not letting this one get me down. I feel in control of myself. You know what I mean?

Mark: You've been out in the sun too long.

Susie: No, I'm not kidding, Mark. It's not just the term paper. I've kind of been thinking about how most of the time I let myself be controlled by the things around me. I worry about term papers, grades, who likes me, who doesn't like me, and stuff like that. Right now, I've talked myself into not worrying about those things, and I feel great!

Mark: Man, I've never seen you so excited. I think you're really on the level.

Susie: Well, I always feel like I tell you about my frustrations and failures, so today you're hearing about my triumphs.

Example 2

Maureen, a woman who was in one of my (John) classes, came into my office and told me that she was "getting *very* uncomfortable in that class."

I had asked class members to divide themselves into ongoing "family groups" in order to work on some of the material. Maureen said that the last time her family group met, she'd become very upset at one person who seemed insensitive to her feelings, almost to the point of brutality.

"I have hardly said anything all quarter in that group," Maureen said, "because I felt I didn't have anything important to say. Yesterday, I really felt strongly about the discussion we were having. We were talking about being forced by institutions we were in to treat people impersonally, and I told them about some of my experiences at the Legal Aid office. Pam interrupted to say that these little stories were just fine, but that they were really beside the point the group was supposed to be discussing. She was really abrupt about it. I was so frustrated and mad at her that I couldn't say anything for the rest of the time we were together."

I was surprised to hear that about Pam, and I said so to Maureen. I also asked Maureen if there was anything I could do to help her and Pam work through their difficulties with each other. After we talked a while, Maureen said that since the group was going to spend that Saturday together, maybe things would work out so that she could bring it up with Pam in a meeting sometime later in the week.

I told Maureen that the situation sounded a little like something I'd recently experienced with Gene Ann. Gene Ann and I both knew we should be talking about a problem we had, but we weren't. I had found that it was really easy to put off dealing with the problem. When Gene Ann and I finally discussed it, however, I'd discovered that the process wasn't as scary as I had thought it would be. Once things got out in the open, it was relatively easy to deal with them.

As I told Maureen, "It's easy to avoid something like this, so I think it might be a good idea to bring it up as soon as there's time to deal with it, and not to wait until next week. I've also been afraid to bring up something like that, but I've found that anticipating that kind of talk is often worse than doing it. The most important thing—and the hardest for me—is to express *my* feelings about the situation without labelling the other person."

Maureen said she'd give it a try and that she'd let me know how it came out.

If you look at those two dissimilar examples, we think you can begin to see what we mean—and don't mean—by sharing some of your self. In the first place, note the lack of references to sex, religion, or politics. Sharing some of your self does *not* necessarily mean discussing your sex life or some other soul-stirring, deep-seated, profound experience or feeling. Sometimes, those kinds of things are important, but the vast majority of the time, what you share is neither deep nor heartrending. That doesn't mean that your sharing is silly or trivial, just that it isn't necessarily heavy.

Nor does sharing mean unloading only your negative or depressed feelings. Two people can often come much closer together just by sharing some things they feel *good* about. The dialogue between Mark and Susie is an example of that. The positive things Susie shared with Mark definitely helped him see her humanness and helped their communication be interpersonal.

We're also *not* suggesting that you should blurt out everything that you're thinking and feeling in a nonstop stream of self-centered disclosures. As Buber puts it, *being* "does not depend on one saying to the other everything that occurs to him, but only on his letting no seeming creep in between himself and the other."[3] In other words, you don't say everything, but what you do say is genuine.

The main point is that sharing needs to be appropriate to the context and the relationship. Most interpersonal relationships take time to grow, and deep, detailed disclosures to a relative stranger will usually succeed only in making the other person uncomfortable. I (John) didn't feel that it would be appropriate to explain to Maureen the details of my discussion with Gene Ann. And I don't think Maureen expected me to. Similarly, she didn't feel compelled to give me a blow-by-blow description of her encounter with Pam. What we shared was relevant and genuine, but the "amount" was appropriate to the situation.

Appropriateness really is important. Sharing some of your self is not just meant to make *you* feel better; it's meant to improve your relationship with other persons. You don't share just to suit yourself, but to facilitate the *relationship*. Remember that what you think is light and relatively impersonal might seem uncomfortably intimate to the other person. In other words, sharing is for you *and* the other person(s); be as sensitive as you can to *their* expectations and feelings.

Finally, we believe that you always ought to be in control of how much of your self you share, with whom, and when. We don't agree with the format of some forced-choice encounter groups in which each person is compelled to spill his or her guts or leave the group. Sharing your self always involves some risk, and consequently you should always retain the right to choose what to reveal and what to conceal.

We have felt that risk in writing this book. We haven't shared anything particularly intimate with you, but we have been more open about some of our thoughts and feelings than we might otherwise have been in this situation. We've done that because we recognize one of the paradoxes of sharing some of your self with another; usually, you don't want to *share* unless you *trust* the other person, because sharing is *risky*. But you can't create *trust* and thus diminish *risk* without *sharing*. In other words, people generally share some of their selves when they trust each other, and they create trust by sharing with each other. Sharing creates trust and trust encourages sharing. We've therefore come to the conclusion that the risks we've taken are worth it. They're worth it because they might help create the kind of trusting relationship that can help us grow. So far, we haven't been disappointed. One or two persons who have read this manuscript have told us we were being too personal or that some of what we wrote was "in questionable taste." But most people have been fairly willing to trust us, and we believe that that trust will make this book much more useful and helpful than a distant, impersonal commentary.

There's another paradox of sharing. The more you find out about another person, the more you realize how relatively little you know about her or him. Or, from the other point of view, the more you share, the more there is left to share. Some people exaggerate the risk of self-disclosure because they're afraid that it means giving up everything that they are—not having anything left that's uniquely theirs. But as many couples who have enjoyed a long-term, intimate relationship have learned, that fear is groundless. You can never succeed in telling someone everything about you, primarily because you're continually changing. As one person becomes more open to another, he or she also becomes more mysterious, and that ever-present mystery is one thing that can keep a relationship exciting over the years.

It would help if you'd remember that when we talk about sharing some of your humanness, we are *not* necessarily talking about a superserious sex rap, a thoughtless gut-dump, a long-winded, self-centered monologue, or an embarrassingly intimate disclosure. We believe that you should always be able to choose what you share and that your choices should be appropriate to the situation and to the relationship. We recognize that sharing is risky, but we believe that the risk is worth it because of the trust that can be built. We've found that the more you learn about another person, the more you realize how impossible it is to know her or him completely.

SOME SUGGESTIONS ABOUT SHARING

First, Become Aware of Your Self

In order to share some of your self, you first have to be aware of what's there to be shared. We're not suggesting that you have to withdraw at this point for a year of contemplating your navel, but it is a good idea to give some thought to the makeup of your self. As we suggested in Chapter 4, one way to do that is to think in terms of your *historical* self and your *present* self.

Your historical self. For some reason it seems that when we look inside ourselves, the negative things are often the ones we notice first. I (John) believe that we've been conditioned to do that in part from many of the educational experiences we've had. The model for education in our culture seems to be "trial and error," with an emphasis on the latter. Too often, education seems to be a process of identifying and eliminating weaknesses or faults rather than a process of becoming aware of and building on strengths. It's certainly not a good idea to develop an unrealistic, pollyanna attitude or to ignore defects and failures. But it's been our experience that if you start by recognizing the positive side of your historical self, you re more likely to be willing to share in ways that can promote interpersonal communication.

We therefore think that it's a good idea to start becoming aware of your self with an inventory of your strengths. It would probably be more complete if you'd write it down, so we'll leave room for you to do that here.* (You might at first feel a little uncomfortable focusing so strongly on what you do well, but give it a try anyway. There's nothing wrong with feeling good about yourself.)

Individual Application: Inventory of Strengths

First, what kinds of manual tasks or jobs are you best at? For example, I (John) was recently surprised to learn that I can hang wallpaper. I (Gary) can handle most house-painting jobs. Are you good at house painting? Gardening? Lawn care? Window washing? Cleaning? Furniture moving? Repair work? Tuning a car? Other?

_____

_____

_____

What is your strongest special skill? Macrame? Cooking? Public speaking? Auto mechanics? Knitting? Woodwork? Electronics? Interior design? Sewing?

_____

*As we said before, if you plan to resell this book, it'd be better to respond to these questions—and to the others in this chapter—on a separate piece of paper.

Photography? Sculpture? Drama? Reading? I (Gary) usually feel comfortable in a public-speaking situation.

_____

_____

_____

What sports or games do you understand or perform best? Volleyball? Pinochle? Bowling? Chess? Swimming? Football? Softball? Soccer? Baseball? Track? Bridge? Basketball? Hockey? Badminton? Billiards? Wrestling? Handball? Driving? Motorcycling? Hiking? Backpacking? Skiing?

_____

_____

Which school subjects were or are easiest for you? Economics? Mathematics? I (Gary) have usually done well in math, although it scares me a little. Biology? Speech? English? Business? P.E.? Drama? Geology? Chemistry? French? Philosophy? That's been fun for me (John). Spanish? Home economics? History?

_____

_____

What do you do especially well as a communicator? Listen? Organize thoughts? Be yourself? Use effective language? Make others comfortable? Understand others' ideas? Treat others as humans rather than as objects?

_____

_____

What are your strongest personal characteristics? Loyalty? Understanding? Thoughtfulness? Cheerfulness? Leadership ability? Enthusiasm? Determination? Even temper? Flexibility? Tact? Carefulness?

_____

_____

_____

Whose love have you been able to return? Parents? Children? Brother(s)? Sister(s)? It's been a revelation to me (John) to grow beyond sister-brother fighting to a really fine relationship with my sister, Barb. Steady date? Spouse? Grandparents? Other relatives? Teacher? Best friend? Boss?

_____

_____

_____

_____

◇◆◇

Obviously, that short list of strengths doesn't completely represent your historical self. But it's a start and, we think, a start in the right direction. Why don't you continue it? Be on the lookout for things you do well, for opportunities to feel good about yourself. Dog-ear this page, if you want, or set aside a notebook page or two and use the space to record your strengths. You might be surprised at the difference it can make in the ways you relate to other people.

◇◆◇

Individual Application: Some of My Other Strengths

_____

_____

_____

_____

_____

Another way that you can help fill in that outline of your self is by looking at what Edmund Byrne and Edward Maziarz call "five polarities of human life."[4] Byrne and Maziarz suggest that you can understand your self in terms of five sets of opposing forces, or "polarities": movement and rest, purposiveness and randomness, growth and deterioration, simplicity with complexity, and immanence and transcendence. Although their language sometimes gets a little abstract, we think the forces they identify can provide some useful "handles" or "focus points" for understanding your self. As they put it: "The various systems by which the human organism is alive are in such a state of constant flow that to be alive as a human being is to maintain a delicate balance between the various polarities of life."[5]

Movement and rest is one polarity. Byrne writes: "I seem never to be fully at rest nor, for that matter, ever fully in motion."[6] If you're like me (John), you sometimes seem to be most completely yourself when all the countless little movements of your breathing, running, straining, stretching, and sensing are unified into one delightful ache—for example, just before I get my second wind in a hard-fought paddleball game. Other times, my movement seems almost completely aimless; I feel about as together as exploding popcorn. In still other situations, I feel most completely myself when I'm at rest—almost in a meditative state. But neither movement nor rest is uniquely or even typically me. I am both or, more accurately, my self is in tension between them.

My self is also both *purposive and random*. Because I am alive, I am continuously in motion—my blood flowing, my foot tapping, my eyes bouncing from one object on the desk to another, my tongue tasting the gum in my mouth, and often my body is moving, either physically or in my imagination. But neither conscious purpose nor pure chance completely explains my movements. Although I have reasons for going to the kitchen and filling my coffee cup, it's difficult to talk about the purpose of my sigh. Much of what I do is done for some reason, but not everything; my self is both spontaneous and planned, purposive and random.

Human selves are also involved simultaneously in *growth and deterioration*, self-realization and withdrawal, life and death. Physiologically, our bodies are continuously generating new cells and sloughing off dead ones. Or, to put it another way, "life is the sum of all those forces that are resisting death, and death occurs when that sum is equal to zero."[7] Interpersonally, we're also in constant tension between growth and deterioration. In the space of a few minutes, we can respond to someone in ways that are facilitative and destructive. We can encourage relationships and discourage them; we're available and aloof, loving and hateful, open and closed. But we're never all one or the other. Our selves include both.

A fourth polarity in terms of which you can see your self is the blending of unity with multiplicity, *simplicity with complexity*. Sometimes, it seems as if I (John) choose to say or do something for a simple, uncomplicated reason. I recently pulled the engine of my Volvo station wagon just to save the $50–$75 labor charge. There was no complex explanation for doing it; I simply wanted to save some money. Other times, whether and how much I work on the car depends on all kinds of things—what meetings I have to attend, whether Gene Ann has to study for a test, whether Marcia and Lisa need a ride somewhere, whether I can borrow the right tools, and what kind of mood I'm in. Similarly, in some ways you might feel that your life is simple—all you want to do is be happy, serve God, be loved, or get rich. But from another point of view, everything depends on everything else, and nothing is uncomplicated or orderly. Maybe you're going to school, for example, partly because somebody expects you to, partly because you're sometimes excited by what you learn, partly because you enjoy the social life, and partly because you want to be able to land a productive and rewarding job. The point of this polarity is that neither the simple nor the complicated explanation alone really captures *you*. Your self is in tension between unity and multiplicity; it's *both*.

A fifth polarity, which in a way unifies the other four, is the tension between *immanence and transcendence*, the concrete and the spiritual, the historically factual and the ongoing. To highlight your self's immanence is to emphasize that you live in an inescapably concrete, natural world. Because you were born a human, you cannot fly without help; if you lean back far enough in your chair, you'll fall over; you can't chew granite. You have a past and you are located in a particular place and time. If you cut yourself, you'll bleed. But immanence is not all there is to you. Transcendence suggests that you're also more than just a physical object in a physical world; you're moving toward fulfilling yourself in the future. You can control some of the forces that affect you; you are free to choose how to respond to what happens; you can change things. You aren't condemned to stay where you are—physically or psychologically. This polarity can remind you that you are always locked, in part, into the concrete, space-time world, but that you're also much more than that. You sweat, but you can also dream. Sometimes, you're closed, but you can also be open to others. You can transcend the concrete and mundane, and one way you can do that is by being willing and able to share some of those *non*spatiotemporal parts of you with another person.

As Byrne and Maziarz suggest, you might want to use these polarities as a five-sided prism through which you can look at your self. Each polarity highlights or focuses on a different dimension of the continually changing you.

Your present self.   Hopefully, your thinking about how your self reflects those polarities can help lead you toward being aware not only of your historical self, but also of your present self. As we said in Chapter 4, since interpersonal communication involves sharing some of your present self, it's important that you develop your ability to get in touch with who you are here and now. Unfortunately, that isn't easy to do. Your present self is always changing, so your awareness has to change, too. It's not so much like learning about an orange—which will sit still and be felt, smelled, peeled, and tasted—as it is like getting to know the wet part of a river. There's no one way to do it, and the job never gets completely done. Being aware of the here and now does get easier, but it never gets finished.

Practice can help, though, so let's try a couple of things here. First, look closely at the picture on p. 156. How do you respond to this picture? What's happening in you as you look at it? Try writing down some present-tense "I" statements about how you're feeling as you look at it. Don't stop with just "I feel angry" or "I don't feel much of anything." Be as specific and as detailed as you can.

As you look at the picture, what's happening—*now*—in your stomach?

I am _____

_____

What's happening in your eyes? I am _____

_____

What emotions are you experiencing? _____

_____

What attitudes about cruelty to children does the picture create or reinforce? _____

_____

Remembering also happens in the here and now. What memories are you thinking of—now? _____

_____

How are you responding to those memories? Is your stomach tight? Are you relaxing? Can you feel reactions in your eyes? What is your breathing doing? _____

_____

What other ways are you reacting *now*? _____

_____

Now, try getting in touch with some of your responses to the following words, which are based on an actual courtroom trial.

"I was driving on highway 90 going to a ski resort. There were three of us in the car. I remember turning to my right and seeing Jill, who was sitting with me in the front seat, half-way out the car window, trying to put the radio aerial up. I grabbed for her and shouted "get the hell in here," and about that time I looked back at the road and it was curving. I missed the curve; we rolled about three times—I'm not sure exactly—but I remember hearing Jill scream. That's all I know . . . .

What's happening now as you respond to those words? What memories does it bring to mind? What are you remembering now?

_____

_____

How is your body responding? _____

_____

What attitudes or feelings do the words create or reinforce? _____

_____

How are you responding to being asked all these questions? Are you skipping over the places where we've asked you to write something down? If so, why? For example, are you feeling rushed now? Too rushed to stop and write? Are you feeling imposed on? "Just let me read; don't ask me to write, too." Are you feeling embarrassed? Discouraged? Defensive? Bored? Impatient? How are those feelings occurring in you— what is happening? Use the space below not to compose a well-worded reply to those questions, but to scribble a scrawl that expresses some of what you're feeling now about our asking you to do these things.

Now try hanging some labels on your here-and-now reactions to this section of this chapter. Circle the words in the following list that you would choose right now to describe this part of this book:

aggressive	energetic	ingenious	logical	persuasive
annoying	foolish	innovative	loving	pompous
bitter	frank	insensitive	malicious	pretentious
calm	friendly	insincere	manipulative	radical
cheerful	gentle	irresponsible	naive	reassuring
cold	giving	serious	negative	rejecting
cranky	happy	silly	organized	scientific
critical	hostile	simple	original	trusting
cynical	idealistic	spontaneous	overconfident	unassuming
derogatory	imaginative	irritable	overconforming	unreasonable
self-conscious	immature	juvenile	overemotional	useful
sensible	inconsiderate	lively	thoughtful	witty
sensitive	thought-provoking	challenging	revealing	threatening

Sometimes the persons in our classes respond to the kinds of questions we've asked you here with a little discomfort and confusion. We've responded that way, too. Our responses are affected by the fact that *we're not used to being aware of our present selves*. It's an unfamiliar thing to be asked to do, and we often react a little negatively when we're asked to do something unfamiliar.

But it doesn't have to be that way. Your self isn't something you need to be afraid to get to know. As Thomas Harris[8] puts it, you *are* "O.K." You feel positive sometimes, and that's O.K; you feel negatively sometimes, and that's O.K., too. It's what you *do* with who you are that's important. We hope that the first part of this chapter has helped you to get in touch with that "who you are." Now, we'd like to talk about what you can do with your awareness of your historical and present self to promote interpersonal communication.

Second, See How Sharing "Works"

Joseph Luft and Harrington Ingham created a diagram that helps explain how the process of sharing some of your self works in human communication.[9] They call the diagram the Johari (Joseph + Harrington) window, and it looks like this:

	Information known to self	Information not known to self
Information known to others	OPEN	BLIND
Information not known to others	HIDDEN	UNKNOWN

The Johari window identifies four kinds of information about your self that play a part in your communicating: the things you are aware of and are willing to share with the other person (open), the things that the other person knows about you but that you aren't aware of (blind), the things you know about yourself that you're *un*willing to share (hidden), and the aspects of your self that neither you nor the other person is aware of (unknown).

In the communication between you and me (John) right now, we both know, for example, that I'm a little uneasy about being the father of two junior-high-age girls; that information about my self is in the "open" square of the Johari window that describes our present communicating. It's important to remember that there's always *something* in this "open" square. Whenever you communicate with another human, you necessarily share *something* of your self; you cannot completely avoid sharing.

As you and I communicate, I'm "blind" to information about myself that you are getting by reading "between the lines" of this book. For example, you might be under the impression that I'm less confident than I'd like to appear or that I'm revealing more about myself than I think I am. There are many things that are "hidden" in my relationship with you—events from my past and my present that I think are irrelevant to our communicating, details about my relationships with others that don't seem to me to be appropriate to share in this context, and so on. There is also for each of us an "unknown" dimension of our relationship. This one's a little difficult to talk about, but it could include, for instance, attitudes or motivations which a psychoanalyst might see manifested in my communication, but which neither you nor I is aware of. The existence of this "unknown" area seems to be proved each time an attitude, fear, or belief that we didn't think we had comes to the surface and affects our relationship with someone.

Theoretically, you could draw a Johari window for each relationship you participate in. The window representing your relationship with your mother or father is obviously different from the one for your relationship with your roommate, lover, or spouse. You can also use the Johari window to diagram what might be called the "sharing status" of your relationship. For example, when two persons first meet, one person's window for that relationship might look like this:

OPEN	BLIND
HIDDEN	UNKNOWN

Some time later, when the same relationship has developed to the point of intimacy, the same person's window would look more like this:

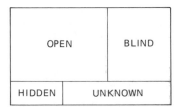

Similarly, some textbook authors' communication with you would probably look something like this:

We've been trying to change that configuration. Hopefully, a Johari window of our communication with you would look more like this:

OPEN	BLIND
HIDDEN	UNKNOWN

The Johari window summarizes much of what we're saying about interpersonal communication in this chapter and the next one. In Johari terms, developing interpersonal-quality communication involves enlarging the "open" area in two ways: (1) moving information from the "hidden" to the "open" area by *sharing some of your self*, and (2) moving information from the "blind" to the "open" area by *being aware of and responding to the other*. In this chapter we're trying to clarify what it means to move information from "hidden" to "open." We think that this movement involves, first, getting in touch with your historical and present self and seeing how sharing works. The next step is to see what to share.

Third, Share Both Your Historical and Present Self

The distinction between the historical self and the present self can also make it easier to talk about the content of your sharing—"what" you share.[10]

Historical self.   In part, sharing involves letting the other person know about some aspects of your historical self that he or she probably wouldn't be aware of unless you revealed them. As we said in Chapter 3, your historical self is made up of those parts of you that are the same today as they were some time ago, the relatively unchanging parts of you that are often thought of as roles—female or male, student, musician, salesperson, chess player, dancer, etc.

Although interpersonal communication cannot be built on just sharing historical selves, that's a beginning, and it can be helpful. It's one thing, for example, to treat someone you're dating like a mannequin whose function is to accompany you to movies, dances, dinner, etc. It's usually much more pleasant if the two of you can at least share enough to find out that you have in common your student status, work experience, political beliefs, or interest in skydiving. That kind of sharing can move you in the direction of interpersonal communication.

Each person reveals some indirect cues about his or her historical self *nonverbally*. The clothes you wear, the style of your hair, whether you wear jewelry and what kind, the setting you're in (office, house, apartment, expensive restaurant), the way you get around (bicycle, sports car, motorcycle) are all ways of revealing something about your historical self. But with the exception of uniforms, nonverbal cues about your historical self are generally vague and indirect. Most information about your historical self comes primarily from *verbal* cues.

You learned something about us from the nonverbal cues in our pictures and from your nonverbal image of us as college teachers — you might visualize us in a classroom, office, or hallway, not far from a stack of books of one kind or another. But you can learn about our families, our experiences, our attitudes, and our beliefs, only from the *words* we write. Your nonverbal picture is general and indirect; our words help specify directly who we are. The same goes for you. The persons you're talking with are probably not going to know that you have been a Young Democrat, have taught swimming, can't stand beer, spent a year in France, and have always wanted to go to law school unless you *tell* them. In *words.*

Remember the six functions of words we talked about in Chapter 2 (refer, perform an action, evoke emotion, affect perception, reduce uncertainty, bring people together)? When words are used to share historical self, they're functioning primarily to *refer.* They point your listener to characteristics you have or to events you have experienced. As such, sharing your historical self is usually not very risky. It is relatively easy to refer to the past from a distance. The words you use can objectify, rationalize, and omit uncomfortable details. In short, sharing your historical self can help you become more than an object for the other person, but in order for you to reveal your humanness in any complete way, you need to share some of your present self.

Present self.   Sharing also involves letting the other person know about some aspects of your *present* self that she or he probably wouldn't know unless you revealed them. When you share some of your present self, both verbal and nonverbal cues are important. The psychologist Sidney Jourard has probably done more research on interpersonal sharing than anyone else, and he highlights the importance of verbally sharing present self:

> I don't want to belabor the point, but I think it is almost self-evident that you cannot love another person, that is, behave toward him so as to foster his happiness and growth, unless you know what he needs. And you cannot know what he needs unless he tells you.[11]

As Jourard points out, if you don't *say* "where you're at," the person you're talking with has only two alternatives: to ignore your needs or to guess them.

You can often tell whether what's shared is historical or present self just by listening to the words that are used. Someone who is sharing present self almost always uses first-person pronouns—it's about *I* and *me*, not about you or they. In addition, this kind of sharing is usually in the present tense. The most accurate and effective sharing of present self is also specific and concrete; the person doesn't hide behind generalities, but shares relevant and graphic details. The statement "People sometimes get upset when they hear things like that" is *not* sharing present self. Comments like "I feel relaxed when we can talk with each other this frankly" or "I feel uncomfortable because I don't feel like you're listening to me" *are*.

Another characteristic of the verbal language of this kind of sharing is a little more difficult to explain. If a person is accurately sharing part of what he or she is *presently* experiencing, the words that person uses cannot be "statements of external facts."[12] Statements like "That tree is green," "Volkswagens are noisy," "He is stupid," "You are brilliant" or "She is the best gymnast in the state" are not direct expressions of present experiencing. Those statements do reflect indirectly something about the person saying them. But present self is always expressed as perceptions, feelings, and meanings from an *internal* frame of reference. As Carl Rogers[13] explains:

> I never *know* that he is stupid or you are bad. I can only perceive that you seem this way to me. Likewise, strictly speaking I do not *know* that the rock is hard [or the tree green], even though I may be very sure that I experience it as hard if I fall down on it. . . . If the person is thoroughly congruent then it is clear that all of his [or her] communication would necessarily be put in a context of personal perception.*

We think that Rogers is making an important point. We've found that it's helpful to interpersonal-quality communication when people are willing to take enough responsibility for what they say to recognize that "You're crazy" actually means something like "I disagree with you," "I don't understand," or perhaps "I'm afraid of you." Similarly, "She's impossible to get along with" means "I can't seem to get along with her," and "This class is worthless" means "I'm not finding anything worthwhile in this class right now." And since labels are actually almost always reports of personal perceptions, it's very helpful to learn to state your perceptions accurately. Your communicating can improve significantly, we think, if you'll just do this one thing: stop labeling others and start taking verbal responsibility for what you say. Try replacing "You're mixed up" with "I don't understand." Try "I'm uncomfortable when you say that" instead of "Shut up!" or "Get outa here!" In order to develop your ability to share present self verbally, you might also try the following individual application.

Individual Application: Description of Feeling

We display feelings in many different ways, e.g., by

Commands:	"Get lost!" "Shut up!"
Questions:	"Are you sure it's safe to smoke this stuff?"
Accusations:	"You're always giving your damn job first priority."
Judgments:	"You're a fantastic songwriter." "You're a snob."

Note that although each of the examples *displays* strong feeling, the verbal statement does not describe or say what the feeling is. In none of the sentences does the speaker refer to himself or herself or to what he or she is feeling.

Sometimes, however, sentences do contain the emotional state of the speaker. Such sentences are *descriptions of feeling*. They share present-self feeling by referring to the speaker and naming or identifying what the speaker feels. "I am really furious!" "I'm afraid to smoke this stuff!" "I feel disconfirmed."

When you use *descriptions* you can share your feelings accurately in ways that will probably be less hurtful than commands, questions, accusations, or judgments.

In each of the following sets of sentences, all the statements display feeling; i.e., any of them could have been spoken by the same person in the same situation. Each sentence, however, may be either of two different ways of communicating feelings by words. Put a *D* before each sentence that shares present-self feeling by *describing* the speaker's feeling. Put a *No* before each sentence that displays feeling, but *does not describe* what it is.[14] (Our answers and explanations begin on p. 166.)

1. a) Shut up! Not another word out of you!
   b) Please be quiet; you're getting awfully loud.
   c) I'm really annoyed by what you just said.

2. a) Can't you see I'm busy? Don't you have eyes?
   b) I really resent your interrupting me so often.
   c) You have no consideration for anybody else; you're completely selfish.

3. a) I feel discouraged because of some things that happened today.
   b) This has been a lousy day.
   c) Who me? Oh, I'm fine.

4. a) You're a wonderful person.
   b) I really respect your opinion; you're so well informed.

5. a) I feel comfortable and free to be myself when I'm around you.
   b) We all feel you're really great.
   c) Everybody likes you.

6. a) If things don't improve around here, I'm going to look for another job.
   b) I'm afraid to admit that I need help with my work.

7. a) This is a very poor exercise.
   b) I feel that this is a very poor exercise.
   c) I feel uncomfortable doing this exercise.

8. a) I feel inadequate to contribute anything in this group.
    b) I am inadequate to contribute anything in this group.
9. a) I'm a born loser; I'll never amount to anything.
    b) That teacher is awful; he didn't teach me anything.
    c) I'm depressed because I flunked that test.
10. a) I feel warm and comfortable in my group.
    b) I feel that everyone values my contributions to this group.

Our Answers

1. a) No Commands like these exhibit strong emotion, but do not name the feeling that prompted them.
    b) No This suggestion is more thoughtful than (a), but it doesn't describe the speaker's feeling, either.
    c) D   Speaker says she or he feels annoyed.
2. a) No These are questions that express strong feeling without naming it.
    b) D   Speaker states that he or she feels resentment.
    c) No This is accusation that displays strong negative feelings. Because the feelings are not named, you don't know whether the accusations originate from anger, disappointment, hurt, or something else.
3. a) D   Speaker says he or she feels discouraged.
    b) No The statement appears to describe what kind of day it was. In fact, it expresses the speaker's negative feelings without saying whether he or she feels depressed, annoyed, lonely, humiliated, rejected, etc.
    c) No It might appear to describe a feeling, but "fine" is too vague to help someone understand the speaker, and this kind of statement is often a way to hide feelings rather than to describe them.
4. a) No This value judgment displays positive feelings about the other person, but does not describe what they are. Does the speaker like, respect, enjoy, admire, love, value the other person, or what?
    b) D   The speaker describes his or her positive feeling as respect.
5. a) D   A clear description of how the speaker feels when with the other person.

b) No You can describe only your *own* feelings; here, the speaker
does not speak for himself or herself, but hides behind the
phrase "we feel." In addition, "you're really great" is a *value
judgment* and does not name a feeling.

c) No The statement does name a feeling ("likes"), but the speaker
attributes it to everyone and does not make clear that the feeling is within him or her. A description of feeling must contain
"I," "me," "my," or "mine" to make clear that the feelings are
the speaker's.

6. a) No This statement displays negative feelings by talking about the
condition of this job. It does not describe the speaker's inner
state.

b) D A clear description of how the speaker feels about this
problem. He or she feels afraid.

7. a) No Negative criticisms and value judgments often seem like
expressions of anger. In fact, negative value judgments and
accusations often stem from the speaker's fear, hurt feelings,
disappointments, or loneliness. This statement is a negative
value judgment that displays negative feelings, but it does not
state what type they are.

b) No Although the person begins by saying "I feel. . . ," the speaker
does not then name the feeling. Instead, the speaker passes a
negative value judgment on the exercise. Note that merely
placing the words "*I feel*" in front of a statement does not
make the statement a description of feeling. People often say
"I feel" when they mean "I think" or "I believe."

c) D The speaker describes his or her feeling when doing this
exercise.

8. a) D Speaker says that she or he feels inadequate.

b) No This sounds much like the previous statement. However, it
says that the speaker actually *is* inadequate—not that he just
currently feels this way. The speaker has evaluated himself—
has made a negative value judgment and has labeled himself
inadequate.

9. a) No The speaker has evaluated himself again—passed a negative
judgment on himself by labeling himself as a born loser.

b) No Instead of labeling himself a failure, the speaker blames the
teacher. This is another value judgment and is not a description of a feeling.

    c) D   The speaker states that he or she feels depressed. Statements (a) and (c) illustrate the important difference between passing judgment on yourself and describing your feelings.

10. a) D   The speaker says she feels warm and comfortable.
      b) No Instead of "I feel," the speaker should have said, "I believe." The last part of the statement really tells what the speaker believes *others feel* about him and not what she or he feels.

We hope that this exercise stressed the idea that one important aspect of sharing your present self is the kind of words you use. They should include first-person pronouns, present tense, active voice, concrete specifics, and the language of present experience. Carl Rogers uses this kind of language as he discusses the process of sharing.[15] Near the beginning of his book *On Becoming a Person*, he writes:

> I might start off these several statements of significant learnings with a negative item. *In my relationships with persons I have found that it does not help, in the long run, to act as though I were something that I am not.* It does not help to act calm and pleasant when actually I am angry and critical. It does not help to act as though I know the answers when I do not. It does not help to act as though I were a loving person if actually, at the moment, I am hostile. It does not help for me to act as though I were full of assurance, if actually I am frightened and unsure. Even on a very simple level I have found that this statement seems to hold. It does not help for me to act as though I were well when I feel ill.
>
> . . . I would want to make it clear that while I feel I have learned this to be true, I have by no means adequately profited from it. In fact, it seems to me that most of the mistakes I make in personal relationships, most of the times in which I fail to be of help to other individuals, can be accounted for in terms of the fact that I have, for some defensive reason, behaved in one way at a surface level, while in reality my feelings run in a contrary direction.*

Note that Rogers talks about the way he "behaves," not just the words he uses. That's because although verbal language is important,

---

   * *On Becoming a Person,* by Carl Rogers. Copyright © Houghton Mifflin Company, 1961. Used by permission of the publisher.

the *nonverbal* part of sharing your *present* self is just as important as the verbal part. As we've said before, you cannot stop "giving off" nonverbal cues. Written words include the nonverbal elements of spacing, typeface, paper color, and so on. Spoken words are made up in part of tone of voice, rate, volume, and vocal quality and are accompanied by facial expression, posture, muscle tone, bodily movement, etc. In short, since your nonverbal cues are always "there," the persons you're communicating with are always *interpreting* them, making inferences about them, and drawing conclusions—more or less consciously—based on them.

We also mentioned before that when there's a conflict between your verbal and nonverbal cues, people are more likely to notice, remember, rely on, and believe the *nonverbal* ones. That's one reason why nonverbal cues are such an important part of sharing your present self. Whether or not you fully recognize it, you're usually accepting or rejecting what others say to you primarily because of the nonverbal aspects of their communication.

This point presents a problem, and right now I (John) feel a little uncomfortable about it. I'm afraid you might be thinking something like this: "Well! If people believe what I share primarily because of the *nonverbal* parts of my communicating, then, since I want to be believable, I'd better concentrate not on what I say but on *how* I say it. I'd better work on orchestrating my facial expression, tone of voice, posture, and so on so I *look* sincere and honest, whether I am that way or not."

That's a very understandable reaction. In fact, the sociologist Erving Goffman has described human relationships generally as forms of drama or play-acting.[16] Goffman argues that each of us always "presents" one of our repertoire of "faces" to others in order to get them to respond the way we want them to. Although Goffman accurately describes some relationships, we emphatically do *not* think that it's a good idea for you to treat your communicating as just a series of rehearsed scenes and artificial performances. We're convinced that there are better ways to communicate. In the first place, the practical problem of living behind a false front is that it's almost impossible to pull it off successfully. As one team of communicologists puts it," . . . it is easy to profess something verbally but difficult to carry a lie into the realm of the analogic [nonverbal]."[17]

More important, hiding behind a "face" or false front is another form of objectifying other persons, and ultimately it backfires. Since your self grows in your relationships with others, *your* self suffers if those relationships are based on lies. In other words, attempting to lie when you're sharing some of your self is a form of interpersonal pollution. It's much better for both you and the other persons involved to be *congruent*. That is, you won't have to worry about conflicts between your verbal and nonverbal communications if you are always trying to be on the outside what you're being on the inside. Once again, Carl Rogers[18] makes the point well:

> I used to feel that if I fulfilled all the outer conditions of trust-worthiness—keeping appointments, respecting the confidential nature of the interview, etc.—and if I acted consistently the same during the interviews, then this condition [trustworthiness] would be fulfilled. But experience drove home the fact that to act consistently acceptant, for example, if in fact I was feeling annoyed or skeptical or some other non–acceptant feeling, was certain in the long run to be perceived as inconsistent or untrustworthy. I have come to recognize that being trustworthy does not demand that I be rigidly consistent but that I be *dependably real*. The term "congruent" is one I have used to describe the way I would like to be. By this I mean that whatever feeling or attitude I am experiencing would be matched by my awareness of that attitude. When this is true, then I am a unified or integrated person in that moment, and hence I can *be* whatever I deeply *am*. This is a reality which I find others experience as dependable.* (Italics added.)

We're not sure that any of us can achieve total congruence—total agreement between what's going on "externally" and "internally." In the first place, we're seldom completely in touch with our own feelings. Also, we're changing too rapidly. In many situations, we need to withhold some feelings just to keep from being overstimulated. As the Johari window illustrates, there are always some things that are "hidden" and "unknown"; total congruence is humanly impossible. But it's very important to enlarge the "open" square as much as possible—to be

---

* *On Becoming a Person*, by Carl Rogers. Copyright © Houghton Mifflin Company, 1961. Used by permission of the publisher.

as congruent as you can. When you want to communicate interpersonally, it's vital to work hard to develop the willingness and ability to share as much of your humanness as the situation will allow.

We hope you've got the idea at this point that sharing your present self can promote interpersonal communication partly because of its verbal possibilities and partly because of how it works nonverbally. There are also some other characteristics of this kind of sharing that explain why it does so much to help make interpersonal communication happen. First, sharing your present self is almost always interesting. As Gerard Egan explains, some people bore others by continually talking about themselves. Such people are boring because they are usually sharing their historical selves rather than their present selves. As Egan puts it, they "speak in generalities poorly disguised under the pronoun "I." Sharing present self, on the other hand:

> is always engaging, for it means that the speaker has to "blow his cover," lower his defenses. . . . People are seldom, if ever, bored with sincere self-revelation, because they intuitively realize its importance for the one revealing himself and respect him for what he is doing. . . . I think perhaps that it might be impossible to dislike someone who [shares present self], for it is an act of humility, a manifestation of a need to move into community. . . .[19]

It is also more risky to share present self than to share historical self. It's relatively easy to refer to the past from a comfortable distance, but it's more difficult when you're brought face to face with the changing, never completely understood here and now. As Rogers says, permitting your observable communication behavior to be congruent with whatever feeling or attitude you are experiencing requires courage. But your willingness to take the risk can move you closer to others, because sharing your present self "is always an implicit request for human support."[20] In fact, unlike sharing historical self which can become a nonmilitary version of the "name, rank, and serial number" monologue, sharing present self almost always invites response. It is, as Egan puts it, "a signal for others to move into one's experience."[21] When you share something of what is presently going on in you, you show in a concrete way your desire to become involved with the other persons present on more than a superficial level. That does *not* mean, as we said at the beginning of this chapter, that you are automatically signaling the beginning of some overintimate, weighty, and serious disclosure. It just means that you're demonstrating your willingness to be more than an object for the people present. You're sharing some of your humanness, and that's one of the first steps toward interpersonal-quality communication.

CONCLUDING THOUGHTS

We've been saying throughout this book that when you get right down to it, communicating interpersonally means *sharing* some of your humanness and *being aware* of the humanness of others. We hope that this chapter encourages and prepares you to try the kind of sharing that can promote interpersonal-quality communication. That kind of sharing is not necessarily negative or heavy. It isn't a nonstop, thoughtless, monological gut-dump. It isn't even a recitation of every single thing that's on your mind.

Instead, it is the kind of communicating that helps someone else see the human *you* a little more clearly. It's appropriate for the persons involved and the situation. It's intended to promote the relationship between you and others, not just to relieve your own anxieties; consequently, it is never motivated by a feeling of "I'm just being honest—you should be able to take it." And it can often be positive, as Kahlil Gibran suggests:[22]

> . . . let the best be for your friend. If he must know the ebb of your tide, let him know its flood also. For what is your friend that you should seek him with hours to kill? Seek him always with hours to live. For it is his to fill your need, but not your emptiness. And in the sweetness of friendship let there be laughter, and sharing of pleasures. For in the dew of little things the heart finds its morning and is refreshed.*

In short, the kind of self-sharing that's necessary for interpersonal-quality communication is made up of sensitive verbal and nonverbal responses to the relationship between you and the others involved, responses that let the other person(s) see some of your humanness, some of your uniqueness, some of the nonspatiotemporal parts of you—your

---

*Reprinted from *The Prophet*, by Kahlil Gibran, with permission of the publisher, Alfred A. Knopf, Inc. Copyright 1923 by Kahlil Gibran; renewal copyright by Administrators C.T.A. of Kahlil Gibran Estate, and Mary G. Gibran.

moods, feelings, hopes, dreams, fears—some of the chooser in you; that is, the part that acts rather than just reacts to the world, and some of your consciousness—your awareness of your self as a being in tension between movement and rest, purposiveness and randomness, growth and deterioration, simplicity and complexity, immanence and transcendence.

Sharing some of your self can be as simple as saying, "I'm in education, too," or "I feel good now." It can be as subtle as wearing a tiny Greek-lettered pin or quietly bowing your head before eating. Or, it can be as explicit and complete as a thoughtful letter that helps a friend understand why you haven't called him or her, or an open, complete response to your parents' question, "What do you think you want to do with your life?" But whatever it is, if sharing doesn't happen, your communication will not be interpersonal communication. A relationship that's interpersonal in quality can happen only when each person is able clearly and fully to *see* the other person. As Hugh Prather succinctly puts it, "In order to see, I have to be willing to be seen."[23]

EXERCISES

Group Application: Three-Minute Sharing

In order to get to know some persons in your class or group, you might want to try the following. Divide into groups of four to six. Each group should have a three-minute egg timer or some other unobtrusive way to keep track of approximately three minutes. Start with whoever has the timer first, and have each person use the three minutes to share with the group his or her responses to the following:

1. What's a particularly happy experience that you remember?
2. What was an especially significant experience that happened to you?
3. What animal do you admire or identify with?
4. Who are you?
5. How are you feeling now?

All the group members should feel free to ask questions of the person talking, but you should also work to stick to the time limit. After each person in the group has had a chance to respond to the five questions, the group as a whole might discuss the following questions.

1. Did you enjoy doing this? Why or why not?
2. Which of the persons' five responses did the most to help you get to know them?
3. How did the structure of this exercise—the time limits, size of group, type of questions, etc.—affect what happened?
4. What similarities did you notice among the responses to the five questions?
5. What points made in this chapter were illustrated, qualified, or contradicted by this experience?

Group Application: An Object That's Me

Another way to share something of your self with others is to bring to class an object that represents some aspect of how you see yourself and to explain to the others what the object "says" about you. I (John) once brought a copy of the play "The Diary of Anne Frank" because I admire and identify with Anne's optimistic view of human beings. For me (Gary), a light switch is an appropriate object for a couple of reasons. First, it seems incomprehensibly complex if you're unfamiliar with electricity, but it's pretty understandable if you take some time to get to know it. Second, one of the things I'd like to be able to do is to help people come alive with discoveries about themselves and their communicating. We've had other persons bring things as diverse and intriguing as a gyroscope, a collage, an x-ray of a rose, a painting, and a brightly decorated box that only one person knows how to open.

Group Application: Sharing Questionnaire

Are you aware of how you share your historical and present selves with others? You might want to respond to the following questions about your verbal and nonverbal sharing behavior and to then get together with two other persons whom you've communicated with before in order to get each other's reactions to your perceptions of your sharing behavior and to talk about what you've learned about yourself, about each other, and about how sharing works in communication.

1. If you feel bored with what is going on in a discussion, how do you usually let others know what you're feeling?

   Using words _____

   Without using words _____

2. If you feel friendliness for someone you don't know very well, how do you share how you're feeling with that person?

Using words _____

Without using words _____

3. If another person does something that hurts your feelings, how do you express your hurt?

Using words _____

Without using words _____

4. If you've had quite a bit of experience with something that would help the group you're in solve a problem, how do you communicate your expertise?

Using words _____

Without using words _____

5. If you feel that a group is wasting time and should move on to discuss more important topics, how do you communicate your perceptions to the group?

Using words _____

Without using words _____

◇━◆━◇

NOTES

1. Martin Buber, "Elements of the Interhuman," in *The Knowledge of Man* ed. Maurice Friedman, trans. Ronald Gregor Smith and Maurice Friedman, New York: Harper & Row, 1965, p. 77.

2. Carl Rogers, "The Interpersonal Relationship: The Core of Guidance," in *Person to Person: The Problem of Being Human,* Carl R. Rogers and Barry Stevens, New York: Simon and Schuster, Pocket Book Division, 1971, p. 87.

3. Buber, *op. cit.,* p. 77.

4. Edmund Byrne and Edward Maziarz, *Human Being and Being Human,* New York: Appleton-Century-Crofts, 1969, pp. 56–61 (Chapter 3). Although this book gets kind of deep at times, it's got some excellent things to say

about human selves—both as objects and as persons. Chapters 10, "The Self in Society" and 11, "Authentic Communication," are especially relevant to interpersonal communication.

5. *Ibid.*, p. 61.

6. *Ibid.*, p. 56.

7. *Ibid.*, p. 59.

8. Thomas Harris, *I'm O.K. — You're O.K.*, New York: Harper & Row, 1969.

9. Joseph Luft, *Group Processes: An Introduction to Group Dynamics*, Palo Alto, Calif.: National Press, 1963. Cf., Luft, *Of Human Interaction*, Palo Alto, Calif.: National Press, 1969.

10. Our discussion of this point reflects much of what we learned from Gerard Egan in his two books, *Encounter: Group Processes for Individual Growth*, Belmont, Calif.: Wadsworth, 1971, and *Face to Face: The Small-Group Experience and Interpersonal Growth*, Monterey, Calif.: Brooks/Cole, 1973. Chapter 5 of *Face to Face* was especially helpful.

11. Sidney M. Jourard, *Transparent Self*, New York: Van Nostrand Reinhold, 1964, p. 3.

12. Carl Rogers makes this point in his essay "A General Law of Interpersonal Relationships," in *On Becoming a Person*, Boston: Houghton Mifflin, 1961 p. 341.

13. *Ibid.*

14. This exercise was adapted from material by John L. Wallen, Northwest Regional Educational Laboratory, Portland, Oregon, and by David W. Johnson, *Reaching Out: Interpersonal Effectiveness and Self-Actualization*, Englewood Cliffs, N.J.: 1972, pp. 90–98.

15. Rogers, *On Becoming a Person*, op. cit., pp. 16–17.

16. Erving Goffman, *The Presentation of Self in Everyday Life*, New York: Doubleday Anchor Books, 1969.

17. Paul Watzlawick, Janet Helmick Beavin, and Don D. Jackson, *Pragmatics of Human Communication*, New York: Norton, 1967, p. 63.

18. Rogers, *On Becoming a Person*, op. cit., pp. 50–51.

19. Egan, *op. cit.*, p. 47. Reprinted by permission.

20. *Ibid.*, p. 46.

21. *Ibid.*

22. Kahlil Gilbran, *The Prophet*, New York: Alfred A. Knopf, 1965, p. 59.

23. Hugh Prather, *Notes to Myself*, Lafayette, Calif.: Real People Press, 1970.

ADDITIONAL RESOURCES

Three books talk in detail about sharing some of your self:

1. Gerard Egan, *Face to Face: The Small-Group Experience and Interpersonal Growth*, Monterey, Calif.: Brooks/Cole, 1973. Chapters 5, "Self-Disclosure," and 6, "The Expression of Feeling and Emotion," are particularly related to this topic. We don't agree completely with everything Egan says, but we think his book can be *very* useful.

2. John Powell, S.J., *Why Am I Afraid to Tell You Who I Am?* Chicago: Argus Communications, 1969, Chapters 1–4. This book can also be a helpful introduction to your understanding of sharing in communication.

3. Sidney Jourard, *The Transparent Self*, New York: Van Nostrand Rinehold 1964. In both this book and *Disclosing Man to Himself* (New York: Van Nostrand Rinehold, 1968), Jourard deals with sharing from the viewpoint of a psychologist interested in interpersonal relationships. Jourard is sometimes a little technical, but there's much research to back up his conclusions.

You can also find treatments of sharing some of your self in other books about interpersonal communication.

1. David W. Johnson, *Reaching Out: Interpersonal Effectiveness and Self-Actualization*, Englewood Cliffs, N.J.: Prentice-Hall, 1972. See especially Chapter 2, "Self-Disclosure," Chapter 5, "The Verbal Expression of Feelings," and Chapter 6, "The Nonverbal Expression of Feelings."

2. John Keltner, *Elements of Interpersonal Communication*, Belmont, Calif.: Wadsworth, 1973, chapter 3, "Who Is Talking to Whom? The Many Faces of You."

3. Leda Saulnier and Teresa Simard, *Personal Growth and Interpersonal Relations*, Englewood Cliffs, N.J.: Prentice-Hall, 1973, part one, "The Self."

4. John R. Wenburg and William W. Wilmot, *The Personal Communication Process*, New York: Wiley, 1973, Chapter 14, "Personal Modification: The Impact of Self-Disclosure."

Psychologist-counselor Haim Ginott sees congruence as a central element of effective communication in families and schools. For example, Chapter 4 of his book *Teacher and Child: A Handbook for Parents and Teachers* (New York: Macmillan, 1972) is called "Congruent Communication." You might also enjoy reading Ginott's *Between Parent and Child: New Solutions to Old Problems* (New York: Macmillan, 1965).

Two films about encounter-group experiences also illustrate how sharing some of your self works in communication. One is called "Journey into Self," (Western Behavioral Sciences Institute, 1968). This is kind of a heavy film—quite a few tears and conflict—but it shows sharing of selves in action.

"Because That's My Way" (Western Behavioral Sciences Institute, 1971) is another. It is a more recent film of an encounter group led by Carl Rogers, a group that begins by talking about drugs, but ends up dealing mainly with communication problems among the participants. There are several examples of sharing in this film.

6

Being Aware of the Other: Responsive Listening

One of the challenges of talking about human communication is that everything is related to everything else. In the last chapter we talked about sharing; in this chapter we talk mainly about responsive listening. But in face-to-face communication, listening can't really be separated from sharing. As you probably realize, when you're talking with someone in a face-to-face situation, you're actually sharing and responding at the same time. When you're speaking, you're making verbal and nonverbal cues available to the other person and at the same time, even though the other person is not talking, he or she is making nonverbal cues available to you—facial expression, eye contact or lack of it, personal space, body position, head movements, etc. So when we write a chapter on sharing and then write a separate chapter on being aware, it sounds almost as though we consider them to be independent processes. We don't and they aren't. They're happening simultaneously and they're *interdependent*. What you share and how you share it affects the other person's sharing and responding behavior, and the other person's verbal or nonverbal response to your sharing affects your responding and sharing, too.

In short, as you read this chapter we think it'll help if you realize how listening relates to some of the things we've talked about in previous chapters.

Cannot not respond.   In Chapter 2 we said that whenever someone is perceptually aware of you, it's impossible for you to stop communicating. Even if you refuse to talk, even if you walk away—these behaviors will be interpreted to mean something. Consistent with that idea, you cannot stop responding to someone. In other words, if you choose not to say anything, your nonverbal behavior "talks" for you.

Context.   What we said about context applies here, too. The context in which you are communicating can almost control your listening behavior if you let it. It's important *not* to allow that to happen. One of the characteristics of your humanness is that you have some freedom in the way you choose to respond to contextual cues. You aren't likely to listen interpersonally to someone if you let things within the context unduly frustrate or irritate you—things such as temperature, room size, furniture, lighting, personal space, noise, the other person's dress and posture, and so on. Our experience with ugly rooms, hot days, uncomfortable furniture, and noisy activities has taught us that the more we let these things control us, the less we listen and respond to people in an interpersonal way.

Interdependent contexts.   Remember that your communication occurs continuously across interdependent contexts. This means that prior experiences and future expectations to some extent affect your listening behavior. In other words, the person you're talking with isn't the single cause of your present feelings. For example, if you feel angry at someone, your anger probably results from a combination of your experiences in earlier contexts, the present situation, and your future hopes or expectations. A poor exam grade, an earlier argument, a confusing lecture, sexual frustration, money problems, fatigue—all can contribute to your anger at any given moment. If you remember this, you'll probably be less likely to take out your anger on the person you're listening to.

Interpretation.   In Chapter 3 we explained that as you communicate, you pick up raw cues and then interpret those raw cues into something meaningful, something that makes sense to you. We also emphasized that your interpretations reflect your biases and that no interpretation duplicates reality exactly. Your listening responses are based on these contextually bound interpretations. When I (Gary) communicate with someone, I try to remember the differences between raw cues and my interpretation of them. When I can do that, I find that I tend to listen more carefully to the other person, I'm able to avoid harsh, judgmental responses, and the inferences I make are tentative rather than permanent.

Negotiation of selves.   As we said in Chapter 4, being aware of the other person is half of what we mean by "negotiating." The way you communicate depends in part on how you define the other person and how you see the other person defining you. These definitions come partly from your awareness of the other. Your awareness can be controlled by the conviction that the other person is out to get you or isn't worth listening to. Or, you can approach the other person with the willingness and commitment to listen well and the skills to do it effectively. The approach you take will affect how you define the other person and how you define yourself in relationship to him or her. And those definitions of self and other are what make your communication impersonal or interpersonal.

In short, when we talk about interrelations between this chapter and others, we mean that here we're trying to describe a way of responding to other persons that:

> sees humanness in others
> reveals humanness in self,
> confirms the other,
> allows for disagreement without deteriorating the relationship,
> encourages openness and sharing,
> enhances understanding,
> is nonthreatening
> is nonmanipulative.

These are the kinds of things we'd like to have happen in your communicating. But as we said early in this book, we don't want to impose mechanical techniques on you and claim that they'll work in all situations. As you read the rest of this chapter and go through the exercises, and as you relate to your experience outside the classroom, you'll discover whether this listening approach works for you. We think it will. But it can be difficult. You'll have to adapt our suggestions to fit your own unique personhood and, if your experience is anything like ours, you'll find that effective listening is not a passive process; it's hard work. A good listener makes a commitment to listen and gets mentally ready to do it.

MENTAL SET: WIN/LOSE AND WIN/WIN

Two nights ago a married couple talked to me (Gary) about arguments they'd been having. The husband felt generally uncomfortable with the way he and his wife communicated. His wife was more specific; she complained that her husband always "seems to know what to say in response to my arguments and he always seems to win. It's frustrating as hell!"

I tried to explain to them the difference between win/lose and win/win attitudes. Win/lose communication is characteristic of a debate or political campaign. Opposing parties or adversaries do whatever they can to come out the winner. They're not concerned about building a relationship. In fact, if they want to win badly enough, they won't mind doing things that damage or even destroy the relationship. Usually, a severe win/lose confrontation is characterized by self-serving listening, i.e., listening that prepares you to tear down your opponent's argument, listening that avoids sharing information, and listening that helps you make the other person's ideas seem inferior to yours. In other words, the primary objective is to *win* while the other *loses*—to communicate that "I am right and you are wrong"; "I am strong and you are weak"; "I am smart and you are dumb"; "I am likeable and you aren't."

Sometimes, win/lose communication is required. Political campaigns, courtrooms, and minority-rights movements are instances in which some win/lose communication is often necessary and appropriate. But when two persons continually communicate as if they were opposing attorneys in a courtroom, their relationship will suffer. In other words, as we said in Chapter 1, not all communication can be interpersonal-quality communication, but when you want to communicate interpersonally, a win/lose orientation won't help.

One of the problems with win/lose communication is that it can very easily lead to manipulation of the other person. When you respond from a win/lose mental set, it becomes easy to use listening techniques only as a strategy for taking advantage of others. You may listen carefully, you may concentrate on what they're saying, you may try to understand exactly how they feel—but you do those things to find weaknesses so that you can ultimately win your point.

It was difficult for the married couple I mentioned to build a strong relationship. Even though the husband won his point most of the time, he still didn't feel satisfied with the communication between himself and his wife, and the wife was developing strongly negative feelings, along with her frustration, toward her husband. If people establish a strong relationship, a few win/lose encounters won't destroy it. But not many relationships can withstand continual competitive communication in which one person is trying to downgrade the ideas or the personhood of the other.

You've probably experienced win/lose communication much of your life. From the time you began to develop a sense of self—at age two or three—it has been important to define yourself, and one of the ways you established an identity was by emphasizing the difference between you and others. Your junior high school years might have been a time when winning contests for attention, recognition, and prestige was especially important. Sometimes, the confrontations you experienced were probably stimulating and challenging—vigorous mental and physical exercises.

Hopefully by now, however, you're seeing that being yourself doesn't require putting down someone else. Being unique, different from others doesn't necessarily mean being better than they. *For you to win, somebody else does* not *have to lose,* and this means that you *can* adopt a win/win attitude in your communication with others.

A win/win listening attitude is concerned with building a relationship that promotes growth for all the persons involved. When you have a win/win mental set, your listening behavior works toward that end. You feel cooperative, not competitive. You don't attempt to produce the strongest argument, to win your point, or to cause someone to feel inferior. With a win/win attitude, you're willing to give others a full hearing. You're willing to concentrate on what the other person is saying—verbally and nonverbally. You're willing not only to observe the other person accurately, but also to *feel* some of what he or she seems to be feeling and to verbalize your conclusions in order to verify them. Finally, you diminish as much defensiveness as you can. These are the goals of the listening approach we're about to describe.

We want to emphasize that this listening approach becomes genuinely *non*manipulative *only* within a win/win atmosphere. When it's used as a device or strategy for winning *at the expense of the other person,* then it becomes manipulative. This kind of listening will work for manipulators, but that's not our intent.

Individual Application: Win/Win and Win/Lose

This exercise should give you some idea of how well you understand the differences between win/lose and win/win communication. We'll give you two situations; for each situation, try to explain what the communication would be like if it were win/win and what it would be like if it were win/lose.

Situation: Two students writing a term paper together.

Win/Win	*Win/Lose*
Both perceive a common goal of trying for a high grade. Both are open to all possible ways of getting it. They share ideas, listen carefully	Neither cares about the other's succeeding; each wants a high grade, but each is more concerned about getting her or his ideas

to each other, and even when they disagree, each respects and tries to understand the other's ideas. Etc.

accepted. Each tries to convince the other that "my idea is better than yours." Neither person really listens to the other; while one person is talking, the other is thinking about what to say next. Etc.

Situation: Family talking about where daughter or son should go to college.

Win/Win   *Win/Lose*

_____   _____

_____   _____

_____   _____

_____   _____

_____   _____

Situation: An employer is trying to get an employee to slow down, so that the quality of the employee's work can improve.

Win/Win   *Win/Lose*

_____   _____

_____   _____

_____   _____

_____   _____

_____   _____

Situation: A student and her or his instructor are talking about whether or not to change the student's grade from "C" to "B."

Win/Win   *Win/Lose*

_____   _____

_____   _____

_____   _____

_____   _____

_____   _____

LISTENING TO CONFIRM

One of the basic things you can do as a listener to encourage interpersonal communication is to *confirm* the person who's talking. Verbal and nonverbal confirming behavior say to the other person, "I'm listening; I might not agree or accept your point of view, but I care about what you're saying, and I'm aware of what's going on." Disconfirmation, as we said in Chapter 4, is the process of communicating as if the other person didn't even exist. People perceive disconfirming behavior to mean that you're not listening—that whether you might agree or disagree, you're ignoring what they are saying and that you're not really interested in taking the time to pay attention to their thoughts and feelings.

It's pretty difficult to continuously confirm the other person. At one time or another, we all lose track of what other people are saying to us. Especially in lengthy conversations, we sometimes daydream or find ourselves thinking about something completely unrelated to what's being discussed. There's nothing abnormal about that; our ability to concentrate for a prolonged period of time is limited. If you want your communication to be interpersonal, however, you should concentrate as much as you can, because it isn't easy to really hear and understand another person. But when you find yourself "tuning out," there's no reason to fake it and pretend that you were listening. In fact, it's much better to let the other person know when you've missed something: "While you were talking just then, my mind was out on a tangent and I missed some things. Would you say that again?" That kind of honesty usually elicits positive reactions from the other person, because it reaffirms your commitment to your communicating and to the other person. And that's confirming, too. In short, communicating confirmation instead of disconfirmation is the first step in listening interpersonally, and there are several nonverbal and verbal ways you can do that.

Nonverbal Confirming

Have you ever tried to talk to someone while she or he was involved in some unrelated activity? Your father reads the paper while you talk with him; your employer opens his/her mail during a conference with you; your friend cleans his or her desk while you try to carry on a conversation. These people may be listening and they may think you realize it, but it's difficult to interpret their behavior that way. Our image of the interested, attentive, and confirming listener isn't the person who reads the mail, washes dishes, shuffles papers, or picks lint off a cuff while we're talking. Few of us believe that a person can listen to what we're saying and at the same time concentrate on some unrelated activity. We tend to believe that attention is going to be on us *or* on the activity. Especially when what we're saying is important to us and when we want the other person to be listening fully to us, we'll interpret those "extra-curricular" nonverbal activities as disconfirming.

Your face is important, too. You may be maintaining natural and consistent eye contact with someone; your posture may be relaxed and your body attentive, but your facial expression may say, "I'm not interested." People generally assume that when you're excited, in doubt, in deep thought, or interested, your face shows it. Consequently, when they look at your face and there seems to be almost no muscle movement, they'll probably infer that you're not feeling anything. You may be, but not from their point of view. The nonverbal facial cues you make available are interpreted by the other person as indicating something about how you're listening. If you're "plugged in," then your face should somehow reflect that fact.

More specifically, one way to let people know you're paying attention is through eye contact. We don't mean that you should fix the other person with a constant glare or stare; that obviously can be intimidating and can make him or her feel very self-conscious. But in virtually all American subcultures, reasonably consistent and natural eye contact is a sign of recognition and acknowledgment. When you look someone in the eye while you're listening to her or him, you say in effect, "I'm tuned in; I hear you."

We recognize that when someone's maintaining eye contact with you, it doesn't *necessarily* mean that he or she is listening. But when you contrast a situation in which a person who's listening to you is also looking at you with a situation in which your listener hardly ever looks at you, you'll get an idea of what we're saying. Comfortably consistent, natural eye contact can be confirming to the other person; the absence of eye contact can be disconfirming.

Your posture and the movements of your body can also affect a person's perception of you as a listener. If you're in continual motion—tapping a foot, fiddling with a pencil or paper clip, drumming your fingers, etc.—people often get the impression that you're anxious to "get

on with it" or to get away. If, on the other hand, you focus on them and
nod affirmatively, people generally see that as confirming. Two people
standing and talking together can also confirm a third person and invite
him or her to join them, just by turning their bodies toward the third
person.

You can also suggest confirmation or disconfirmation with posture,
as are the persons in the picture below.

Remember, though, that cultural context affects the interpretation of
these cues. All the persons shown on the next page are listening, and all
feel that their posture confirms the other people.

The history and setting of a relationship can also be important contextual factors. Two close friends who are talking while listening to music may not care at all about each other's eye contact or posture. But in another setting, in which the friends are concerned about being listened to, each may focus quite a bit on the other's nonverbal confirmation or lack of it. Counselor–teacher Larry Brammer suggests that in most situations, the most clearly confirming posture is leaning *toward* the other person in a *relaxed* manner.[1]

Finally, you can listen to confirm by using nonverbal vocal cues— noises that indicate you're keeping up with what the other person is saying and that you're interested in having him or her continue. This can become affected and phony, as when the pseudolistener responds to every phrase with an artificial "mmmnnuhh?"or "Ahhuummmnn!!" or "Uhhhnmmmh." We're *not* suggesting that you do this. But whether you're on the telephone or in a face-to-face situation, it can often be reassuring for the other person to hear some confirming noises just to reinforce the fact that you're there and listening.

Verbal Confirming

Eye contact, appropriate posture, active facial expressions, and vocal sounds don't always suggest to people that you're listening. Think about how you'd feel if you were in this slightly exaggerated situation:

> You: That game was somethin' else!
> Friend: (looks at you, nods head affirmatively, says nothing)
> You: I couldn't believe how often they ran that same quarter-
>   back draw play, and it worked almost every time!
> Friend: (looks at you, nods head, says nothing)
> You: I can't wait to see what happens when they go up
>   against Southern Cal!
> Friend: (looks at you, smiles, nods head, says nothing)

That conversation includes important nonverbal confirmation: eye contact, affirmative head movements, and facial expression. But without verbal response from your friend, you might feel as though you are talking to a machine. If the conversation continues with just one person talking, that person is almost certainly going to feel frustrated and disconfirmed. To put it another way, silence, even with confirming nonverbal cues, can be disconfirming. When your listener says nothing verbally, it's sometimes easy to believe that you're being ignored.

In addition, people usually believe that nonverbal behavior is less consciously controlled than verbal behavior. For example, a listener's nods and smiles are often viewed more as habit or mechanical move-ments than as evidence of genuine listening. People are capable of smiling and nodding their heads even though they're daydreaming about something completely unrelated to the conversation. On the other hand, when we respond verbally, people perceive that we're committing more of our conscious selves to the relationship, especially if our verbal response relates directly to what the other person has just said. Our verbal responses can confirm the person in ways which even the best nonverbal behavior can't.

In the next section we'll talk specifically about the kinds of verbal responses that can promote interpersonal communication. For now, we'd just like to suggest that verbal confirmation occurs when as a listener, you carry the conversation in a direction closely related to what the other person has said. Changing the subject or going off on some tangent without some good reason usually evokes a feeling of disconfirmation in the other person.

LISTENING TO UNDERSTAND

Although confirmation is important, paying attention doesn't always lead to genuine understanding of what's being said. It's also important to use listening skills that increase your chances of accurately interpreting the other person.

If people had exactly the same experiences and if they interpreted all words and nonverbal cues in the same way, there would be no need to talk about understanding or misunderstanding. When I used a word, I'd know what it meant to you and you'd know what it meant to me. Unfortunately, that's not the way things are. We interpret the same raw cues differently, and sometimes those differences are extreme. As a result, we need to find ways of reaching each other, of understanding better how we interpret each other's cues.

Genuine understanding doesn't necessarily mean agreement. Understanding involves grasping fully what the other person is trying to say—from her or his point of view—and how he or she feels about it. It comes about when you're able to interpret accurately and empathically the cues the other person makes available.

Accurately understanding the other person's ideas and feelings usually requires you to "listen" with your ears, your eyes, and all of your other sensory equipment. You hear the words being spoken, but you also listen to the tone of voice, pauses and sighs, and you watch for body movements, facial expressions, eye movements, spatial relationships, and so on. In other words, to understand someone, you sometimes have to "hear" both what they're saying and what they're *not* saying in words. People don't always reveal verbally that they're frustrated, afraid, anxious, excited, or depressed. An insightful and understanding listener, though, frequently detects feelings in another person without words being said.

But when the person doesn't express in words certain feelings and ideas, it's not always fair to make inferences from the nonverbal communication. After all, nonverbal cues can mislead. We think that this point is important: you can't develop understanding entirely nonverbally. You probably realize that there are usually many more nonverbal than verbal cues available. But that situation shouldn't lead you, as a listener, to rely exclusively on smiles, gestures, and eye contact, important as these factors are. We believe that when you're listening to understand, it's best to emphasize verbal cues at least as much as nonverbal ones. The best idea is to let the other person know what your interpretation is and to give him or her a chance to respond to your interpretation. The label attached to this process of listening is *perception checking.*

When you're perception checking, you verbalize your interpretation or inferences about what was said—or left unsaid—and you ask the other person to verify or correct your interpretation. Few people use this kind of listening in social conversation. As Larry Brammer says, "We are conditioned to chatter onward socially, even to deliberately confusing the meaning with innuendo, humor, and metaphor. We rarely check with one another about what we are really trying to say."[2] To the extent that what Brammer says is true, very little genuine understanding occurs in most social conversations. But interpersonal communication goes beyond that kind of superficiality, and it does that in part through perception checks.

Paraphrasing.   There are at least two dimensions of perception checking you might want to familiarize yourself with. The first is simple paraphrasing. When paraphrasing, *you say in your own words how you've interpreted the other person's ideas and feelings.* Obviously, this kind of response isn't always appropriate. When you hear someone whistling, you don't stop and say, "Pardon me, but do I hear you saying that you're happy?" And if a friend says, "I gotta go; I'm late for class," you don't grab her arm and respond with "Are you saying you have to go because you're late for class?"

Paraphrasing also feels a little mechanical when you first try it. You'll find yourself repeating phrases like "I hear you saying . . ." and "Are you saying that . . .?" At first, it may seem incredibly redundant.

But if your mental attitude as a listener is one of really wanting to understand, you'll find that paraphrasing comes almost naturally. Also, you'll quickly discover that genuine paraphrasing is more than un-necessary redundancy or "word swapping." The two dialogues that follow help illustrate the difference between inadequate and useful paraphrasing:

Bob: My parents are really great!
Marc: You mean you like your parents?
Bob: Yeah, I like my parents.

Bob: My parents are really great!
Phil: Sounds to me like your parents have either given you something or they've really treated you like a human being recently.
Bob: Well, not exactly that. They've decided to quit pushing my sister about going to college. She wants to stay out of school for awhile and get a job so she can put some money away. Three days ago my dad was really upset. Right now, he's helping her look for a job, and he's giving her moral support at the same time. He's really helping her.

In the first dialogue, Marc doesn't give Bob much to respond to, and Marc's words merely repeat what Bob has already said. In the second dialogue, Phil says enough for Bob to know how his statement was interpreted, giving Bob a chance to verify or correct Phil's interpretation. Also note that in neither dialogue does the listener approve or disapprove. Paraphrasing doesn't mean approving or disapproving of what you hear. The goal is simply to give the other person a clear indication of "This is my understanding of what you said and how you feel about it. Are my interpretations accurate?"

Parasupporting.   We've labeled the second dimension of perception checking *parasupporting.* In parasupporting, *you not only paraphrase the other person's comments, but also carry his or her ideas further by providing examples or other data that you believe help to illustrate and clarify those ideas.* Here's an example we think will help explain paraphrasing and parasupporting:

A: College is oppressive.
B paraphrases: Are you talking about the fact that stu-

	dents don't get to make very many choices about their education?
A goes into more detail:	Yeah, partly. It's true we're told which courses to take, how many hours, and things like that. But I'm thinking about specific courses and how my profs and T.A.s tell me what I should know, what I should remember, how I should write term papers, what I should write even. I'm just feeling squashed. I can't sit down to study without worrying about what I have to know for a test instead of what I *want* to know.
B parasupports:	There's a course in humanities—201 I think—where they tell you how many times you can miss class and that you have to write three ten–page papers, and they give you topics for the papers and the books you have to use for research. Is that the kind of thing you're talking about?
A verifies B's parasupport:	Yeah, exactly. I'm not taking that course, but I've got some just like it.
B senses A's feeling:	Really, I know what you mean when you say "frustrated." *And* "squashed," too. I think one follows from the other. But sometimes it's the other way around. I've got a couple of courses where we choose our own assignments, and each day in class we decide what we want to talk about. Sometimes, I think that's too much freedom.
A paraphrases:	Sounds like you're not so sure about wanting more freedom in your classes. Like, you wonder whether or not we're able to make decisions if we get the chance to?

Besides the paraphrasing and parasupporting, note two other important characteristics of this dialogue. First, both A and B are motivated by a win/win attitude. Neither person is trying to "put down" the other's ideas. Neither seems to be concerned about who is right and who is wrong. The win/win atmosphere is evidenced in part by B's parasupporting of A, i.e., a person who wants the other person to lose usually won't parasupport the other's idea. In addition, there are no judgmental responses. Neither directly nor indirectly does B say that A is uninformed, misled, naive, or wrong. Neither does A tell B that. Both persons are concerned about understanding what the other is thinking and feeling.

This leads to a second characteristic of the dialogue: mutuality. Note A's last statement. Up to that point, the primary focus of the conversation was on B trying to understand A. Then, B relates an experience and belief, and in response to that, A tries to understand B. In other words, even though the two persons don't completely agree, *both* are willing to reciprocate listening for understanding.

In Summary:
(so far)

Perception Checking

Paraphrasing
1. Say in your own words what you heard the other person saying.
2. Try to include some of what you perceive the other to be *feeling*, too.
3. Don't just "word swap."
4. Give the other person a chance to verify your paraphrase.

Parasupporting
1. Paraphrase *and* carry the ideas and feelings you perceive further in the same direction.
2. Use examples from similar experiences you've had.
3. Use additional data that illustrate the other person's point.

Individual Application: Perception Checking

You can practice perception checking realistically only in live situations, because your perceptions rely heavily on nonverbal cues. But maybe the following examples will help you see how comfortable you are with these two listening skills.

Try to respond appropriately to the following statements as if they were made by the persons pictured.

"That class is really exciting! I can't believe some of the things that came up today! I'm really learning a lot in there!"

Your paraphrase of the nonverbal:_____

_____

_____

_____

_____

_____

"You're finally getting smart about that college stuff. A lot of people waste a lot of time there—and money."

Your parasupport:_____

_____

_____

_____

_____

_____

"If things go on like this, I'm afraid we're going to have a problem. Your work has to improve or you're definitely going to suffer for it at the end of the term."

Your parasupport: _____

_____

_____

_____

_____

_____

_____

"I hate this place! I don't know why I ever came here!"

Your paraphrase: _____

_____

_____

_____

_____

_____

_____

_____

LISTENING TO DIMINISH DEFENSIVENESS

There's one more major challenge for the person who wants to listen in ways that promote interpersonal communication. Confirmation and understanding need to be supplemented with listening behavior that keeps other people—so far as you can—from feeling defensive.

After studying group discussion over an eight-year period, Jack Gibb reported that *defensiveness* is one of the major barriers to interpersonal communication. He defined defensive behavior as behavior "which occurs when an individual perceives threat or anticipates threat."[3] He noted that person A's defensiveness usually creates defensiveness in person B, which in turn creates the same thing in person C, and so on to the point where a group's communication can become unproductive and even hostile. Gibb pointed out that one major cause of defensiveness is "speech or other behavior which appears *evaluative*"[4] (italics added). Note that Gibb says *speech* or *other behavior*. Both verbal and nonverbal cues can be evaluative. You may say verbally to someone, "You've gotta be kidding; how can you believe something as stupid as that?" Or, you might accomplish essentially the same thing by covering your face with your hands, taking a deep breath, sighing, and shaking your head negatively. People are sometimes careful about not making evaluative verbal statements, which are relatively easy to control, but at the same time they evoke defensiveness in others through their nonverbal evaluative behavior, which is not so easy to control.

Steve Stephenson (a friend and faculty member in our department) and I (Gary) studied this same phenomenon, and we identified a similar link between evaluation and defensiveness. We found that listeners who were strongly evaluative—who interrupted, disagreed, and continually corrected the other person—evoked significantly more defensiveness than listeners who were less evaluative—who agreed, didn't interrupt, paraphrased, and encouraged the other person.[5] It seems clear, in short, that evaluative listening increases defensiveness and that defensiveness can destroy interpersonal communication.

These conclusions suggest that if you want to communicate interpersonally, you shouldn't be evaluative. But in an important sense that's *impossible;* you *cannot not evaluate* the things—and people—you perceive. Right now, you're probably perceiving the pressure of a chair against your bottom, the fit of shoes around your feet, and the weight of clothes on your shoulders. Yet before you read that sentence, you probably weren't aware of any of those perceptions. You're continuously *selectively* perceiving, as we said in Chapter 3, and your selection is based on some kind of value judgment: one thing is relevant to you, another is irrelevant; this is important, that's unimportant; this is interesting, that's boring, or whatever. Your evaluating goes on at different levels of awareness, but it's always there; you cannot not evaluate.

So what do you do? If evaluation creates defensiveness but you can't stop evaluating, what can you do as a listener to help, rather than hinder, interpersonal communication? We think this is a really important question, the answer to which could have a significant effect on the ways in which you listen to other people. We want to respond to that question with six suggestions for listening to diminish defensiveness:

1. Be generally positive
2. Postpone specific evaluations
3. Limit negative evaluations
4. Own your evaluations
5. Keep your evaluations tentative
6. Actively solicit responses

Be Generally Positive

First, we think it's important to recognize that evaluation can be both positive and negative, but that interpersonal-quality communication is based on a generally optimistic, positive approach to other persons. If you honestly believe that it's a dog-eat-dog world, you'll naturally be unwilling to take the steps toward sharing and being aware that can help make interpersonal communication happen. If you are absolutely sure that the other person will get you if you don't get him or her first, you probably won't be able to adopt a win/win attitude, and it's unlikely that you'll ever be able to give enough to communicate interpersonally with someone else.

We are definitely *not* saying that you should go around with your head in a pink cloud, oblivious to the fact that people sometimes deliberately treat others in thoughtless and even inhuman ways. We do *not* mean that you have to be simple-minded or naive to communicate interpersonally. We recognize that human beings have the potential for evil as well as for good.

But we *are* suggesting that your basic, general evaluation of the persons you meet can be positive. You might reject parts of their *behavior* or some of their *attitudes*, but one characteristic of humanness is that persons have intrinsic worth—they are worthwhile just because they are human. You'll be better able to listen interpersonally to them when you keep this in mind.

It might encourage you to know that there's some evidence to support this positive point of view. The assumption that human nature is essentially evil, malicious, or cruel has *not* been supported by psychological studies.[6] As Abraham Maslow puts it, psychologists are finding out that "history has practically always sold human nature short."[7] Counselor-therapist Carl Rogers also reports that in more than 25 years of reaching into the core of being of hundreds of "pathological," "antisocial," and "disturbed" persons, he has yet to find one who is not, at this very basic level, moving in *positive* directions.[8]

Our experience supports the validity of this positive general evaluation of persons. We are still occasionally disappointed to meet someone whose needs we are unable to understand or who feels pressure to abuse or take advantage of our relationship. But the overwhelming majority of the time, we find that every person whom we can allow ourselves to meet is very much worth knowing. In other words, we're finding that our optimism is seldom inappropriate or misplaced. Persons *are* intrinsically worthwhile, and it "works" to treat them that way.

More specifically, we find that our positive general evaluation helps us listen more effectively. We don't pretend to be "nonevaluative," but we do try to listen from a positive, accepting point of view. When we're able to do that, the people we're communicating with don't seem to get defensive, and our communication is generally growth-promoting and productive.

Individual Application: Seeing Persons Positively

If it's difficult for you to feel positive about persons, you might want to try the following exercise. Write the name of a person you dislike or have strong negative feelings about—acquaintance, co-worker, classmate, politician, educator, celebrity.

_____

Now try listing that person's *strengths*. Identify the positive character-istics that person has. List as many as you can. If you have trouble, try the following:

1. Role-play that person's close friend. How do you think this close friend might reply if asked "What do you particularly like about that person?"

2. Get in touch with the feelings in *you* that contribute to your negative reactions to the person:

    a) Are you afraid of that person?

    b) Do you feel inferior around him or her?

    c) Do you feel ignored by that person?

    d) Do you enjoy feeling more powerful than that person?

    e) Do you feel stupid around that person?

    Try to *own* those feelings; recognize that they're *yours*. Does that help you see the person differently?

3. How do you see the other person defining you? What effect do you think that definition has on your evaluation of the person?

4. How did you find out what you know about that person? (What we're suggesting by this question is that if you had more information, you might be able to see the person more positively.)

Postpone Specific Evaluations

Our second suggestion is to postpone any specific positive *or* negative evaluations until you're sure you understand clearly whatever you're evaluating. Virtually everyone has had the experience of violently disagreeing with the first few words they hear, only to discover two or three sentences later that their "enemy" is really their friend. That's an easy mistake to make, but one which you can avoid by hearing what the other person is really saying before assuming that you disagree. In a classroom discussion recently, a student said: "Doctors are overpaid." Another student, whose father was a general practitioner, violently disagreed and evaluated that statement harshly. Later, we discovered that the first student was actually referring to her home-town physician. who reputedly makes over $75,000 a year. As it turned out, both students believed that *some* doctors overcharge for *some* services, but they didn't mean that all doctors are guilty. As we say in the next chapter, mutual understanding occurs when each person is able to adequately limit the range of possible interpretations of what the other person is saying. You need information to do that, and if you make specific evaluations too soon, you may misinterpret what's being said.

Early evaluation can also stifle conversation. Committees sometimes fail to work because they spend too much time evaluating suggestions and too little time generating them. "Brainstorming" is a technique to avoid that. The purpose of a group brainstorming is to come up with as many ideas as possible without evaluating any of them. The technique is based on the recognition that when evaluating starts— no matter whether it's positive or negative— creative thinking often stops. That's another reason why communication can often be improved when a listener postpones his or her specific evaluations.

Limit Negative Evaluations

There's an important difference between "You're a stupid person; it's dumb to think that studying history will ever help you get a job" and "Your interruption right then sure seemed to kill the conversation." When you feel that a negative evalution is warranted, i.e., that you've got enough information and you can't honestly be positive, it can make a big difference whether you evaluate *behavior, attitudes,* or *persons.* We think that whenever possible, it's important to limit negative evaluations to *behavior.* Negative evaluations of behavior are least likely to create defensiveness, because people generally recognize that behavior is something they can change. It's pretty difficult to do anything about a statement like "You're hopelessly clumsy." That evaluation is almost always going to create defensiveness. But you *can* do something about the evaluation in a statement like "It seems to me that when you try to paint that fast, you don't cover the area very evenly."

Negative evaluations of behavior can create defensiveness, too—all evaluation can. But people are less likely to respond defensively to negative comments about their behavior than to negative comments about their *attitudes* or *ideas.* The main reason is that attitudes often seem harder to change. They're somehow more a part of us, and it's more threatening to give them up or modify them. So when our attitudes are challenged, we're likely to feel more strongly the "perceived or anticipated threat" that causes defensiveness.

Evaluating another person's attitudes is also dangerous because you can't really be accurate. You can never know for sure what another person is thinking; you can only make inferences based on the behavior you observe. As we said in Chapter 3, inferences are often inaccurate. I (John) made some inferences about Lisa's ideas regarding dating when she was a sixth grader. Lisa talked about "going steady," came home with a ring that belonged to a guy in the neighborhood, and did everything she could to spend time with him. I inferred that her idea of "going steady" was like mine, but mine was an archaic relic of the late 1950s and early 1960s, when that term was used for a serious, potentially preengagement commitment. When Lisa and her "steady" "broke up" two days later, I recognized that the idea I was upset about wasn't anything like Lisa's idea of "going steady." I felt just about as silly as I probably looked to her, but at least I stopped complaining about her behavior.

Evaluating *persons* negatively will almost always create more defensiveness than will evaluating behavior or even attitudes negatively. Each of us needs security, acceptance, and self-esteem; when someone says that we are "stupid," "a bigot," "clumsy," "a hypocrite," "lazy," "a doper," "conceited," "a liar," or whatever, we will virtually always feel threatened enough to react very defensively. But if the point we've made about human worth is true, none of those statements can be accurate. Persons might—and often do—*behave* in ways that are "bigoted," "clumsy," "hypocritical," and "conceited." But the same persons also behave in ways that are "supportive," "thoughtful," "generous," and "loving." So it's hardly accurate to conclude that they "are" one set of behaviors and "aren't" another.

It's very difficult not to evalute some persons negatively. Adolf Hitler is almost always cited as one such example. The Jewish philosopher Martin Buber wrote emphatically and extensively about the intrinsic worth of human beings, yet he was never able to fully accept the personal worth of convicted Nazi Adolf Eichmann. Some persons feel the same way about contemporary political or religious leaders. Fortunately, it's usually much easier to accept the inherent worth of the persons you communicate with from day to day. When you can do that—when you can limit whatever negative evaluations you feel you have to make to the other person's *behavior* or, in extreme cases, to his or her *attitudes*—you can diminish the defensiveness that ruins interpersonal communication.

Own Your Evaluations

It also helps to reduce defensiveness when you identify your evaluations as just that: *yours* and *evaluations*. Thinly veiled comments such as "Is it safe to drive this fast? I'm just *asking* . . ." or "Most people don't do that" and nonverbal cues, e.g., a scowl, a sarcastic smile, or looking away, often masquerade as "descriptions" or "neutral reactions." They aren't, and usually everybody knows it. But often, everybody doesn't know exactly *who's* reacting (you, "the group," etc.), *how* they're reacting (you're frustrated? angry? bored? threatened? etc.) or *why* (the language you're hearing? nonverbal cues you're interpreting? etc.).

When you explicitly verbalize your evaluations in first-person terms, you can avoid these problems. (You might want to check back on the "Description of Feelings" exercise, pp. 164–166.) Try to move from disowned pseudodescriptions to owned evaluations:

Disowned pseudo-descriptions	*Owned evaluations*
Is it safe to drive this fast?	I don't like the thought of being arrested for speeding. I'm frustrated with you, and I'm looking for something to criticize you about. I'm scared.
You only think about yourself.	I'm envious of the clothes you just bought. I don't like losing an argument, and I think I lost. I don't want to baby-sit the kids, either.
You're too bossy.	I feel inferior to you. I want to play poker more than I want to take you to a movie, but I feel threatened by your insistence that we go out.
(With exaggerated inflection) Oh, I don't care. Go ahead and go!	You're damn right I feel left out! I understood we had planned to go together, and now I hear you saying I'm not invited.
Never mind. Just forget it!	I feel frustrated even *trying* to discuss it with you. I feel ignored by you—like you don't listen even when I try to explain. I don't want to hassle it any more.

Keep Your Evaluations Tentative

The approaches to perception and communication that we've followed throughout this book suggest two final characteristics of defense-reducing evaluative responses. The first is tentativeness. Since you interpret perceptions in your own, unique ways, you can never be absolutely sure that you fully understand another person or are completely clear about his or her intentions. Consequently, your evaluations of another person's attitudes or ideas almost *have* to be tentative.

You might label a person a racist because you see her or him putting down a person from another ethnic group, a person with whom he or she has had a long-standing, nonracial argument. You might conclude that someone is a hopelessly naive radical because he or she is Marxist, without learning for yourself the pragmatic and politically conservative dimensions of Marxism. In short, your evaluations of persons and attitudes can easily be wrong, so it's fairest to keep them tentative and open to change.

We believe that you can be more firm in your evaluations of another's *behavior*. But the trick is to keep your firm evaluations limited to *behavior*. That's one of the hardest things for parents to do. It's easy—and justifiable—to reject a child's tantrum-throwing behavior, but it's not so easy to keep from moving from behavior-rejection to person-rejection, i.e., from "No, you're not going to throw your shoe through the window!" to "You're a bad girl!" or "Calm down or I'll whack you good, you worthless brat!" Adults have the same problem with other adults. A teacher might justifiably react negatively to a student's continual absence or tardiness. But this doesn't mean that the teacher should necessarily conclude that the student is "defiant" or "doesn't care." Similarly, a supervisor might very well criticize an employee's rate of work; it might actually be too slow to keep up with the rest of the production line. But the employee's behavior might be explained in a variety of ways—insufficient training, poor tools, bad lighting, inadequate materials, etc. So the supervisor *isn't* justified in concluding that the employee's behavior proves that she or he is "lazy" or "incompetent."

In short, you don't have to compromise your own values to the point where you accept everything everybody does; you can, we believe, justifiably reject some kinds of *behavior*. But you're on pretty shaky ground when you firmly reject attitudes or persons. As a result, it's a good idea to keep in mind the inherent error factor of *all* evaluations and to keep you evaluations as tentative as you can.

Actively Solicit Responses

Our final suggestion is that you communicate your tentativeness and make it real by perception checking, i.e., by actively soliciting responses to your evaluations so that the person you're talking with has the chance to tell you how he or she is reacting to your judgments. Then you have the opportunity to change your evaluation if it needs changing.

It's usually pretty difficult to be genuinely open to change after you've evaluated someone's behavior or ideas negatively. It's easy to feel as though you've made a public commitment to a point of view and that you'd look like a fool if you were to change your mind. It's hard not to feel the need to defend your evaluations—and along with it, your self-respect.

But that kind of (literally) self-centeredness doesn't make sense if you: (1) remember how human communication works, and (2) want to encourage interpersonal communication. You know that your evaluations are based on your interpretation of cues you perceive. It's obvious that the person you're evaluating might both perceive and interpret the cues differently and that he or she might be as "right" or as "wrong" as you. So when you ask for responses to your evaluations, i.e., when you use perception checking in this situation, it's an indication that you actually do understand how human communication works.

Asking for responses to your evaluations also shows a win/win rather than a win/lose attitude. In other words, this kind of perception checking reveals your genuine willingness and ability to share some of your humanness and to be aware of the humanness of the other. The other person might have changed since you perceived whatever you're evaluating. He or she might be conscious of the behavior you're noticing and have good reasons for continuing it. You might be unaware of all kinds of nonspatiotemporal factors that contribute to the behavior or attitudes you disagree with—emotions, past experience, hopes, fears, and so on.

The point is, communication that involves negative evaluating should be mutual and interdependent, as should any other human communication. But negative evaluation tends to stifle response. So it's often important for the person doing the evaluating to actively solicit responses to decide whether or not the evaluations need changing.

CONCLUDING THOUGHTS

In this chapter we've said a great deal about listening, probably too much to absorb in one reading. We've said that your listening behavior will be affected by many things, including contextual cues, your prior experiences, expectations about the future, the attitude with which you listen—win/lose or win/win—your perception and interpretation processes, and your willingness and ability to *apply* what you know about human communication and about interpersonal communication. We've also tried to lay out three important interpersonal listening skills—confirming the other, listening to understand, and listening to diminish defensiveness—all of which work together to help create an atmosphere in which interpersonal communication can happen.

By itself, good listening won't necessarily solve your communication problems, nor will it guarantee interpersonal communication; good listening does, however, make an important contribution.

EXERCISES

Individual Application: Owning Your Evaluations

Change the following "disowned" judgmental statements into "owned" defense-reducing responses. In other words, verbally describe as explicitly as you can the feelings that are probably behind each judgment.

Disowned judgments	*Verbal description of feeling*
Person 1: You're wrong about that!	I don't see it the same way you do; my experience with . . . etc.
Person 2: Oh, come on! How can you say that?	I feel frustrated by what you just said; I'm worried that you're trying to make what I say seem inferior.
Person 3: Only an ignoramus would believe that.	_____. _____

Person 4: You haven't looked at
the facts. Your opinion
isn't worth anything
because you haven't
researched the issue.

_____

_____

_____

Person 5: That was a boring
meeting.

_____

_____

_____

Person 6: His lectures are absolutely irrelevant to any-
thing.

_____

_____

_____

Individual Application: Alternative Responses

You might want to try this for practice. Write four different responses to the
following statement:

Parent:

"This younger generation scares me. They have no moral values. They
smoke dope, believe in premarital sex, rebel against our government.
I'm afraid of what's going to happen when they become our leaders."[9]

1. Write an evaluative-judgmental response.

_____

_____

_____

2. Write a paraphrase.

_____

_____

_____

3. Write a parasupporting comment.

_____

_____

_____

_____

4. Verbally describe the feelings you had as you read the statement.

_____

_____

_____

_____

Group Application: Responsive Listening

Break your class or group into dyads. Spends about 20–30 minutes discussing a controversial issue that the two persons in each dyad disagree about. Try to listen to each other with: (1) a win/win attitude, (2) confirming behaviors, (3) paraphrasing and parasupporting (perception checks), (4) defensiveness-reducing responses. After your conversation, respond individually to the following questions:

How did you see your partner during the conversation?

1. "I felt confirmed   __:__:__:__:__:__:__   "I felt disconfirmed
   by him/her"   1 2 3 4 5 6 7   by him/her"

2. "He/she was un-   __:__:__:__:__:__:__   "He/she was
   derstanding"   1 2 3 4 5 6 7   judgmental"

3. "He/she was non-   __:__:__:__:__:__:__   "He/she was defen-
   defensive"   1 2 3 4 5 6 7   sive"

4. "He/she had a   __:__:__:__:__:__:__   "He/she had a win/
   win/win mental   1 2 3 4 5 6 7   lose mental set"
   set"

How did you see yourself during the conversation?

5. "I confirmed him/   __:__:__:__:__:__:__   "I disconfirmed him/
   her"   1 2 3 4 5 6 7   her"

6. "I tried to under- __:__:__:__:__:__:__   "I was judgmental"
   stand him/her"   1 2 3 4 5 6 7

7. "I was non-   __:__:__:__:__:__:__   "I was defensive"
   defensive"   1 2 3 4 5 6 7

8. "I had a win/win   __:__:__:__:__:__:__   "I had a win/lose
   mental set"   1 2 3 4 5 6 7   mental set"

There are several things you might want to do with the information from the eight questions.

1. Turn in your questionnaire to your instructor who will summarize the results for you.

2. Compare your perceptions with those of your partner. Did your partner see you the same way you saw yourself? What verbal and nonverbal cues led you to answer the questionnaire the way you did? Discuss with your partner the differences in your perceptions.

3. Divide the questionnaires from all class members into two groups. Place in the first group all questionnaires which have scores of from one to three on items 1 and 2. Place in the second group all questionnaires which have scores of from five to seven on items 1 and 2. Now check to see which group has the highest scores on the defensiveness scale (item 3). Group 1 should come out the lowest; that is, members of that group should have felt the least defensive if the scores on items 1 and 2 are accurately reported.

NOTES

1. Lawrence Brammer, *The Helping Relationship: Process and Skills*, Englewood Cliffs, N.J.: Prentice-Hall, 1973, p. 82.

2. *Ibid.*, p. 86.

3. Jack R. Gibb, "Defensive Communication," *Journal of Communication*, **XI** (September 1961): 141.

4. *Ibid.*, p. 142.

5. Stephen J. Stephenson and Gary D'Angelo, "Relationships Among Evaluative/Empathic Listening, Self-Esteem, Sex, and Defensiveness in Dyads," unpublished manuscript, University of Washington, 1973.

6. A.H. Maslow, *Motivation and Personality*, 2nd ed., New York: Harper & Row, 1970, p. 118.

7. *Ibid.*, p. 271.

8. Carl R. Rogers, *On Becoming a Person*, Boston: Houghton Mifflin, 1961, p. 26.

9. Exercise adapted from David Johnson, *Reaching Out: Interpersonal Effectiveness and Self-Actualization* (Englewood Cliffs, N.J.: Prentice-Hall, 1972).

ADDITIONAL RESOURCES

You'll find some really good information about listening in both experimental and nonexperimental writings. For example, in his experimental work, William S. Verplank found that paraphrasing acts as a reinforcement and that it encourages the other person to express opinions. His article "The Control of the Content of Conversation: Reinforcement of Statements of Opinion" is reprinted in Dean Barnlund's book, *Interpersonal Communication: Survey and Studies* (Boston: Houghton Mifflin, 1968). That same article is also in the *Journal of Abnormal and Social Psychology*, 51, 1955, pp. 668–676.

You might also enjoy Charles M. Kelly's article "Empathic Listening," pp. 251–259 in Robert S. Cathcart and Larry A. Samovar, eds, *Small Group Communication: A Reader*. Kelly helped us in our thinking by his clear differentiation of *deliberative* and *empathic* listening.

There is also some material in Chapter 2 of *Bridges Not Walls: A Book About Interpersonal Communication* (ed. John Stewart, Reading, Mass.: Addison-Wesley, 1973). See especially the articles by Ralph R. Greenson, "Personal Involvement," and Jack R. Gibb, "Defensive Communication."

David W. Johnson presents a practical, humanistic view of interpersonal communication with a variety of structured experiences in his book *Reaching Out: Interpersonal Effectiveness and Self-Actualization* (Englewood Cliffs, N.J.: Prentice-Hall, 1972). Chapters 5, 6, and 7 relate especially to listening.

The counselor-teacher Carl Rogers identifies responsive listening as an important part of his theory and practice of interpersonal communication. He explains his approach in several places, e.g., his book *On Becoming a Person* (Boston: Houghton Mifflin, 1961), and his article "Communication: Its Blocking and Facilitation," *Harvard Business Review*, XXX (1952): 46–50. You might also enjoy watching him communicate with a counselee in the film "Three Approaches to Psychotherapy: Part I."

Thomas Gordon has elaborated a primarily Rogerian approach to listening in his book *Parent Effectiveness Training: A No-Lose Program for Raising Responsible Children* (New York: P.H. Wyden, 1970).

7

Interpersonal Clarity

Sometimes, being *unclear* can be an advantage. For example, if Zonker can type a paper that's general and ambiguous enough, he can use it for several different classes. You might say that Zonker is using "purposeful ambiguity." But students aren't the only ones who use purposeful ambiguity.

COPYRIGHT/1972. G.B. TRUDEAU/DISTRIBUTED BY UNIVERSAL PRESS SYNDICATE.

Some politicians do:

"Senator, what is the government doing to discourage large companies from taking advantage of energy shortages?"

"My position on this aspect of the energy crisis is the position I have taken since it became apparent that a supply shortfall was emerging due to international market conditions in the Southern Hemisphere and Middle East. We should continue to move ahead, emphasizing exploration and international cooperation, while protecting our energy independence."

Some educators do:

Student: What are the practical applications of what you just said?

Teacher: It's practical in the sense that the element purports to relate to existence in the same way that your behavior relates to the behavior of others.

Some advertisers do:

". . . cleans whiter, brighter, faster, yet is more gentle to your hands."

Some children do, too:

Mother: Where've you been?
Son: Out.
Mother: Out? Out is big! Where's out?
Son: I've been out. That's it.

The object of purposeful ambiguity is to be *mis*understood; this kind of language is used as a diversion or as a ploy. Most of the time, however, you'd rather be *understood* than misunderstood. At least that's what we're assuming as we write this chapter. We're also assuming that not everyone you communicate with will have learned to listen interpersonally and that some persons you talk with won't regularly paraphrase and parasupport what you say. We're predicting, in other words, that you'll need to be as clear as possible in many situations, because you won't get a second chance to explain yourself.

This has been a difficult chapter for us to write. We've talked about it a lot, written notes to ourselves and to each other, and made several beginnings that we threw away. Part of the problem was our feeling that we haven't always been able to comfortably and effectively fit a discussion of clarity into our interpersonal-communication teaching. Because of our ineffectiveness, some persons in our classes often seem to get the impression that interpersonal communication is mostly a matter of good vibes, open selves, and warm feelings, and that any discussion of how to be clear and accurate is artificial and inappropriate. In other words, we believe that clarity is important, but we've had some trouble explaining why.

We've also been affected by some of the feedback to my (John) book, *Bridges Not Walls*. One student wrote that the chapter on clarity in that book "had a lot of true points in it, but reading it was like reading a textbook full of facts. I found it hard to react and to get interested." Another student put it succinctly: "[It was] tedious, like learning bones and muscles." We're concerned about that, too. We definitely don't want to "be tedious," but we do want our suggestions to be useful enough so that your communicating will be better understood in a variety of contexts.

Another thing we've thought about is that on the one hand, we know that human perception is subjective, as we talked about in Chapters 4 and 6; we can't *cause* you to see or hear something exactly the way we want you to. In that sense, we *can't* "be completely clear" (or "tedious") on our own. And you can't either. Clarity, like every other aspect of human communication, happens between persons—it's affected by cues made available by a speaker, as well as how those cues are interpreted by a listener. On the other hand, we have experienced enough communicating—as you have—to *know* that sometimes we can understand what another person intends to say and sometimes we can't. In that sense, it seems like some communication *is* clear and some *isn't*. So we sometimes feel like we're caught between a rock and a hard place.

We hope you don't interpret our explanation as an apology for what we're about to say. We just want you to know where we're coming from. We realize that many people wonder how a discussion of organization, channel utilization, restatement, and the effective use of examples and analogies relates to a study of interpersonal communication. We've wondered that, too. But we think we have some answers. We've worked through these questions and apparent contradictions, and we'd like to try to explain how we think they relate, i.e., how being clear *can* help you to promote person-to-person communicating.

BY WAY OF DEFINITION

As we've already said, since nobody ever perceives things exactly as you do, you'll never be able to get somebody else to think and feel precisely what you're thinking and feeling. But that doesn't mean that you'll never be able to communicate clearly. First, you *do* affect what the other person is perceiving. You can't *cause* her or him to think a certain way, but you are part of the context that affects the way she or he interprets raw cues.

Second, we think that interpersonal clarity will make the most sense if you think of it as *limiting the range of possible interpretations*. Humans can't usually achieve direct mind-to-mind hookups—at least not yet. But you can communicate in such a way that you *adequately reduce the range of possible interpretations of the cues you're making available* so that the other person interprets your cues close to the way you interpret them. And that's what it means to communicate clearly.

For example, have you ever been in a conversation like this?

You: What do we have to know for the exam?
Friend: Oh, just understand the basics.

Or, maybe you've been involved in an interchange like this one, more detailed but no less confusing:

You: How do you get to the stadium from here?

Friend: Just go down that street over there for several blocks until it kind of divides into three ways down by a couple of brick buildings just over two or three streets from the place where the McDonald's used to be. You should be able to see the gym flagpole than and take that street about five blocks toward the pool until you get over by that line of trees, and then look for where the other road takes off so you can turn in on it.

Obviously, neither of your friends' responses is clear. That is, neither response adequately limits the number of different ways you could interpret what he or she said. In neither case is your communication with your friend likely to be interpersonal.

There are two reasons why it's pretty difficult to communicate interpersonally in situations like those. First, failing to adequately limit the range of possible interpretations can be another form of the objectifying we talked about in Chapter 1. Second, when someone can't understand what you're saying, that person may lose whatever desire or willingness he or she had to communicate; and without personal involvement, interpersonal communication can't happen. So being clear *can* help you promote person-to-person communicating.

Objectification

One of the problems with both of the examples is that your friend isn't seeing you as a unique individual. There seems to be an implicit assumption that since he or she knows what "understand the basics" means, you will, too. But you could interpret that phrase in a number of ways. You could infer that the exam will be all short essay questions; therefore, it might be enough just to memorize the general definitions you've studied. Or, you might conclude that there'll only be a few multiple-choice questions and that they'll be limited to the ideas outlined in the chapter summaries. It might make just as much sense, however, to interpret your friend's response to mean that the exam will be all problem-solving questions; if so, you primarily need to know how to apply the main concepts. But from what your friend said, there's no way to tell which of these interpretations—if any—is accurate.

Your friend might have decided to be unclear on purpose. He or she might feel unwilling to share with you information that it took long hours and hard work to accumulate. Maybe that feeling is justified. But in refusing to share the feeling with you because "You wouldn't understand," or "You'd just get mad," your friend is assuming that you can't deal with those feelings; he or she is stereotyping your probable response. And that's a form of objectifying, too.

Similar things are happening with the directions to the stadium. Your friend apparently has a clear picture of what he or she is describing. But you may be much less familiar with the neighborhood than your friend is. The point is, so long as your friend's assuming "Since *I* understand it, you will, too," he or she is not recognizing your individuality. And in that sense you're being objectified. As we'll talk about below, one of the principles of clear communication involves putting yourself in the psychological shoes of the listener. When you do that, you develop your ability to respond to the listener's humanness, and you help make interpersonal communication possible.

Involvement

When others have trouble deciding how to interpret your message, they often break psychological contact with you. That can happen for a variety of reasons: they may not want to work hard enough to listen interpersonally; they may infer that you're being purposely ambiguous for strategic or manipulative reasons; they may infer that you don't know what you're talking about; or they may "tune out" because they're confused and bored. Look for a minute at the directions to the stadium. How do you usually respond to communication as confusing as that? Sometimes, you may find yourself not listening— ignoring what the person is saying while you try to think of another way to get the information. Unclear communication often works that way. As you've read this book, you might have found yourself breaking contact with us because we weren't making sense to you. When that happens, you're responding to the uncertainty of having too many interpretations to choose from. When we don't adequately limit the possible interpretations, we make it more likely that others will break contact with us. That's another reason why being clear can affect your ability to promote interpersonal communication.

You can respond to these two problems by working to adequately reduce the number of ways others can interpret your verbal and non-verbal cues. You can do that, that is, you can work toward "being clear" by:

1. Being sensitive to the effects of the *context*
2. Letting others know where you're coming from (*content sharing*)
3. Putting yourself in their psychological shoes (*content responding*)
4. Giving what you say a sense of *wholeness*
5. Trying to communicate in verbal and nonverbal *pictures*, and
6. Remembering to use *reminders*.

BEING SENSITIVE TO THE EFFECTS OF CONTEXT

Noise

We mentioned before that all human communication is contextual and that the context you're in affects how people interpret your message. Many of the contextual elements can create what information theorists call "noise." Broadly speaking, anything that interferes with another person's understanding of your communication is "noise"—from fatigue or a headache to high humidity or depressing colors, from a squeaky or harsh voice to constant pacing or repetitive "Y'know"s.

There are at least three kinds of noise. When someone's bad headache, heartburn, hunger pangs, etc., prevent effective listening, he or she is experiencing *physiological discomfort* noise. A second type is *psychological* noise, which includes, for example, a strongly biased opinion that keeps a person from listening accurately to any message that contradicts that opinion. Sometimes, psychological noise is so strong that it prevents genuine communication. For example, a worry about grades causes gamesmanship between instructor and student; a fear of losing his job contributes to an employee's high anxiety level, and he's unable to hear accurately the work instructions given; a strong prejudice against women prevents a male hospital patient from listening to a female dietitian about proper diet. *Physical*, or environmental, noise—the third type—includes things like a hot stuffy room, an uncomfortable chair, cramped physical space, and so on.

The problem, however, is that one person's noise is another person's information. What may be a "cramped" space to another person may be a comfortably intimate environment to you. Since noise often originates "in" the persons with whom you're communicating, you can't always know when or how it's operating. But you can do two things. First, you can take the time and effort to get in touch with and then do something about the potentially distracting elements of your communication contexts. Do you need to stop playing with the ball point pen in your hands? To quit twisting and tugging the rings on your fingers? To stop the continual shifting of your weight from foot to foot? Do you need to close the door? Open the window? Turn down the heat? Move closer together? Sit down? Go somewhere else? Rearrange the furniture? Talk more quietly? Relate what you're saying to what was being discussed before you began? Comment on why you're dressed as you are?

Remember that you have the ability to control many of the elements of a communication situation. Even in fairly formal situations, you can change some of the contextual factors that you think might be distracting. For example, if you're late, you can mention why, thus limiting the number of ways in which your nonverbal message might be interpreted. Or, if you're talking with a small group of persons in a large room, you might ask them to move closer together so that they feel less anonymous and perhaps more willing to contribute.

I (John) remember one situation in which I was extremely insensitive to contextual noise. When I was teaching at Stout State University in Menomonie, Wisconsin, our offices were crowded into one corner of the basement of Old Main; whenever we wanted privacy or quiet, we had to move to another part of the building. Down a dark hall from my office was the drama director's costume room, a large, gloomy place filled with racks of clothes, long tables, and storage boxes. Since it was convenient and quiet, I often used it to listen to student speeches or readings. A woman named Adrienne had asked for some help with an oral-interpretation presentation she was working on, and we had made a late-afternoon appointment. As soon as she arrived, I started heading toward the costume room, babbling about the class, Adrienne's reading, the weather, and I don't know what else. I unlocked and opened the door, flicked on the dim lights, and motioned for her to go in. She looked at me strangely, so I mumbled something about" . . . bad facilities. . . practice . . . good acoustics." Adrienne just about exploded with relief. "Oh brother! You don't know *what* I was thinking!" For Adrienne, the dim lights, secluded hall, and locked door all added noise to the context by interfering with my naive interpretation of the communication situation. I still feel embarrassed remembering it.

Communication Modes

Within any context you have control over several different modes, or ways, of communicating. For example, when you're talking on the telephone, your tone of voice can influence the other person's interpretation of your mood and feelings, your relationship to him or her, and your interest in the conversation. You also have control over your rate of speaking, pronunciation, and articulation. Each of these factors can contribute to confusion or clarity. When you're writing a letter, you don't have control over auditory cues, but you do have a variety of visual modes: the quality, size, and color of paper, the kind of pencil or pen, whether you type, print, or write, the style of your writing, your choice of words, and the informal or formal structure of your sentences or paragraph layout. If you're applying for a job and you want to address your prospective employer formally, you wouldn't want to use pink perfumed paper and a lavender felt tip pen. Similarly, we've learned that most of our friends respond differently when we type a letter to them on formal, University of Washington stationary from when we write the letter in longhand on notebook paper.

In face-to-face oral communication, there are a tremendous number of modes you have available to inform or confuse your listeners. You have not only the same auditory cues that are available in a telephone conversation, but also visual cues and, in some situations, touch and aroma cues, too.

One research team investigated the comparative effects of faces and voices by creating a situation in which communicators' faces indicated one attitude—positive, neutral, or negative—while their voices indicated a different attitude. Not surprisingly, they found that people tended to believe the attitude they *saw* in the communicator's face more often than the one they *heard* in the communicator's voice. But the researchers also found that when information in the two modes was consistent—when face and voice agreed—listeners perceived the attitude communicated to be significantly more *intense*. Using more than one channel definitely made a difference.[1]

The same research team also came to some conclusions about the relative importance of three different face-to-face modes. When they combined results of the face-voice study with some data about how words work,[2] they concluded that when you use all three modes— words, tone of voice, and facial expression— words contribute 7%, tone of voice 38%, and facial expression 55% of the total meaning. Or to put it another way, listeners tend to rely on your facial expression most heavily, your tone of voice next, and your words last. These findings are obviously incomplete, because they don't indicate the impact of any of the several other modes that are operating. But they do suggest that the number and kind of modes you use can significantly affect how others understand you.[3]

Few people take full advantage of the visual modes available to them in face-to-face contexts. Some use gestures to describe size and shape, but often those gestures are too "quick" and not "definite" enough. Instead of just "talking" about their models of communication, students in our classes sometimes sketch diagrams on overhead projectors, blackboards, sketching pads, or whatever is available. If they aren't comfortable with their own art work, they'll ask friends to do the sketching for them. Some of the clearest explanations have included models, pictures, objects, and the use of different color schemes. One group of students decided to present a report on how context influences nonverbal behavior. But since they didn't want to give just a verbal report, they dressed a person in a weird "spaceman" uniform and took Super 8 films of him walking at a shopping center, a cemetery, a science center, and outside a classroom window. The camera focused on the observer's nonverbal responses to the spaceman in each of those contexts. That report, with the film used to illustrate the verbal comments, was very effective and successful.

If you wanted to talk to your class about different body postures, you could use magazine pictures, slides, sketches (e.g., of stick figures), cartoons, etc. Or, if none of those is available, you could ask the persons around you to demonstrate the various postures you're talking about. If that's not possible, you could demonstrate the postures yourself.

In short, as we said in Chapter 2, people are always interpreting the nonverbal cues that they observe in a communication context. It therefore makes sense to try to have those cues work *for* you, to have them help you reduce the range of possible interpretations of your message. If you avoid looking at the other person and talk in a listless monotone, or if you ignore what's communicated by facial expression, movement, and proximity, you're reducing your chances to help others interpret you accurately. Your communicating can "be clearer" when you make available consistent cues in as many modes as you can, and when you're also aware of all the modes through which the other person is communicating.

Individual Application: Communication Context Checklist

Your residence. What kind of communication context do you presently live in? What are some potential *noise* factors in that context? Check the ones that apply, and add others in the blank spaces.

room size	temperature	degree of privacy
sound level	light level	furniture arrangement
type of floor	rules and regulations	color scheme

_____   _____   _____

_____   _____   _____

You might want to circle the contextual factors in that list which you can alter or control, and to think of how the changes you could make might affect the quality of your communicating.

What communication *modes* are available to you at your residence?

word choice	tone of voice	rate of speaking
volume	vocal quality	gestures
dress	facial expression	furniture
bodily movements	proximity or distance	posters, signs,
written notes and letters	wall colors	bulletin boards
_____	_____	floor covering

Again, you might want to circle the channels you most frequently use and to consider how using other channels might affect the quality of your communicating.

Your place of employment. What are some potential *noise* factors where you work?

_____   _____   _____

_____   _____   _____

Which ones can you change or control?

_____   _____   _____

_____   _____   _____

What *modes* are available to you at your place of employment?

_____   _____   _____

_____   _____   _____

Which ones do you use most? Which other modes could you use to improve the quality of your on–the–job communicating?

_____   _____   _____

_____   _____   _____

Your classroom. What are some potential *noise* factors in your classroom?

_____   _____   _____

_____   _____   _____

Which ones can you change or control?

_____   _____   _____

_____   _____   _____

What modes are available to you in your classroom?

_____   _____   _____

_____   _____   _____

Which ones do you use most? Which other modes could you use to improve the quality of your classroom communicating?

_____   _____   _____

_____   _____   _____

_____   _____   _____

◇━◆━◇

CONTENT SHARING—LETTING OTHERS KNOW WHERE YOU'RE COMING FROM

In Chapter 5 we said that sharing some of your self is necessary in order to establish and maintain interpersonal communication. We suggested that it would be helpful for you to get in touch with both your historical and your present selves and for you to make some of both available to the persons you're communicating with. A closely related kind of sharing can also help others understand more clearly what you're saying about some topic or content. The need for this sharing-for-clarity is suggested by the same studies of communication defensiveness that we mentioned in the last chapter (Jack Gibb's studies to identify causes of and cures for defensive communication).

Gibb found that two important causes of defensiveness are *strategic* and *controlling* behaviors. As he explains, "no one wishes to be a guinea pig, a role player, or an impressed actor, and no one likes to be the victim of some hidden motivation"[4] Consequently, when listeners believe that the speaker has some kind of manipulative strategy and is purposely "hiding" his or her intent, the listeners become defensive. Similarly, Gibb writes, "speech which is used to *control* the listener evokes resistance (italics added)."[5] But when a speaker is open about her or his attempts to control, that provokes less defensiveness than if he or she is suspected of having hidden motives.

These studies suggest—and, more important, your own experience probably confirms—that the more the other person knows about your motivation, your intent, and the reasons behind your position on a topic, the less likely he or she will be to misinterpret what you say about it. The more someone knows where you're coming from regarding the topic, the more accurately that person will be able to interpret your communicating about it.

For example, Nancy, a student who sees herself as a dedicated but quiet Christian, was upset by some vague generalizations a radical Christian named John was making about the church attendance and the general state of salvation of the people in our class. Nancy said that she really felt uncomfortable when she perceived what she thought was John's thinly veiled, obviously strategic desire to control one aspect of her behavior. She said that she found herself feeling defensive and attributing all kinds of undesirable motives to John. But when John let her know where he was coming from, when he openly shared his attitudes about Christianity and his concern for people he thinks are non-Christians, Nancy found it much easier to listen to him. She didn't accept everything he said, but she did make fewer unfair interpretations of his position, and she felt comfortable talking about her Christian commitment.

In other words, just as sharing some of your historical and your present selves can help others understand *you*, sharing some of your attitudes toward and experiences with your content or topic can help others understand *what you're saying*. If you verbalize some of where you're coming from, you'll be able to reduce the number of inaccurate ways others might interpret what you say, and that way you'll be able to communicate more clearly.

Individual Application:
When You Know Where I'm Coming From . . . [6]

Here are some simple statements about different topics. *Before* you read the material printed upside-down, write out a quick, subjective statement about how you feel about the statement. Try to express your "now feelings" in immediate response to the statement. Then read the material printed upside down and see if your immediate statement still reflects your feelings.

1. "I don't believe people in this class should look each other in the eye when they're talking. I don't want to do that, and I don't want others to do it to me."

_____

_____

_____

(In my Asian culture, direct eye contact is appropriate only for intimates.)

2. "This equality stuff is a myth. In every human organization there are always leaders and followers, and I'm gonna be a leader."

_____

_____

_____

(My dad has been a career Naval officer for 30 years. I enlisted at age 18, I've served five years, and I plan to career the Navy, too.)

3. "I never stay in the dorm over the weekend."

_____

_____

_____

(My parents are ill and I have to go home every chance I get.)

4. "I hate teaching! It's a waste of time! Teachers are nothing but glorified babysitters!"

_____

_____

_____

(I'm a 27-year-old WASP who grew up in the suburbs, and I've just finished my first semester of teaching in the remedial English program of an urban ghetto junior high school. _I'm scared_.)

5. "Hitchhiking is ugly! There ought to be strict laws against it! It's dangerous, especially for women and young people. In fact, the legislators who allowed it ought to be shot!"

_____

_____

_____

(Two days ago my daughter was raped and shot by someone who picked her up hitchhiking.)

CONTENT RESPONDING—PUTTING YOURSELF IN THEIR PSYCHOLOGICAL SHOES

When we were discussing negotiation of selves Chapter 3, we made the point that human communication involves both giving and receiving, both showing and seeing, both sharing and responding. The same applies to "being clear," too. Sharing is important, but so is responding. Your responses to the persons you're communicating with can also help you adequately narrow the range of interpretations of what you say.

Generally, it's a good idea to apply what's been called the principle of adaptation.[7] The principle of adaptation says that you can communicate more clearly if you continually try to put yourself in the psychological frame of reference of the other person. It's pretty difficult to effectively limit the range of possible interpretations if your communication behavior is affected by unexamined assumptions about the persons you're talking with. Try to see the communication situation from their point of view. Try not to assume, for example, that people always respond in a way that *you* would call rational. I (John) think that it makes very good sense (i.e., is "rational") to get up early and write while your mind is fresh—even before breakfast. I (Gary) think that getting up early for almost *any* reason is a waste of good sleep time. I work better late at night.

Other assumptions can also create problems. We've come to realize that just because we're talking, it doesn't mean people should automatically listen. We're often reminded not to assume that other people care about the same things we do or that most problems have a simple cause and a simple cure, or that there's only one way to look at a problem and that it's our way.[8] Perhaps most important, we always try to remember that not everybody defines words the way we do. We've found, in short, that unexamined assumptions can really get in the way of mutual understanding.

In order to do something specific about the problem of assumptions, you might think in terms of applying the *principle of prior definition:* define before you develop; explain before you amplify. In other words, if you're using words which have several possible interpretations (even the simplest words can be interpreted in a number of ways), define those words before you develop or elaborate further. For example, where would you go if your friend left you a note saying that he or she would meet you at the "side" of the building you live in? Similarly, it wouldn't do much good for us to talk with you about something like "analogically coded metacommunicative cues" until we defined or explained those terms. The following example illustrates how misinterpretation of cues can sometimes be embarrassing.

An English lady, while in Switzerland, looked at several rooms in a large apartment house. She told the schoolmaster who owned the house that she would let him know about renting one of the rooms later. However, after arriving back at the hotel, the thought occurred to her that she had not asked about the water closet (bathroom), so she immediately wrote a note to the schoolmaster asking about the "W.C.," being too bashful to write out the word water closet.

The schoolmaster, who was far from being an expert of English, did not know what the initials "W.C." meant. He asked the parish priest, and together they decided that it meant Wayside Chapel. The schoolmaster then wrote the following letter to the very surprised lady:

Dear Madame,

I take great pleasure in informing you that the W.C. is located seven miles from the house in the center of a beautiful grove of pine trees. It is capable of holding 229 people and is open on Sunday and Thursday only. I recommend that you come early, although there is plenty of standing room. This is an unfortunate situation, especially if you are in the habit of going regularly. You will, no doubt, be glad to hear that a good number bring their lunch and make a day of it; while others, who can afford it, go by car and arrive just in time. I would especially suggest that your ladyship go on Thursday when there is social music. Acoustically, the place is excellent. It may interest you to know that my daughter was married in the W.C. and it was there she met her husband. I can remember the rush there was for seats. The newest attraction is a bell donated by a wealthy resident of the district. It rings joyously every time a person enters. A bazaar is to be held to provide plush seats for all, since the people think it is a long-felt need. My wife is rather delicate and does not go regularly. Naturally, it pains her very much not to attend more often. If you wish, I shall be glad to reserve the best seat for you where you will be seen by all. Hoping I have been of service to you, I remain, the schoolmaster."[9]

One final suggestion about content responding: one way social, professional, and political groups define themselves is by creating their own *jargon* or in-group vocabularly. I (John) have seen it happen in the Campfire Girl group Marcia and Lisa belong to. "Wohelo," "Horizon," "Tawanka," and "Discovery" are words with special meaning for Campfire Girls. Auto mechanics have special words, e.g., "detent spring" and "socket ratchet," and special uses for many common words, e.g., "stand," "come-along," "mike," and "drift." Interpersonal communication teachers also create their own jargon. For example, we talk about "symmetrical escalation," "overrigid complementarity," "relationship cues," "structured experiences," "congruence," "imagining the real," "negotiation of selves," "parasupporting," etc. You probably use some jargon terms, too, and generally there's nothing wrong with them. In some situations, they can increase both clarity and interpersonal cohesion. But jargon can confuse and frustrate someone who's not in your group but who wants to understand you clearly. Explaining or defining unusual terms before you use them to develop your ideas can help. Recognize, too, that you're not always able to rely on *prior* definition. Especially if the terms or concepts are quite unfamiliar to the persons you're talking with, you may want to *re*define or *re*-explain to help them stay with you, and you may want to give them a chance to paraphrase or parasupport your definitions in order to check their interpretations.

We hope that the point about content responding is fairly clear. Each person is unique, and that means, in part, that she or he sees the topic differently from the way you do. In order to adequately limit the number of ways others might interpret what you say, try to put yourself in their psychological shoes.

GIVING WHAT YOU SAY A SENSE OF WHOLENESS

If your experience is anything like ours, people have been telling you to "get organized" ever since you were in diapers. Your toy box was to help you learn to organize your room. School and work taught you to organize your time. And invariably, one goal of English, speech, philosophy, and science classes is to teach you to organize your thinking and the ways to express yourself. Sometimes, I (John) wonder whether we tend to go a little overboard. Gary's got a cartoon on his office door that shows a high-school-age girl deep in thought, and the caption is: "Sometimes they teach things out of me. And I feel like saying, "I wanted to keep that." We sometimes wonder whether spontaneous chaos is one of those things that schools "teach out of us" that we might enjoy—and profit from—keeping.

On the other hand, as we said in Chapter 4, most psychologists believe that we *naturally* structure our world, i.e., that order is more characteristically human than is disorder. But whether structure is natural or is an artifact of Western culture, it's here. We *do* tend to see things and people in wholes made up of parts that are somehow related to one another. Therefore, communication that has a sense of wholeness is usually easier for us to comprehend clearly than is communication that doesn't.

When people perceive something that's "incomplete" or "disordered," they sometimes fill in or add details so that it makes more sense to them. For example, as you watch a television program you may see an actor put a coffee cup to his lips and make drinking movements. Even though you don't actually see the coffee itself, you mentally "put" coffee in the cup —you fill in the detail. This same kind of process can occur when you're talking with another person. If you don't provide a "whole" message, the other person may fill in missing details or examples and in so doing may make your message into something you didn't intend. To the extent that you don't come across as a "whole" person, the other person may fill in or infer things about you that don't adequately characterize you as an individual. In short, giving a sense of wholeness and some structure to your communication gives you some control over how *you* and your *ideas* are perceived by others.

The more formal the communication context, the more obvious that sense of wholeness can be. Persons listening to a public speech usually expect the talk to be clearly structured. As we'll discuss in Chapter 9, a public speech doesn't have to sound as if it's coming from a robot; the speaker can still promote some person-to-person contact. But the speech should usually be pretty clearly organized. Your contribution to a group discussion should also have fairly clear structure, although it can be less formal than the organization of a speech.

An informal conversation, however, is obviously different from both a speech and a group discussion. You don't sit down beforehand to organize a conversation—not usually, anyway. (Your first date might have been an exception to that rule. Both of us remember frantically trying to plan topics of conversation for our first major boy-girl social engagements. You know how well that worked.)

Yet structure is important, even in conversational communication. For example, have you ever had a conversation like this?

Fred: How many Christmas presents do we have left to get?
Wilma: Just a couple. You have any ideas for your brother? I don't remember what we got him last year.
Fred: That reminds me, I forgot to call that woman.
Wilma: Hunh? Should we call Ann and ask her? I always feel like. . . .
Fred: *Damn*, that makes me mad! Oh, well, he still does a lot of hunting.
Wilma: She remembers *Halloween* even.
Fred: Who?
Wilma: Was it you who told me about that guy who killed one of the six remaining animals of that one species?
Fred: Yeah, but how does *that* relate to Sam's present?

In a conversation like that, the problem is *not* that there's a total lack of structure. Fred's contributions make all kinds of sense to him, and so do Wilma's—to Wilma. *The problem is that the implicit structure is not made explicit.* Fred knows the connections among his own statements, but he doesn't bother to show Wilma those relationships, and Wilma doesn't bother to explain anything to Fred.

For example, when Wilma mentions Fred's brother (Sam), Fred pictures Sam on the job—Sam counsels handicapped children—which reminds Fred that he forgot to call a psychologist he works with—"that woman." Wilma hears "that woman" and assumes that Fred is talking about Sam's wife, Ann. Wilma feels uncomfortable around Ann and so begins to say to Fred, "I always feel like. . ." Fred doesn't even hear her. He's thinking that they might get Sam something he can use while hunting; when Wilma hears the word "hunting," she remembers a story Fred told her that she's been wanting to share with a friend, but forgot about until now, and so on.

The point we're trying to make is that there's structure even in an informal conversation, in the sense that each person's contributions "fit in" or "follow logically" or "make sense"—in short, connect—*for that person.* Problems arise when two (or more) persons' structures don't merge or fit together. Then you get the kind of confusing exchange Fred and Wilma had. You can avoid such confusion by thinking of the other person as unique, as someone who doesn't structure the world or the conversation as you do. Your thought patterns, the connections you see between ideas, are different from his or hers. So if you reveal your thought patterns, if you make them explicit by bringing them to the surface with verbal cues, then the structure of each person's contributions to the conversation becomes apparent to the other, and there will be less room for misinterpretation.

In other words, there are ways to structure even informal conversation so that it makes sense. You don't necessarily have to give your conversation a beginning (introduction), middle (body), and end (conclusion). It would sound a little phony if you said to someone in an informal conversation: "Hi, I'm really glad to be talking with you today. As our conversation progresses I'd like to talk about three things: (1) the weather, (2) the movie I saw last night, and (3) our relationship." That kind of organization or structure fits many public speeches, but most people prefer spontaneity in informal conversation.

Even in an informal conversation, however, you can verbalize the implicit structure, that is, talk about the links you're seeing between ideas. When you don't, you leave open the possibility for all kinds of misinterpretation. When you do, you significantly improve your chances of adequately limiting the range of interpretations, i.e., you improve your chances of "being clear."

Below are two conversations between a doctor and her patient. In the first conversation, we've tried to illustrate a situation in which the participants are *not* verbalizing the links between ideas. Here, the patient has so many different things he wants to talk or ask about that his conversation "skips" all over without explicit reason.

Doctor: That's my analysis. All the tests on your respiratory system came out negative. Overall, you're in good health.

Patient: Why would I get a sharp pain in my back when I go to bed at night?

Doctor: Could be a variety of reasons. For example, it could be because of something as simple as your mattress or pillow. I'm not prepared to answer specifically right now. We could try to find out.

Patient: You know my eight-year-old son Billy—he seems so
            tired all the time. You think I should bring him in?
Doctor: When was Billy's last physical?
Patient: Doctor, how often should a woman get a Pap test? I've
            been trying to convince my wife for months now to get
            one. Doesn't the American Cancer Society recommend
            once a year?

Here, the patient doesn't seem to be "in tune" with his doctor. It
wouldn't be suprising if the doctor were a bit confused.

In the second situation, the patient is helping to create understanding by explaining how what he says fits into the conversation, by
bringing to the surface the structure he is seeing, and by letting the
doctor know how a comment relates to what preceded it.

Doctor: That's my analysis. All the tests on your respiratory
            system came out negative. Overall, you're in good
            health.
Patient: Well, that sure doesn't fit with how I'm feeling some-
            times. If I'm in good health, I don't understand why my
            back hurts just about every morning when I get out of
            bed.
Doctor: Could be for a variety of reasons. For example, it could
            be because of something as simple as your mattress or
            pillow. I can't specifically say right now. We could try to
            find out.
Patient: That makes sense. I'll try to work that out myself
            because I know your time is limited right now—you've
            got other patients to see. But when you mentioned
            "mattress," it reminded me that I wanted to ask you
            about my eight-year-old Billy. He seems to be tired all
            the time. Never wants to do anything. His mattress is
            very old and sags like a hammock. You think I should
            bring him in for a checkup, or could it be he's not
            sleeping well at nights?
Doctor: When was Billy's last physical?
Patient: He was in three months ago. I remember that because
            at that same time my wife had an appointment to have a
            complete physical, too, including a Pap test. But she de-
            cided to forget it. I've been trying to convince her for

three months now to get a physical. I'm wondering now if I should get both Billy and my wife to make appointments. What do you think?

TRYING TO COMMUNICATE IN VERBAL AND NONVERBAL PICTURES

The differences between the following two examples of *written* communication are pretty obvious:

Example 1

"The nurse is at the door of the glass station, issuing nighttime pills to the men that shuffle past her in a line, and she's having a hard time keeping straight who gets poisoned with what tonight. She's not even watching where she pours the water. What has distracted her attention this way is that big red-headed man with the dreadful cap and the horrible-looking scar, coming her way. She's watching McMurphy walk away from the card table in the dark day room, his one horny hand twisting the red tuft of hair that sticks out of the little cup at the throat of his work-farm shirt, and I figure by the way she rears back when he reaches the door of the station that she's probably been warned by the Big Nurse. ('Oh, one more thing before I leave it in your hands tonight, Miss Pilbow; that new man sitting over there, the one with the garish red sideburns and facial lacerations—I've reason to believe he is a sex maniac.')"[10]

Example 2

"The atomistic psychology, which analyzes the stream of consciousness into separate units and accounts for the course of the stream by the interplay of these units, in now obsolete. The physiological evidence is against such a theory. The brain functions cannot be broken up into elementary units, occurring in distinct areas. The specific character of any brain process involved in any particular activity of the organism is a quality of the total process, a peculiarity of the total field and not a putting together of specific processes occurring in special areas. The *Gestalt* psychology holds that the stream of consciousness is not a sum of elements but a configuration in which every distinguishable part determines and is determined by the nature of the whole. Thoughts and their relations are unified wholes of subordinate parts and not mechanically added sums of independent units."[11]

Example 1 is full of concrete words—"pills," "water," "big redheaded man," "dreadful cap," "horrible-looking scar," "card table," "dark day room," "one horny hand," "red tuft of hair," "work farm shirt," and so on. The passage moves in a narrative, or storylike, way—like you'd see it and describe it if you were there. Its structure grows out of tangible and specific things, people, and movements. As you read the passage, you can't help but "see" or imagine the looks of the persons and places described. You think of it in terms of *pictures*.

The second example, by contrast, is full of abstract words— "consciousness," "interplay," "physiological evidence," "theory," "brain functions," "elementary units," "brain process," " total field," "configuration," "thoughts and their relations," and so on. The text moves in a logical order—contrasting, defining, and developing—an order with few links to tangible objects or persons. It discusses general rather than specific functions, fields, and processes. As you read and think about the passage, it's pretty difficult to "see" a picture or image of what's being discussed.

In your high school or college experience, one or more of your English-composition teachers probably made a major point of writing in concrete rather than abstract terms, and that's important in spoken communication, too. People will never interpret what you say exactly as you want them to, but they'll almost always understand you better if your communication helps them think of verbal and nonverbal *pictures*. To put it another way, when the words you use—along with your tone of voice, facial expressions, gestures, rate of speaking, etc.—suggest technicolor movies, your communicating is likely to be not only more interesting, but also clearer.

Think for a minute about the differences between a movie and an abstract written message. Films, whether they're travelogues or musicals, documentaries or porno, have impact partly because, they're made up of concrete events, happenings, or occurrences. In other words, movies are both tangible and dynamic, specific and in motion. Example 1 at the beginning of this section is like a movie in that something is happening (it's dynamic, moving) to specific place. It's pretty hard *not* to "see' something when you hear or read the words ". . .big redheaded man with the . . . horrible-looking scar," and "she rears back when he reaches the door. . . ." On the other hand, it's almost impossible to imagine any pictures that might make vivid the meaning of the words, "the specific character of any brain process involved in any particular activity of the organism is a quality of the total process. . . ." In that sentence there's no event going on and almost no concrete objects involved. As you read those words, you might imagine the typical picture of a brain—a lumpy, convoluted, gray tissue mass—but that's not really appropriate, because the excerpt talks about "brain process," not "brain." So you're left without any pictures at all. The theater is dark.

The same thing happens in spoken communication. Look at and listen to the differences in concreteness and movement between these two excerpts from student-teacher conferences:

Example 1:

John: How much do you see yourself having given to the other persons in the class? What I'm asking is how much do *you* think you participated in their growth?

Peter: Pretty much.

John: How so? Were there some times you remember especially?

Peter: Oh yeah. I'm a good listener, and I think they noticed that. I felt like I listened a lot in class. I also gave feedback a lot of times. People listened when I did, and they seemed to appreciate what I said. I think I felt okay about how much I helped others. Yeah, I did.

Example 2:

John: How much do you see yourself having been willing and able to give to other people in the class? How much do you think you helped them grow?

Tom: Quite a lot. Bill and I've become pretty good friends. We had coffee after class one day last week and he mentioned that when I talked about his never looking at people, that helped him. He said he had never realized how little he actually looked at the person he was talking with.

John: Great!

Tom: Yeah. I said that talking to him was sometimes like kissing a brick—or like trying to talk to some professor or salesman who makes you feel like he's too busy to bother with you. He was able to tell me some things about my communicating, too—we were pretty open with each other.

John: It's good that you were able to say that to him. I've mentioned it to him, too.

Tom: I also talked to Julie after that listening exercise we did in
       class. She said she felt you were really down on her be-
       cause she didn't say enough in class.
John: Ouch.
Tom: Yeah. I told her that I thought participation meant more
       than just saying things, and that I thought she'd partici-
       pated quite a lot. And I gave her some examples of when I
       thought she'd helped Bruce understand the negotiation of
       selves and when she'd worked out the role-playing stuff
       we did for the responding chapter. . . .

The main difference between Tom's responses and Peter's is important. Tom talks about examples, illustrations, analogies, and specific
instances, but Peter doesn't. Tom's responses enable his listener to
picture images—of Tom and Bill having coffee, of kissing a brick, of a
disinterested professor or salesman, of Tom and Julie, of Julie talking
with Bruce, etc. And, to get back to the point of this chapter, Tom's
responses more effectively limit the range of possible interpretations
than do Peter's. John will probably understand that Peter feels generally
okay about his involvement in class, but he won't know much more
than that.

Tom's response narrows the number of ways John might think Tom
sees himself. John might conceivably disagree that the examples Tom
cites are really responsive to the question, but at least he can accurately
interpret what Tom means, i.e., he can understand Tom pretty clearly.

So try to use examples and analogies. Help others understand you
by using illustrations of what you're saying and by explaining how your
topic or point is "like," i.e., analogous to, something else. Let your
imagination paint pictures of what you're saying, and share them with
your listeners. Help others to "see" what you mean by talking about
examples and specific instances. Try to make your communicating like
film—vivid, visual, concrete, and in motion.

REMEMBERING TO USE REMINDERS

All of us live in complex communication environments; we're continually interpreting raw cues from a variety of sources. Our sensory limitations make it impossible for us to pick up and remember
everything we hear; we select only fragments of the cues available to us.

When you realize that the other person's communication occurs continuously across dynamic and interdependent contexts, you can understand why he or she might not catch what you say the first time you say it or why someone might not remember what you say. Our final suggestion is that you give people signposts and reminders to help them accurately interpret what you're saying. This is a simple process, but one which often seems to be ignored or forgotten. We tend to forget that written messages can be read and reread, but that speech communication comes by only once. And, as with almost everything else, you can't expect to do a perfect job the first time.

In one study, communication researchers found that just inserting an appropriate signpost or pointer, e.g., the words "this is important" or "now get this," significantly increased the listeners' retention of what was said. In fact, they found that in a public-speaking situation, a verbal reminder was a more effective means of emphasis than a pause, increased volume, or repetition.[12]

It's also often helpful simply to repeat or restate what you say. The last paragraph of the "Communicate in Pictures" section of this chapter (p. 238) is an example of restatement. The paragraph makes one fairly simple point: use examples and analogies. But we tried to clarify and emphasize that idea by restating it, i.e., by saying it in a number of different ways.

In a face-to-face situation, you can often see what needs repeating by the look on your listener's face. Try to respond to it. Stay plugged into the nonverbal feedback so you can recognize the need to go back over something. But whether or not the other person looks puzzled, remember that humans can process only a limited amount of information at a time. We need reminders in order to keep up with you— repetition of key phrases, reuse of important names or terms, restatement of crucial ideas.

CONCLUDING THOUGHTS

Almost every instance of human communication involves persons in relationship *and* a topic. So, just about every time you communicate, you're involved in *two* processes: negotiation of selves and content development. Although you can distinguish between these processes, they're very closely related. In this book we've chosen to emphasize negotiation of selves, and we've focused on that process in most of the first six chapters. In this chapter we've shifted that focus to the other important process, content development. We've tried to show how effective content development relates to negotiation of selves and more specifically, how clarity can help promote interpersonal-quality communication.

We started with the reminder that nobody can actually "be clear," because understanding is a mutual thing, just like the rest of human communication. But we can improve the understandability of our communicating by working to *adequately limit the range of possible interpretations of the cues we make available to others.* That's what we mean by interpersonal clarity.

We also said that when you work to adequately limit the range of possible interpretations, you promote interpersonal-quality communication by decreasing objectification and increasing involvement. Then, we offered six suggestions for improving your understandability:

1. It helps to be sensitive to the effects of the communication context; specifically, to the impact of *noise* and to the communication *modes* available to you.

2. Content *sharing* is also important. If you let others know where you're coming from, they don't tend to misinterpret your attitudes toward and experiences with your topic.

3. Content *responding* also helps create understanding. Work to put yourself in the psychological shoes of the other person.

4. Since people tend to perceive and think in terms of patterns or wholes, it also helps to give your communicating a sense of *wholeness.* You needn't build a formal, artificial structure for your communication, but you should make *explicit* the organization that's *implicit.*

5. You can often make your communication more interesting and less ambiguous by using *examples* and *analogies.* These kinds of specific illustrations can help your listeners "see" or "picture" what you're saying.

6. Since speech communication can't usually be reheard and since most things aren't interpreted completely accurately the first time, don't be afraid to use *signposts* and *restatements* to help adequately limit the possible interpretations of what you say.

EXERCISES

Group Application: Who Understands You?[13]

Think about the persons you communicate with — regularly or infrequently — and try to determine the one person who understands you better than anyone else does. Of all the persons you know — immediate family, relatives, friends, co-workers, superiors, roommates, subordinates, casual acquaintances — who seems to misinterpret you the least?

Try to determine why. Think about a *specific communication situation* which that person understood you well and see if you can pinpoint what helped him or her understand you. What specifically did you do to adequately limit the other person's range of interpretation of the cues you made available?

Jot down a few notes so you can share your conclusions with others. You might also want to notice whether or not they identify the same factors as you do. What does your discussion suggest about interpersonal clarity?

Group Application: Being Clear

One way to discuss what we've said in this chapter is to begin by having someone try to "be completely clear." Whoever volunteers should stand in front of the rest of the group and describe a diagram. The diagram might look like one of the following:

The task is to verbally describe the drawing as clearly as possible so that the others can replicate it without asking questions or interacting with the speaker. After about ten minutes you might want to discuss the following questions as specifically as you can:

1. How closely did the listeners' drawings match the original in shape, size, placement on paper, etc.?

2. In what ways was the speaker unclear? That is, what got in the way of clear communication?

3. In what ways was the speaker clear? That is, what did the speaker do that helped others understand her or him?

In your discussion try to come up with some generalizations about what it takes to "be clear." Then you might want to try applying those generalizations by having someone describe a person, event, belief, or feeling as "clearly" as possible.

NOTES

1. Albert Mehrabian and S.R. Ferris, "Inference of Attitudes from Nonverbal Communication in Two Channels," *Journal of Consulting Psychology,* **XXXI** (1967): 248–252.

2. The data on words are from A. Mehrabian and M. Weiner, "Decoding of Inconsistent Communications," *Journal of Personality and Social Psychology,* **VI** (1967): 108–114.

3. In another study, K.K. Neeley found that listeners could understand speakers significantly better when they could see the speaker's lips: K.K. Neeley, "Effect of Visual Factors on Intelligibility of Speech," *Journal of Acoustical Society of America,* **XXVIII** (1956): 1275–1277.

4. Jack R. Gibb, "Defensive Communication," *Journal of Communication,* **XI** (September 1961): 145.

5. *Ibid.,* 144.

6. This activity was suggested by a similar one in *The Dynamics of Human Communication* by Gail E. Myers and Michele Tolela Myers; New York: McGraw-Hill, 1973, p. 261.

7. This suggestion—and others we'll offer—was first identified for us by David Mortensen, a friend and ex-colleague, who called it a "Key to the Kingdom of Clarity."

8. Thomas R. Nilsen, "Some Assumptions that Impede Communication," *General Semantics Bulletin,* **XIV** (Winter–Spring 1954): 40–44.

9. Source unknown. A student shared this with me (Gary) about six years ago. I've been unable to locate the original source.

10. From *One Flew Over the Cuckoo's Nest* by Ken Kesey. Copyright © 1962 by Ken Kesey. Reprinted by permission of The Viking Press, Inc.

11. Sarvepalli Radhakrishnan, *An Idealist View of Life,* 2nd ed., George Allen & Unwin, 1941. Reprinted by permission.

12. Ray Ehrensberger, "The Relative Effectiveness of Certain Forms of Emphasis in Public Speaking," *Speech Monographs,* **XII** (1945): 94–111.

13. This exercise is a modification of one suggested by Gail E. Myers and Michele Tolela Myers in *The Dynamics of Human Communication: A Laboratory Approach,* New York: McGraw-Hill, 1973, p. 260.

ADDITIONAL RESOURCES

Paul Roberts writes humorously about clarity in a short, readable essay called "How To Say Nothing in Five Hundred Words." You'll find it in his book *Understanding English* (New York: Harper & Row, 1958), pp. 404–420.

Stuart Chase wrote an essay called "Gobbledygook" in which he talks about the problems of "jargon," "using big words," and "using too many words." It's in his book *The Power of Words* (New York: Harcourt Brace Jovanovich, 1954), pp. 249–259.

Sometimes, our communication is "unclear" because we assume that the other person knows more than he or she really does. Edgar Dale talks about this in his essay "Clear Only if Known." That essay is reprinted in Joseph DeVito's *Communication: Concepts and Processes* (Englewood Cliffs, N.J.: Prentice-Hall, 1971), pp. 190–194.

You may want to look at a few original research articles that deal directly or indirectly with clarity. Here are three to start with: Albert Mehrabian and S. R. Ferris, "Inference of Attitudes from Nonverbal Communication in Two Channels," *Journal of Consulting Psychology*, **XXXI** (1967): 248–252; A. Mehrabian and M. Weiner, "Decoding of Inconsistent Communications," *Journal of Personality and Social Psychology*, **VI** (1967): 108–114; K.K. Neeley, "Effect of Visual Factors on Intelligibility of Speech," *Journal of Acoustical Society of America*, **XXVIII** (1956): 1275–1277.

8

Handling Conflict Interpersonally

When we began this chapter, we were concerned about what *seemed* to be a contradiction. On the one hand, we knew that the economist-philosopher Kenneth Boulding was accurate when he said that:

> conflict is an activity that is found almost everywhere. It is found throughout the biological world, where the conflict both of individuals and of species is an important part of the picture. It is found everywhere in the (human) world . . . and all the social sciences study it. Economics studies conflict among economic organizations—firms, unions, and so on. Political science studies conflict among states. . . . Sociology studies conflict within and between families, racial and religious conflict, and conflict within and between groups. Anthropology studies conflict of cultures. Psychology studies conflict within the person. History is largely the record of conflict. . . .[1]

Our experiences at home and at school reinforce what Boulding says about conflict occurring almost everywhere.

On the other hand, while writing this book we've personally experienced almost two years of a close working relationship that has included disagreements and misunderstandings, but that has been completely free of "fights." As we started this chapter, we reviewed the past 20 months of our relationship and discovered that at various times we've disagreed about what to say in this book and how to say it, and several times we've experienced conflict and misunderstandings about content, about who agreed to do what, when he'd finish it, and so on. Yet we have not "had a fight" with each other—not even an encounter either of us would classify as an "argument." We've also experienced that kind of relationship with other persons. That doesn't mean we haven't argued with anyone; we've been in disputes with spouses, students, and friends.

But we've concluded that although it's certainly unrealistic to expect to avoid interpersonal conflict completely, it is *not* unrealistic to believe that you can create and sustain relationships in which conflict is almost always dealt with in positive and productive ways. In other words, conflict is, as Boulding says, all around us, but it doesn't have to inhibit the development of interpersonal-quality communication. You can learn to handle or manage conflict in human-to-human, person-to-person ways.

We think that you can learn to do that best by first recognizing what human conflict is and generally why it arises, by then identifying some of the things that often keep people from handling conflict productively, and finally by developing some communication skills that can help you deal interpersonally with the disagreements you experience.

WHAT IT IS AND WHERE IT COMES FROM _(human conflict)_

We've said several times already that each human is unique. Genetically, each of us is one-of-a-kind, and each person experiences the world in a unique way. Although we share many things in common—general physical make-up, biological and psychological needs, etc.,—each person is significantly different from every other person.

Simply stated, conflict can occur whenever these human differences meet. In other words, conflict can be seen as synonymous with disagreement; whenever a manifestation of one person's or group's uniqueness encounters a manifestation of another person's or group's uniqueness, conflict can happen. The disagreement might be over such manifestations of uniqueness as different needs, attitudes, beliefs, desires, conclusions, or points of view. It might be anywhere from crucially important to almost irrelevant to the persons involved. But whatever the form they take: (1) conflicts or disagreements happen all the time, and (2) there is nothing inherently destructive, and there doesn't have to be anything inherently threatening, about them. _The important thing is how disagreements are handled._

In short, humans are both unique and are choosers; our uniqueness means that disagreements will inevitably happen, and our ability to choose means that we _can decide_ to handle our disagreements interpersonally. When you experience a conflict, you can choose to respond to it in a number of possible ways—by ignoring it, actively denying its existence, running away, attacking the other person, giving in, agreeing to meet the other half way, postponing the confrontation, or working through the problem until you either resolve your differences or mutually "agree to disagree." The quality of your communication will depend on the choices you make, i.e., on the ways you handle or deal with the conflict you experience.

From the point of view of interpersonal communication, there are three kinds of conflict: disagreements about content development, disagreements about definitions of selves, and disagreements about basic values or philosophies. In practice, these three categories overlap, and one sometimes looks like another. But we think it can be useful to distinguish among them.

Content Conflict

Disagreements about content development are often expressed in such statements as "That conclusion doesn't follow from those statistics" or "Just because that happened when they changed the law in Sweden doesn't mean it's going to happen when they change the law here" or "The problem's not going to be solved that way." This kind of disagreement reflects different interpretations of objects, events, or phenomena separate from the persons involved. One kind arises from a conflict about the *accuracy* of perceptions or statements—"Was the car really going 50 miles an hour in the school zone or was it closer to 30 m.p.h.?" "Were there actually three thousand students at the rally?" Another kind grows out of differences in *definitions*—"I see what you mean, but I think that's an advantage rather than a disadvantage"; "I didn't lie to you; I just omitted some things"; or "That's not cheating, that's just carelessness." Content-development disagreement can also focus on *reasoning* processes—"I don't think that conclusion follows from your evidence"; "There's no cause-effect relationship between education and income"; "You can't compare her job to mine; the analogy is invalid"; and so on. Content disagreement doesn't focus directly on the persons involved, but rather on information or reasoning about objects or events separate from them.

Definition-of-Selves Conflict

This kind of disagreement is frequently the most damaging and difficult to resolve. It often comes out as some form of the question: "Who the hell do you think you are?" which says indirectly, "I disagree with the way you are defining yourself." Sometimes, the conflict will focus on whether a person is informed or uninformed. "You don't know what you're talking about" is a common way of saying "I disagree with your definition of yourself as 'competent,' 'informed,' or 'an expert.' " It can also work the other way around. Sometimes, positively motivated comments from a parent or a teacher can reflect a disagreement over definitions of selves, e.g., when a child complains, "I can't do this; I don't know how," and the teacher responds in an exasperated tone, "What do you mean, you don't know how? You've been doing that kind of problem for six weeks now!" In that case the child is defining himself or herself as uninformed or in need of help and the teacher is disagreeing, implying that the child *is* capable and informed and may be lazy or obstinate.

Disagreements about self-definitions can also center on who has what kind of authority in a given situation. Not long ago, almost all college and university administrations believed that they had the authority to operate *in loco parentis*—in the place of parents—and to regulate the personal lives of their students. Many students disagreed— violently, on some campuses—with that definition of self. Coeducational dorms, open visiting hours, and other relaxed living regulations are some outcomes of that disagreement. On a job, you might agree that your supervisor has the authority to determine your working hours, but you might disagree with his or her definition of self as custodian of your hairstyle, unless it interferes directly with your work. Conflict can also arise when one person defines the other as having more authority than the other wants or thinks he or she has. The accountability that usually accompanies decision-making authority often encourages people to insist: "I'm just a peasant here, don't ask me!" or "You always tell the kids to ask me. You decide for once."

Conflicts in power relationships can also be understood as differences in definitions of selves. Power is usually defined as the ability of one person to provide something another person wants and can't readily get anywhere else.[2] In other words, if Jack wants something, and can get what he wants only with Jill's help, Jill has power over Jack. Conflict over a power relationship can arise, for example, when Jill disagrees with Jack's definition of her as capable of helping him get what he needs—"I can't get that for you; I don't have the power you think I do"—or when Jill defines herself as more capable of meeting Jack's needs than Jack thinks—"I have more control over your destiny than you're ready to admit." Especially when the stakes are high, disagreements over power relationships can be very difficult to handle.

Conflict about definitions of selves can also focus on questions of duty or obligation. War-crime trials often center on the question of whether a soldier has the duty to follow orders or whether he or she is free to question an immoral command. Honor codes define students as having the obligation to be honest and to report any dishonesty they observe. Obligation also goes with other role definitions. Most parents believe that they have the duty to protect their children from danger. Conflicts often arise when a child sees that duty interfering with his or her right to decide what experiences are meaningful or which situations to avoid. "I can't let you do that" or "I can't go along with that" often means something like "I see myself as duty-bound to prevent that." And sometimes the other person disagrees.

Finally, people sometimes disagree about definitions of *present* selves. Occasionally, one person believes that he or she knows what another is thinking or feeling better than the other person does. Examples of this kind of disagreement might sound something like the following:

> "Let's quit for now; I'm tired."
> "You can't be tired, we just started. You're just afraid to go on."

> "I don't care who she goes with."
> "Baloney. You're ticked off because she won't go with you."

> "It really makes me mad to see people get away with things like that."
> "You're just jealous because you got caught and she didn't."

> "Don't get so defensive."
> "Who's getting defensive?! I'm not defensive! I'm never defensive! You're the one who's defensive! Not me!"

Each disagreement over definitions of selves has the potential of preventing interpersonal communication. But, as we'll suggest later, this kind of conflict can often be resolved.

Conflicts over Basic Values

Some disagreements between persons just can't be *resolved*. But that doesn't mean that they can't be handled in person-to-person ways. It's unrealistic to expect a strong Christian and a strong atheist to work through all their religious differences and to agree on everything. But it's not unreasonable to expect them to handle their conflict positively and productively.

We want to emphasize that relatively few interpersonal conflicts are of this kind. Most of the time we disagree with others about content development or about definitions of selves. But sometimes we encounter persons whose belief structure, value system, or basic philosophy is so different from ours that the best possible relationship we can have with them is peaceful coexistence.

We know that human perception is subjective and that human knowledge is fallible, so we believe that it's important to continually challenge, question, and validate the values and beliefs you hold. In addition, as we've already said, we believe that it's important to work hard to understand the other person and to keep your evaluations of him or her as tentative as possible. But given those qualifications, we don't think that it's necessary to be willing to compromise away your basic values or beliefs. We're strongly committed, for example, to our beliefs that we are becoming human interpersonally and that it's better to treat persons as humans instead of as objects. When we encounter a person who has arrived at different basic beliefs, we work toward meeting that person as a person while "agreeing to disagree" about our different points of view. More about that later.

In Summary
(so far)

Conflict can occur whenever human differences meet.
   Disagreements are unavoidable.
   But most of them can be handled interpersonally.

Content conflict can include
   disagreements about the accuracy of perceptions or statements
   differences in definitions of terms
   disagreements about reasoning processes.

Definition-of-selves conflict can focus on
   historical selves
      whether a person is informed or uninformed, competent or incompetent
      who has what kind of authority
      who is more powerful
      who has what duties or obligations;

present selves
     how a person sees himself or herself at the present moment.

Conflict over strongly held basic values
     is often irresolvable, but
     is relatively infrequent, and
     can be handled interpersonally.

THE PROBLEM

As we've said, the existence of conflict is not the problem. Conflict over content, disagreements about definitions of selves, and even opposing basic beliefs would present no difficulties if they were handled interpersonally. But they're usually not. The problem is that most conflicts of all three kinds are handled in objectifying rather than in humanifying ways. The chart on the next page shows the conditions under which conflict arises.

Somebody says something like . . .	and even though we realize . . .	we often say something like . . .	instead of something like . . .
"I don't want to go if *they're* gonna be there. I can't stand to be around them!"	**Each human is unique**	"You're just like the idiots I knew in high school—you never want to do anything with anybody but the people in your own juvenile little clique!"	"It sounds like you're really down on them. What happened?"
"I still think it's better to wait until next week to talk to her—I've got the feeling that things will work out better then."	**A person is made up of more than just his or her measurable parts**	"Oh, come on—you're just stalling. We can't put this off just because of your weird 'feeling'!"	"What kind of feeling? I admit I'm anxious to get this finished, but I haven't noticed anything that makes me feel like we should put it off. What are you seeing?"
"I'm going out for awhile with Bob."	**Humans act, not just react**	"No you're not! He'll have you out until 2 in the morning! I won't let it happen!"	"I don't trust Bob with you. I don't like the idea because I'm afraid you'll go along with whatever he says."
"I don't know why I did so badly this quarter—it just didn't seem like there was any big reason for studying."	Humans are conscious, self-reflective	"Well, dammit, stop daydreaming on my money! As long as I'm paying your way, I expect you to put out!"	"Sounds like you're questioning whether you even ought to be in school right now. Is there someone you can work that through with, or would it help for us to talk about it?"

And as a result, things get worse instead of better

There are several ways to explain *why* that happens—why we tend to handle disagreements in objectifying rather than in humanifying ways. Sometimes, we fear the intensity of feelings generated in a conflict, so we objectify the other person in order to keep him or her at a distance. So long as we're dealing with an object, we figure, we don't have to get close enough to get hurt.

On the other hand, sometimes, as David Augsburger explains, anger is more directly related to feeling personally threatened.

> When I feel that another person is about to engulf or incorporate me (assuming ownership of me, taking me for granted, using me, absorbing me into his or her life-program), I feel angry.
>
> Actually, I first feel anxious. "Anxiety is a sign that one's self-esteem, one's self-regard is endangered," as Harry Stack Sullivan expressed it. When my freedom to be me is threatened, I become anxious, tense, ready, for some action. Escape? Anger? Or work out an agreement?
>
> Escape may be neither possible nor practical. Agreement seems far away, since I see you as ignoring my freedom, devaluing my worth, and attempting to use me. Anger is the most available option.[3]

Identifying causes of anger is important, but we would like to concentrate more on how to handle disagreements as *communicators* in order to promote more profitable responses to fear or threat. And we think that several suggestions we've made earlier in this book can help.

SOME SUGGESTIONS RELATED TO PREVIOUS CHAPTERS

Context

In Chapter 2 we talked about the contextual nature of all human communication. We think that when you're experiencing a disagreement, it can help to recognize how the context might be affecting that conflict. For example, the time and place you choose to work through a disagreement can significantly affect what happens. A social evening with friends is usually not the time or place for a husband and wife to confront each other with money-management problems or dissatisfaction with their sex life. Similarly, you probably won't accomplish much if the person you want to talk with is preoccupied with other people, a job, or a different set of serious worries. At school, I (John) find it helps to get away from my office with its "you're on my turf" implications and its telephone calls and visits. A quiet spot outside—when it's not raining—usually puts everyone in a better frame of mind. In short, when and where you choose to handle a disagreement can contribute significantly to your success or failure. Sometimes, you can't postpone or ignore a confrontation. But when you can, try to choose as comfortable and nondistracting a context as you can.

In other words, choose a context that's free enough of distractions to allow all the persons involved to concentrate on the issue. Try to pick a time and place where the other person is not likely to feel inferior or threatened. And, very importantly, recognize that handling disagreements interpersonally takes *time*; try to allow for that by raising the issue when you're fairly certain that you'll have the time to work it through.

Another point we made in Chapter 2 is also important. When you understand how human communication works, you recognize that although one person's behavior *is* influenced by other persons, it's never accurate to assume that a disagreement is *caused* by one action or by one person. When someone decides that "he started all this" or "it's all her fault," that person has *punctuated* the ongoing sequence of communication events that he or she is experiencing. As we said in Chapter 2, that means that the person has divided his or her communication experiences into isolated segments, just as periods and commas punctuate words. Then, the person tends to assume that whatever comes "first" in the series of events (as he or she punctuates it) *causes* what comes after it.

Usually when there's a disagreement, the other person punctuates the situation differently—he or she sees it as beginning sometime or somewhere else. Also, both persons tend to see their own behavior as responses caused by the other:

Husband: Sure I nag her, but what can I do? She never says anything to me. If I don't keep at her, she just sits there and pouts! (Translation: It's *her* fault; I'm just responding to her. She's the cause; I'm the effect.)

Wife: Listen. I'll tell you why I refuse to say anything. He's always nagging me! I can't open my mouth without him yelling about something. So I shut up just to protect myself! (Translation: It's *his* fault; I'm just responding to him. He's the cause; I'm the effect.)

One of our most important suggestions emerges from an understanding of how communication gets punctuated. *When you disagree, forget the blaming game.* It's almost always a waste of time to try to decide who is at "fault." Get in touch with where you are and work on it from there.

That's often a real challenge. Whenever a problem occurs, there seems to be a natural tendency to ask: "Whose fault is this?" But it's important to remember that the answer you get will almost always depend on who you ask. "Fault" is almost completely a matter of a person falsely assuming that there's a starting point in a continuous sequence of interdependent events.

Personal Perceiving

In Chapter 3 we spent some time talking about the subjectivity of perception. We made the point that not only do people differ in their punctuation of reality, but they also select, organize, and go beyond raw communication cues in subjective, sometimes idiosyncratic, ways. In a conflict, differences in perceptions of things and people can be especially troublesome. As the counselor David Johnson points out, the normal obstacles to "objective" perception are often supplemented in a conflict situation by at least three additional factors that create perception distortion. First, and related to the point about punctuation, there is the "mirror image" problem—both persons or sides tend to feel that they are being unfairly persecuted. Second, both see the other's objectifying, or even vicious, acts while remaining oblivious to identically damaging things they are doing. That is, both sides tend to apply a double standard, accepting what they do but rejecting the others' actions as "unfair." Third, both sides tend to see the conflict in a polarized way, oversimplifying issues and events into right/wrong terms.[4] Later, we'll make some suggestions about how to deal with these problems. For now, we just want to point out that disagreements often escalate when the persons involved forget that this kind of distorted perceiving is happening.

Sharing Some of Your Self

Two points we made when we talked about sharing some of your self are especially applicable to conflict situations. First, recognize that as a human chooser, you are responsible for your feelings and actions; be sure to share your recognition of that responsibility with the other persons involved. Substitute "I am angry" for "You make me angry." Replace "You're always rejecting me" with "I feel rejected." Instead of trying to make the other persons responsible—"You're building a wall between us"—share perceptions and feelings that you clearly own—"I don't like the wall between us." In addition, avoid using "it" as a scapegoat for your attitudes or behavior. When you say "I just can't help it. It makes me mad" or "It's like something comes over me, and I can't do a thing about it," you're obscuring your own responsibility for the way you are. As David Augsburger summarizes:

> "You make me angry," I used to say.
>
> Untrue. No one can make another angry. I become angry at you, I am responsible for that reaction. (I am not saying that anger is wrong. It may well be the most appropriate and loving response that I am aware of at that moment.)
>
> But you do not make me angry. I make me angry at you. It is not the only behavior open to me.
>
> There is no situation in which anger is the only possible response. If I become angry (and I may, it's acceptable) it's because I choose to respond with anger. I might have chosen kindness, irritation, humor, or many other alternatives. . . . There is no situation which commands us absolutely. . . .[5]

There's also an interesting and helpful result of taking responsibility for your feelings and sharing that responsibility with others. As a person discovers that he or she owns his or her feelings and responses, new ways of responding open up. When you become responsible, you become response-able. "A great freedom comes as I own my thoughts, feelings, words, and emotions. (1) I become free to choose my actions, (2) I become free to choose my reactions."[6]

The situation can almost always be improved if *descriptions* ("You've mentioned my shoplifting conviction twice in the last three times I've seen you this week") are substituted for: *generalizations* ("You bring up that shoplifting thing every time you see me!"), *accusations* ("Boy, you must really get off on making me squirm!"), or *inferences* ("The way you keep bringing that up, you must think I'm dirt.") We've talked about descriptions in other chapters. By way of review, when you're describing an event or someone's behavior, you focus on *what* you perceive to be happening and not on your inferences about *why* it was done. So, for example, you say something like: "We've met only five times, and you've been late to two meetings and have missed two others" instead of "You must think this group is really wasting your time" or "You obviously don't give a damn about what we're doing!"

When you're describing your feelings, it's helpful to remember the suggestions in the exercise in Chapter 5: (1) don't confuse specific expressions of feeling with the indirect display of feelings by commands, questions, accusations, or judgments; (2) remember, you can't describe anybody's feelings but your own (avoid "we feel," "he feels," etc.); (3) distinguish between value judgments that masquerade as feelings—"I feel you're great" or "I'm inadequate"—and genuine descriptions of feeling—"I feel excited" or "I feel inadequate"; and (4) name the feeling you're describing as specifically as you can. In short, whenever you substitute specific descriptions of events, behavior, or feelings, for generalizations, accusations, inferences, or other kinds of evaluations, you'll contribute significantly to the process of handling a disagreement interpersonally.

In addition, when you take responsibility for your feelings, words, and behavior, other people stop feeling responsible—and guilty—for them, and the resulting reduction in pressure can often be enough by itself to defuse a disagreement. Even if it isn't sufficient, however, it can be a first step toward creating the *trust* that's essential to handling disagreements interpersonally.

That's another point from Chapter 5 we want to re-emphasize. Sharing creates trust, and trust encourages sharing. So if your communication in a conflict situation is ever going to become person to person, you'll have to share enough of your historical and present selves to enable the other(s) to trust you and the situation enough to reciprocate. That kind of sharing is often risky; it means making yourself more or less vulnerable to the other. But there are two ways you can legitimately justify taking that risk: (1) recognize that it's worth it because you have so much to gain; and (2) realize that to be trusted, you must trust. To receive trust from others, you risk trusting them by opening yourself, to some degree, to them. Risk and trust go together.

Being Aware of the Other

Almost all of what we said in Chapter 6 (responsive listening) is also applicable to handling disagreements. Unfortunately, it's usually *very* difficult to apply. It often seems as though there's nothing harder than

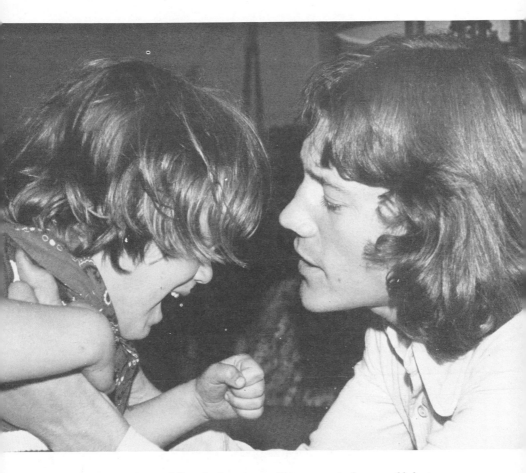

having to stop in the middle of a bitter conflict to remind yourself that this should be a win/win, not a win/lose, situation and that you should strive to listen to the other in confirming, accepting ways and to keep your evaluations tentative and limited to behavior or attitudes. Sometimes, all that seems just plain impossible, and unless the other person is also at least partly willing and able to do those things, you might not be able to work things out interpersonally.

When I (John) am confronted with the kind of situation in which I feel it's important to win at all costs and in which genuinely focusing on the other person seems like the *last* thing I want to do, the only way I seem to be able to think-feel myself into a win/win orientation is by reviewing the philosophy this whole book is based on. I don't do it in detail, out loud, or even consciously sometimes. But it helps me to think through, at least briefly, a rationale something like that given in the following sentences:

> I really am becoming human interpersonally. That isn't just theory, that's the way things actually are. Who I am as a person depends greatly on the quality of my communicating with others.
>
> If I objectify the other person in this situation, I'm gonna get objectified in return. And that won't help me grow. I won't wither up and blow away because of one dehumanizing fight, but it *will*—it *does*—make a difference.
>
> In other words, I've got something at stake here. It's important to me that we handle this interpersonally.
>
> I also believe that it's *possible* to handle it that way. His or her abusiveness, anger, bitterness, sarcasm, or even hate is there for what looks to him or her like a damn good reason. If I'd experienced what he or she's experienced, I might well respond that way, too.
>
> But if I can avoid just reacting in kind, if I can promote a climate of acceptance and trust—without necessarily compromising my own position—it'll be easier for him or her to do the same thing.
>
> That *is* possible. It might not happen here or now, but if a person is not constrained by fear or ignorance, he or she *will* respond interpersonally.
>
> I need to do all that I can to help that happen. (I can't *make* it happen, but I *can help* it happen.)

For us, the goal of that kind of inner monologue is to reaffirm our willingness to be aware of the other's humanness. But willingness alone isn't enough. It's also important to be *able* to be aware, i.e., to practice the skills we talked about in Chapter 6. As we said there, you can confirm the person you're listening to in both nonverbal and verbal ways— by focusing on him or her, showing reactions in your face, by making sounds that indicate you're "tuned in," and by talking with the other person about his or her ideas and feelings, not just about your own. In addition, you can use perception checking—paraphrasing and para-supporting—to increase your understanding of the other person. And finally, you can be aware of the other's potential defensiveness, and you can respond in ways that diminish it. All those attitudes and behaviors can help you handle a disagreement both positively and productively.

In Summary:
(so far)

Context. Whenever you can, choose a comfortable, nondistracting context. Forget the "blaming game"; instead of focusing on whose fault it is, get in touch with where you are and work with it from there.

Personal perceiving. Remember that disagreements escalate when you forget that your perceptions are highly subjective, especially in conflict situations. Recognize that there's a tendency for each person: (1) to feel that he or she is being unfairly persecuted; (2) to apply a double standard, i.e., to see the other person's vicious acts but to ignore his or her own; and (3) to perceive issues and events in oversimplified, right/wrong terms.

Sharing. Take responsibility for your feelings and actions. Use specific descriptions of your feelings instead of generalizations, accusations, and inferences. Remember that sharing creates trust, and trust encourages sharing.

Being aware. Resolving conflict interpersonally is much easier when you listen responsively: confirm, paraphrase, parasupport, and diminish defensiveness.

SPECIFIC SUGGESTIONS NOT COVERED IN PREVIOUS CHAPTERS

In addition to the suggestions in previous chapters that apply to all communication situations, we'd like to offer some additional recommendations that relate specifically to conflict situations. The first suggestion should help in all disagreements; the next three apply most directly to conflicts about content development; and the final five suggestions are mainly for disagreements about definitions of selves.

Imagine the Real of the Other*

We believe that no single step will help you handle conflict more effectively than this one. We strongly recommend that you set as your goal in each specific disagreement to imagine at least once the real of the

---

*Most of the ideas in this section emerged in conversations with Helen Martin Felton.

person you're disagreeing with. We're taking the term "imagining the real" from Martin Buber's writing, and at this point it might sound a little vague. But we think it'll make sense if you just hang on for a few paragraphs.

To understand what we mean, start by thinking back to a specific time when you identified strongly with a character in a book you were reading, a television program or play you were watching, or a "real-life" event you were observing but not participating in. Think of a specific time when you felt that you *really* understood that character or person—you *knew* what she or he was going through. You might have identified strongly, for example, with the boy Demian in Herman Hesse's book; with one of the lovers in the play or movie *Romeo and Juliet*; with Thoreau in *Walden*; with Frodo, Aragorn, Gandalf, or Treebeard the Ent in Tolkien's *Trilogy of the Rings*; or with Billy Pilgrim in Vonnegut's *Slaughterhouse Five*. You might have identified strongly with John-boy, Elizabeth, or Olivia ("Livvy") in an episode of "The Waltons"; with Serpico or Papillon in the book or movie of the same name; or with a swimmer, sprinter, golfer, or tennis player in a crucial match. Or, you might have witnessed a family fight at a friend's house and *really known* what your friend was going through. Stop reading now until you choose a person. Recall some of the features of that particular event.

Person _____

Event_____

_____

Now focus your attention for a minute on the *way in which you were perceiving the other person* in that situation. Although you strongly identified with that person, you did not "become" him or her; no magical transformation of matter took place. You stayed *you*. In that sense, your sharing experience with the other happened "in your imagination." And yet the *kind* of imagining you did wasn't the same as daydreaming about what it would be like to be a successful politician or to fall in love with the person of your dreams or to play in the World Series. One difference is that when you identified with the other person, your act of imagining was limited by the realness of the other. If it wasn't—if you gave the character superpowers, perfection, or purity—

you were imagining, not imagining the *real*. When you imagine the real—whether the character you identify with is in a book, on stage, on a screen, or in person—her or his realness puts bounds on what you imagine. For example, I (John) remember seeing Frodo the Hobbit this way. I really identified with his combination of adventurousness and fear. But I also remember feeling how *his* fear would be anchored partly in his size—he was just over four feet tall—and in the myths he'd been taught, both of which made his fear different from what mine would be.

Note also another feature of that experience. At the moment when you were most in touch with what the other person was going through, you were vividly aware that it was the *other person*—not you—who was going through the experience. For a moment you were in touch with the other's present self. You were recognizing that the other was a unique person, separate and different from you, and the feelings you were experiencing with him or her were not just your feelings projected onto the other person. The experience wasn't like looking into a mirror, where everything appears in relation to *your* point of view. The other person's "position," or "point of view," the reality of the unique other, affected what you were feeling. At that moment of imagining the real, you moved beyond being aware of just yourself to being genuinely aware of the other, beyond letting the other exist only in your own experience to participating with the other in his or her *own* unique world. The difference, as Maurice Friedman puts it, is the difference between "that awareness which turns one in on oneself and that which enables one to turn to the other."[7]

A third, related feature of that experience was the element of surprise. The best way to tell whether you're looking at the other person from his or her point of view or just from your own is to notice whether you're ever surprised by what you "see" or experience. If you're not, you're probably not yet in touch with the *other's* uniquely present self. If your experience is something like: "Yeah . . . I know that feeling. . . ." or "Uh-huh . . . I've felt just like that before . . .," you haven't yet gone beyond reflection. When you imagine the real of the other, you experience part of her or his present *otherness*, and since it is different from your own reality, it's new to you—it's at least somewhat surprising. When you get to the point of "Oh, wow! Yes, *now* I see!" or "Ouch! Migod, I've never felt just like *that* before! Now I really see what she's feeling!" you're imagining the real. The presence of genuine surprise is often the key.

Buber gives several examples of imagining the real. For instance, he says, think of the situation in which one person is criticizing and reprimanding another—is really bawling that person out. The other is remaining quiet. Imagining the real happens when the person doing the criticizing "suddenly receives in his soul the blow which he strikes,"[8] i.e., when the critic experiences receiving one of his or her own blows just as it's received by the one who remains still. As Buber explains, for the space of a moment the person experiences the situation from the other side. Reality imposes itself on him or her. When this happens, the critic will have to do one of two things—either ignore or overwhelm the "voice of the soul" which tells him or her to stop inflicting pain, or reverse the impulse to hurt and to criticize the other.

Or consider another situation:

> A man caresses a woman, who lets herself be caressed. Then let us assume that he feels the contact from two sides—with the palm of his hand still and also with the woman's skin. The twofold nature of the gesture, as one that takes place between two persons, thrills through the depth of enjoyment of his heart and stirs it. . . . The one extreme experience makes the other person present to him for all time.[9]

As Buber summarizes, "Imagining the real means that I imagine to myself what another [person] is at this very moment wishing, feeling, perceiving, thinking, and not a detached content but in his [or her] very reality, that is, as a living process in this [person]."[10] When I'm able to do that, as Buber continues, something like the following happens:

> I become aware of the other person, aware that he or she is differ-ent, essentially different from myself, in the definite, unique way which is peculiar to him or her. I also accept the person I'm aware of, so that I can directly and with full earnestness say to that person whatever I have to say. Perhaps sometimes I have to offer strict opposition to her or his view about the subject matter of our conversation. But I accept this individual as the personal bearer of an opinion, the personal holder of a point of view, and I accept his or her person as the definite being out of which the opinion or point of view has grown, even though I must try to show, bit by bit, the wrongness of this very opinion. I affirm the person I struggle with. I struggle with the person as his or her partner; in other words, I

confirm as a person the one who is opposed to me. At this point it's up to the other person to determine whether mutuality will happen and we will meet in genuine dialogue. I can do no more than all I can do. But if I can give to the person who confronts me his or her legitimate standing as a person with whom I am ready to communicate interpersonally, then I may trust that person and I may legitimately expect him or her also to be ready to deal with me as a partner.[11]

We're convinced that no other specific recommendation will help you to handle disagreement interpersonally as effectively as imagining the real. If opposing parties can imagine the real of the other, for even a moment, they will not necessarily give up their own positions, but they will be much more able to deal interpersonally with the conflict that separates them.

Deal Directly with Content Disagreements

While you're working toward imagining the real of the person(s) you're in conflict with, it's also important to use some common sense about handling the content, or subject matter, of your disagreement. Three suggestions that should help are: (1) limit your disagreement to one issue at a time, (2) remember to be tentative in your evaluation of ideas, and (3) be prepared to offer and explain alternative actions or ideas.

One thing you can do is limit your disagreement as much as possible to a single issue. Partly because most of us fear conflict so much, when it does occur we tend to seize the opportunity to bring up all the bruises we've been nursing for days, weeks, or even years. George Bach and Peter Wyden call that "gunnysacking," and they accurately emphasize its danger.* As they explain, a violent fight between a wife and husband often occurs because the "aggression reservoir" of the couple

> was simply so full that even a slight jar caused it to spill over. Both partners had been keeping their grievances bottled up, and this is invariably a poor idea. We call this "gunnysacking" because when

---

*In transactional analysis (*I'm OK—You're OK, Born to Win,* etc.) it's called "stamp collecting."

marital complaints are toted along quietly in a gunny sack for any length of time they make a dreadful mess when the sack finally bursts.[12]

It's much healthier, as Bach and Wyden point out, to try to deal as much as you can with controversial issues one at a time as they come up. That way, a disagreement triggered by one event doesn't become the occasion to air every doubt and hurt you've carried for weeks.

It's also important to make the specific issue of the disagreement as mutually understood as possible. Be sure that you and the other(s) involved agree about the focus of your disagreement. Apply the principles in Chapter 7 to clarify your point of conflict, and you might discover, as we sometimes do, that when you reach agreement about your "fight topic," there's often nothing left to argue about.

Bach and Wyden also suggest—pretty sensibly, we think—that you restrict arguments to topics that actually mean something to you. Sometimes, it seems as though we're ready to make a mountain out of just about every molehill we encounter. Since conflict takes energy and is sometimes interpersonally risky, it makes more sense to ask yourself before any confrontation whether you really care about the issue involved. In short, limit disagreements to one issue at a time and to a nontrivial issue, i.e., one that means something to you.

A second suggestion is that you work to remain as tentative as you can in your evaluations of the ideas you're discussing. We've talked about tentativeness before. But a tentative mental set is even more important—and more difficult—when you're in the middle of a disagreement than it is in nonconflict situations. It's not easy to reduce your own perceived need to fight-in-order-to-survive enough to entertain the possibility that your ideas may not be 100 percent right and the other person's 100 percent wrong.

It sometimes helps me (John) to do just that when I remind myself of three things. (1) In an encounter with another person, I don't have to win *over* him or her in order to win. In other words, we can both come out on top, and the best communicating happens when we do. My feeling good about myself does not depend on my ideas always being better than the other person's. I can be wrong and/or correct and still "win" in the relationship. (2) Since my perceptions are just that—mine and perceptions, not "realities"—I want to remember that I might be objecting to something I've created myself. I want to be careful about making assertions or arguments until I'm sure I understand the other person's point clearly. I've experienced too often the uncomfortable embarrassment that comes when one person discovers that the idea she or he is wildly attacking is far different from the one held by his or her "opponent." (3) Not only do I try to realize that my perceptions are subjective, I also try to remember that context—including the persons involved—is continually changing. I want to use active listening and perception checking to stay in touch with those changes so that I don't end up flailing away at a windmill or storming a fortress that my "opponent" long ago vacated. In brief, if you can remember that the ideas involved in a disagreement are human products, generated by subjective, continually changing humans in subjective, continually changing contexts, it's much easier to remain tentative about the ideas and to respond interpersonally in the conflict.

Our third suggestion for dealing with disagreements over content development is that you be ready to not only criticize a position or idea, but also offer and explain an alternative point of view. Occasionally, your main goal might be to simply dissuade the other from taking some action, but usually a disagreement involves not just stopping one kind of action or plan, but also starting a different one. Most of the time, consequently, both—or all—persons involved share the responsibility for developing solutions. It's important that each participant remember that. Disagreements often dead-end in such statements as: "Well, you just have to grow up!"; "Stop being so radical!"; "Be nicer to me!" or "Stop wasting so much time!" Those orders are dead-ends not only because their tone tends to create defensiveness, but also because it's next to impossible to comply with them. Do you mean by "growing up" that you think it would help for the other person to try to be on time more often, or to take more responsibility for his or her comments about others, or to stop putting off term papers until the last minute, or what? Try to remember to be ready with suggested alternatives. Even more important, be willing and able to work mutually to reach a choice or compromise.

Work to Handle Disagreements over Definitions of Selves

You can probably remember a number of disagreements you had with your parents when you were between 11 and 15, disagreements that centered on who was the expert. When I (Gary) was 11 or 12, I wanted to learn all I could about football, but I wasn't at all sure that my dad was competent to teach me, even though he'd played as a semipro. Like most of us at that age, I "knew" that parents know almost nothing about anything important. So when my dad showed me how to block and tackle—legally and illegally, as I remember—I paid attention, but not very closely. Sometimes, we'd end up disagreeing, primarily because I defined myself as knowledgeable and my dad as uninformed, and he defined himself and me in just the opposite way.

As we've suggested before, human communication would be relatively simple if it weren't so incredibly human, that is, if the persons' images of themselves didn't play such a significant role in what happens. But they do. So when disagreements over self-definitions occur, we think it can be helpful to remember four suggestions for handling them effectively: (1) get in touch with how you usually define yourself when you're in a conflict; (2) try to identify the triggering events that set off each conflict; (3) include relationship reminders in your disagreement; and (4) develop interpersonal approaches to a deadlock or an apparently insoluble conflict.

Typical responses.   To get in touch with how you respond to a conflict situation, try the following activity.

Individual Application: How You Define Yourself in Conflict Situations

How do you react when you disagree with persons older than you? With superiors? With your spouse or parents? Although generalizations don't accurately represent you as a unique, changing person, you might want to respond to the following questions about your "typical" self-definitions in conflict situations.

1. When I disagree with a friend who is my age, I usually see myself as

    _____more competent than the other
    _____less competent than the other
    _____about as competent as the other

    I tend to respond by

    _____strongly asserting myself
    _____tentatively asserting myself
    _____searching for a compromise

_____tentatively giving in
_____giving in

2. When I disagree with a spouse, lover, or intimate friend, I usually see myself as

_____more competent than the other
_____less competent than the other
_____about as competent as the other

I tend to respond by

_____strongly asserting myself
_____tentatively asserting myself
_____searching for a compromise
_____tentatively giving in
_____giving in

3. When I disagree with my parent or an adviser, I usually see myself as
_____more competent than the other
_____less competent than the other
_____about as competent as the other

I tend to respond by

_____strongly asserting myself
_____tentatively asserting myself
_____searching for a compromise
_____tentatively giving in
_____giving in

4. When I disagree with my job supervisor, I usually see myself as

_____more competent than the other
_____less competent than the other
_____about as competent as the other

I tend to respond by

_____strongly asserting myself
_____tentatively asserting myself
_____searching for a compromise
_____tentatively giving in
_____giving in

You might be able to use this information in a couple of ways. First, it can help you understand the way others behave when disagreeing with you. If you habitually define yourself as more competent, for example, the other person is probably going to notice, and he or she might well respond with fear, stronger antagonism, or capitulation (depending on her or his own definition of self) instead of constructive communication. Your responses to those questions might also help you understand why you dread conflict with your spouse or lover ("I habitually feel inferior and tend to respond by giving in") while welcoming a disagreement with a friend your own age ("I usually feel equally competent and tend to assert myself").

In addition, this kind of analysis can give you information about your self that can allow you, at least in your long-term, intimate relationships, to set "belt lines" below which you and your partner agree not to strike. As Bach and Wyden explain, "Everyone has such a belt line—a point above which blows can be absorbed, thereby making them tolerable and fair; and below which blows are intolerable and therefore unfair.[13] In Bach and Wyden's terms, "the belt line protects the Achilles' heel, and this is no mixed metaphor."[14] In other words, each person has spots of intense vulnerability—Achilles' heels—where a blow can seriously damage his or her definition of self.

One person who reviewed this chapter shared some examples of his own especially touchy topics. "Most of my below-the-belt areas," he wrote, "involve personal characteristics or behaviors over which I have little control: the size of my ears, the fact that I blush, that I tend to get tongue-tied when highly excited. When my 'opponent' points to these things during an argument, I am really wiped out. I see this sort of thing happening often in arguments between people. . . ."

Intimates, Bach and Wyden suggest, should disclose these areas, their Achilles' heels, to each other and should mutually agree on belt-lines so that their arguments will not become person-destroying. They suggest that intimates learn to shout "foul!" whenever a partner hits below the belt. Although that specific technique might not work for you, we think it can help generally to get in touch with how you see yourself in several different conflict situations, so that you can deal with those situations more effectively.

Triggers.   A second recommendation is that in each disagreement, you identify the specific events that triggered, or set off, the conflict. By "triggers" we don't mean "causes." As we said before, trying to decide what or who "started" an argument is almost always either destructive or at least a waste of time. Triggers are precipitating events, the actions or words that mark the *point in time* when a given discussion began, and often they are minor compared to the real problems that need discussing. The problem is that we often forget that they're "the last straw," and we focus on them as if they were "the first straw."* For example, Gene Ann's discovery of a mismatched seam in some wallpaper I (John) was hanging triggered a disagreement between us. But it wasn't really a conflict over the seam. By identifying and talking about the triggering event, we were able, in part, to pinpoint some of the reasons why the disagreement continued—my fatigue, her frustration at not having the time to help with the wallpapering, etc. And that helped us deal with the conflict.

You might have experienced an argument that was triggered when your parents refused to loan you the money for additional stereo equipment, or your son or daughter was out two hours later than he or she promised, or your roommate left her or his part of the room cluttered and dirty again, or your friend forgot to pick you up for the game. It's often helpful to use the triggering event to help you identify the definitions of selves that are involved in the disagreement. That process, in turn, can often help you put the conflict in perspective and can defuse all the participants.

For example, although a son or daughter's coming home two hours late seems like a legitimate cause for disagreement over priorities, the nature of the conflict itself can change if the parent can recognize that part of what's happening is that he or she is defining his or her historical self as (1) responsible for the son or daughter's safety ("I must protect you."), (2) being watched by other adults ("People will think I'm a poor parent."), or (3) enforce of agreed-on family regulations ("There have to be some rules around the house.") In addition, the parent may be defining his or her present self as (1) frightened ("Kids are getting kidnapped every day"; "I was afraid you had a car accident") or (2) rejected ("I see myself as an authority and I feel you're rejecting that."). The son or daughter might also come to understand what's happening more clearly by examining what the triggering event reveals about his or her definition of historical and present selves.

In a similar way, pinpointing the trigger and identifying the definitions of selves suggested by that event can help other combatants

---

*Those terms were suggested by Joe Munshaw of Southern Illinois University, Edwardsville, who helped us a great deal with this chapter.

understand the situation. Do you lash out at your forgetful friend because you feel that he/she has defined you as not-worth-remembering, or because you are defining your friend as incompetent and yourself as competent? Does the trigger of the cluttered room reveal that your disagreement is over the conflict between (1) your roommate's definition of self as easy-going, casual, and concerned about "important" things and definition of you as parental and nit-picking, and (2) your definition of self as organized and tidy and middle class and your roommate as disorganized, thoughtless, and lower class? What definitions of selves are working when there's a disagreement over a parent's unwillingness to loan money to his or her college-age child?

In other cases, the triggering events might be more difficult to spot. You might have so much trouble identifying why you're arguing that you reconsider the need for any conflict at all. Or, you might find that the trigger is so insignificant that it's not worth the energy that the conflict requires.

The point is, you can often focus a disagreement on something specific *and* begin to understand some of the humanness of the persons involved by pinpointing the triggering event and identifying the definitions of selves manifested by your mutual reactions to that event.

Relationship reminders.   Our third suggestion is that in your disagreeing, you remember to include reminders to the other persons of your positive feelings toward them. It's not likely that you feel 100 percent negatively toward a person even when you're arguing with him or her. In a specific conflict, it may seem that way—you may tend to take a microscopic view of your feelings about the other person and see him or her only in terms of the immediate disagreement. Instead of looking only at the other's "disagreeable-ness," however, try to take a broader perspective of your feelings toward that person. Martin Buber often mentions the necessity to, as he puts it, "confirm the one with whom I struggle." As he explains, that means recognizing the other as a whole person, as well meaning, legitimately concerned about his or her point of view, a being who deserves your respect as a person. Even as you confirm the other, Buber points out, you may well disagree with him or her. But if you're confirming, your disagreement does not come out in efforts to force your ideas on that person or to hide the fact that you are trying to "change his or her mind." When you confirm the one with whom you struggle, you make the effort to "find and to further in the soul of the other the disposition toward" something you have recognized in yourself as the right.[15] Or, to describe it from another point of view, you try to plant in the other person's mind the seed of your belief and to let it grow there "in the form suited to individuation," i.e., in a way that fits the other person's uniqueness.[16] You treat the other, in short, as a whole person, not as an object.

As we said in Chapter 6, that kind of confirmation can be communicated by verbal and nonverbal cues that say: "I'm listening," "I recognize your right to your position," and "Although we disagree, I care about you as a person." In some cases it might be best to simply *say* one of those things or something like: "Look, the reason I'm disagreeing with what you're doing is because I'm afraid of what's going to happen to you." In other cases you can indicate your positive feelings nonverbally by your eye contact, smiles, and by touching the other person in nonthreatening ways.

But it's crucially important that relationship reminders be genuine; they can't be a device or gimmick. Most persons are sensitive to this kind of phoniness, can readily spot it, and get angry when it happens. It's easy to see why—phony confirmation is manipulative, and nobody likes to be a puppet on somebody else's strings. So don't try to fake relationship reminders. If you honestly cannot see worth in the other person, it'd probably be best to postpone your discussion until you can.

Results of a study done by the counselor David Johnson indicate that people respond positively when a person they're disagreeing with combines genuine expressions of confirmation and warmth with expressions of anger. Johnson trained persons to express anger and warmth and then asked them to communicate with another person in a negotiating context. Some of the experimenters (trained persons) communicated "all anger"; some communicated "all warmth"; some communicated "anger followed by warmth"; and some communicated "warmth followed by anger." The study generated the following conclusion: (1) The people participating *liked* both the experimenters communicating "all warmth" and the experimenters communicating "anger followed by warmth"; (2) The expression of anger followed by warmth seemed to lead to the *most agreements* on the negotiated topics.[17]

The point both Buber and Johnson make is that genuine positive verbal and nonverbal comments are important in a conflict situation. Confirming the other, indicating your acceptance of him or her as a person, despite your disagreement, can help both of you handle the conflict interpersonally.

Role reversal.   Sometimes, the most effective way for disagreeing individuals to begin treating each other as persons is to try acting out each one's imagining the real of the other by agreeing for a few minutes to take the other's place in the conflict. When you are forced to act out the other person's responses, even though it's "only pretending," you can often get an unusually clear picture of how the other is seeing herself or himself and how she or he is seeing you. Sometimes, there's almost no better way to clarify disagreements in definitions of selves and to begin to work through them.

David Johnson has also studied how role reversal works in a conflict situation. In one study Johnson found that except when two persons' positions are mutually exclusive, role reversal significantly helped the disagreeing persons to understand each other.[18] The results of a later study validated the belief that the accuracy of understanding created by mutual role reversal significantly helps people reach agreement.[19] In other words, role reversal helps antagonists understand each other's position, and when they do, they often tend to reach agreement.

When conflict seems irresolvable.   Finally, we feel the need to say a couple of things about disagreements that "just can't be solved." First, it's often helpful to remember that many conflicts—maybe even most—*look* irresolvable at some point. Especially when definitions of selves are really on the line—and they often are—people may take exaggerated, "hard and fast" positions that they're actually willing and able to move away from. Try to remember to give them the freedom to change— that's part of treating them as a human. Remember, too, that you have the freedom to change. Try *not* to let conflict "scare" you into thinking that people aren't willing to change or that nothing can be done about it.

Instead, try as systematically as you can to apply the suggestions we've offered here that fit the situation. Distinguish content disagreement from conflict over definitions of selves. Recognize and deal with the impact of context, and be aware of different punctuations of the situation. Try to use descriptions in place of evaluations; share some of your self; be aware of the person of the other; especially try "really imagining" his or her thoughts and feelings. Keep the conflict on a specific issue, and be sure to offer positive suggestions for a solution. Get in

PHOTO COURTESY OF UNIVERSITY OF WASHINGTON *DAILY*.

touch with the ways you're defining your self in the situation and with the triggering events that seem to have set off this particular disagreement. And remember to use relationship reminders. When you actually try applying all these suggestions, many apparently insoluble conflicts can get solved.

If all that doesn't help, try a quiet time. Call a moratorium on the disagreement and do something else for awhile—an hour, a day, maybe even several days or a week. Give all the persons involved time to think and feel things through. Don't wait so long that the issue gets ignored or half forgotten—that can create a festering wound that will get harder and harder to heal. But when the situation seems to require it, build into your disagreeing some breathing space, some time to put things into perspective.

If there is still no resolution of the conflict, remember what we mentioned earlier; sometimes, the best you can do is to recognize clearly the point at which you disagree and to do that in a way that's mutually humanifying. Sometimes, the most you can do is interpersonally agree to disagree.

If you reach that point, we don't believe it's necessarily accurate to say that you've "failed." Some differences between unique persons are irreconcilable. But the aspect that is never irreconcilable, the element that is always shared in common, is humanness. And the living possibility always exists for two combatants to meet on that ground.

When Buber talks about the clash of irreconcilable ideas, he distinguishes between the "persons" and the "points of view." A student once asked him whether true interpersonal communication could ever occur between persons whose basic world-views differed. Isn't it true, his questioner asked, that as soon as their radical disagreement becomes clear to each of them, they would have to break off the relationships and to stop talking to each other? Buber said that he didn't think so. "Neither needs to give up his point of view," Buber wrote. But what can happen is that if each person can meet the other as a person, *"they enter a realm where the law of the point of view no longer holds."*[20] Even though each is committed to his or her position, both can "let themselves run free of it for an immortal moment"[21] and in the process can meet the other as a person; the commonness of their humanity overshadows the antagonism of their differing points of view. Their disagreement may remain, but so may their interpersonal relationship.

CONCLUDING THOUGHTS

We began this chapter by recognizing conflict as an inevitable human experience. Humans are significantly different from one another, and whenever their differences meet, conflict can occur. Our motivation for writing this chapter was based in part on that premise—conflict is no myth; as long as humans communicate, they will sometimes disagree.

Conflict, however, is not the same as a person-destroying argument. Disagreement need not damage a relationship. That's the second premise on which we've based our writing of this chapter—there's nothing inherently destructive or threatening about conflict. The important thing is *how* disagreements are handled. That's why we've been discussing how you might deal with conflicts while maintaining your personness and how you might help maintain the personness of the other. In other words, we've tried to develop an approach for dealing with conflict consistent with what we've said throughout this book; one that captures the essential methods of handling conflict *interpersonally*.

In skeleton form, this is what we've tried to say:

Conflict can occur whenever human differences meet.
Disagreements are unavoidable, but most of them can be handled interpersonally.

Content conflict can include
disagreements about accuracy of perceptions or statements
differences in definitions of terms
disagreements about reasoning processes.

Definition-of-selves conflict can focus on
historical selves
whether a person is informed or uninformed, competent or incompetent
who has what kind of authority
who is more powerful
who has what duties or obligations
present selves
how a person sees himself or herself at the present moment.

Conflict over strongly held basic values
is often irresolvable, but
is relatively infrequent, and
can be handled interpersonally.

In previous chapters we've made these suggestions for dealing with conflict:

1. *Context*—whenever you can, choose a comfortable, nondistracting context; forget the "blaming game."

2. *Personal perceiving*—remember that disagreements escalate when you forget that your perceptions are highly subjective, especially in disagreements. Try to recognize that there's a tendency for each person to feel that he/she is being unfairly persecuted, apply a

double standard to what's going on, and to perceive issues and events in oversimplified, right/wrong terms.

3. *Sharing*—take responsiblity for your feelings and actions:
    a) Use specific descriptions of your feelings instead of generalizations, accusations, and inferences.
    b) Remember that sharing creates trust, and trust encourages sharing.

4. *Being aware*—resolving conflict interpersonally is much easier when you listen responsively:
    a) Confirm
    b) Paraphrase
    c) Parasupport
    d) Diminish defensiveness.

Here are suggestions not covered in previous chapters:

1. Try to imagine the real of the other.
    a) Imagining the real involves knowing and understanding what the other person is going through during the conflict.
    b) Imagining the real is limited by the realness of the other:
        1) You recognize the other as a unique person.
        2) The feelings you experience aren't just your feelings projected on to the other.
    c) Imagining the real involves the element of surprise.

2. Deal directly with content disagreements.
    a) Limit your disagreement to one issue at a time; avoid "gunny-sacking."
    b) Try not to let the conflict influence you to exaggerate how relevant the issue actually is to you.
    c) Clarify points of disagreement, in order to avoid attacking a position that the other person isn't maintaining.
    d) Be ready with well-thought-out, specific alternatives.

3. Handle disagreements over definitions of selves by:
    a) getting in touch with how you define yourself when you're in a conflict

b) identifying the "triggers" of the dispute so you can pinpoint the definitions of selves that are operating

c) remembering to use your positive feelings about the other to keep clear the distinction between unacceptable *ideas* and unacceptable *persons*

d) exploring the use of role reversal.

4. If the conflict seems irresolvable:

a) systematically review the ways you've tried to deal with it

b) be sure to leave people room to change

c) suggest a quiet time

d) remember that sometimes the best you can do is interpersonally agree to disagree; when that happens, remember that the other person is a *person*, worthy of your concern and respect.

EXERCISES

You'll be able to handle conflict more effectively when you learn to distinguish between *content* conflict and *definitions-of-selves* conflict. There are several things you might do to increase your understanding of how they differ.

Individual Application: Which Kind of Conflict?

Watch a television drama and pick out two characters who are in conflict with each other. As you observe their nonverbal cues and listen to their verbal cues, ask yourself the following questions:

Content: 1. What facts did they disagree about?
2. Did they disagree about statements made by others?
3. Did they disagree about definitions of terms (e.g., murder, love, responsibility in the home, job description, etc.)?
4. Did they disagree about reasoning processes (e.g., validity of conclusions of inferences made)?

Definition of selves: 1. How did character A define himself/herself in relation to character B? More competent? Less competent? Superior? Inferior? More powerful? Less powerful?
2. How did character B respond to A's self-definition?
3. How did character B define himself/herself in relation to A?

4. How did character A respond to B's self-definition?
5. Which aspects of the self-definitions promoted the conflict or disagreement?

Group Applications: Which Kind of Conflict?

1. Ask several members of your class to role-play a conflict situation. This won't be completely artificial if the participants choose a highly controversial issue to discuss, one which the participants actually differ on. The nonparticipating members of the class will take notes on a sheet of paper divided into two parts: on one side, list the content disagreements; on the other side, list the definitions-of-selves disagreements. Be sure to practice the interpersonal methods of dealing with content disagreement:

a) Limit disagreement to one issue at a time
b) Be tentative in your evaluation of ideas
c) Clarify points of disagreement
d) Be sure you care about the issue
e) Maintain a win/win mental set.

2. Ask three members of your class to role-play a situation in which a counselor is working with a parent and child. The parent and child characters should clearly indicate their definitions of selves in relation to each other, and they should disagree about each other's definition. The counselor will describe for the parent and child what the conflict is about and will suggest ways to handle the disagreement interpersonally. (*Note:* the characters don't have to be parent and child; choose any two persons who might be talking with a counselor.)

Group Applications: Division of Money[22]

The objective of this exercise is to place you in a conflict situation so that you can examine your present style of dealing with conflicts. The procedure for the exercise is as follows:

1. Divide into groups of three. Each person contributes 25¢ to the group. The 75¢ should be placed in the middle of the group.

2. The group has 15 minutes to decide how to divide the money between two individuals. Only two individuals can receive money. It is not legitimate to use any sort of "chance" procedure, such as drawing straws or flipping a coin to decide which two persons get what amounts of money. You must negotiate within the triad to reach a decision. *The purpose of the exercise is to get as much money for yourself as possible.*

3. As soon as your group reaches a decision, write out your answers to the following questions:

   a) What were your feelings during the exercise? Be as specific and descriptive as you can.

   b) What behaviors did you engage in during the exercise? Be as specific and descriptive as you can (e.g., ignoring, attacking, giving in, agreeing to meet half way, working through).

   c) How would you characterize your style of resolving the conflict in this exercise? Again, be as specific as you can.

   d) In your group, give one another feedback about what you perceived to be the feelings, behaviors, and conflict styles of the other group members.

4. In the group as a whole, describe what you learned about yourself and your style of dealing with conflicts.

Group Application: Achilles' Heels and Belt Lines

To make conflict situations more comfortable to deal with, you'll want to: (1) be aware of your most vulnerable spots; (2) communicate those vulnerability lines to the other person; (3) be aware of and understand where the other person is most vulnerable; and (4) avoid hitting below the lines of vulnerability. The first three steps require you to communicate with the other person about vulnerability; that's not always easy to do *during* a conflict, so you might want to try the following:

1. Get together with a person you really care about—someone you'd like to communicate interpersonally with even during disagreements, e.g., a lover, roommate, parent, spouse, etc. Each of you should respond to the following questions in order to get in touch with your belt lines. Then discuss vulnerability with each other until you have a clear notion of how you can avoid damaging the other person and your relationship with her or him.

   a) I usually feel defensive and hurt when you talk about my:

   1) _____

   2) _____

   3) _____

   4) _____

b) Here are some of the nonverbal cues that really get me down:

_____

_____

_____

c) Around you, my *most* vulnerable spot is probably:

_____

2. It can also help to recognize areas of vulnerability around others.
   a) The persons with whom I feel the most vulnerable are:

   _____

   _____

   b) I'm especially vulnerable when it seems to me that someone:
      1) has power over me
      2) is more competent than I
      3) can do things better than I can
      4) is older than I
      5) is more attractive than I
      6) _____

   c) I can handle "put downs" except in the following areas:
      1) my physical characteristics
      2) my athletic ability
      3) my personality
      4) _____
      5) _____
      6) _____

NOTES

1. Kenneth Boulding, *Conflict and Defense: A General Theory*, New York: Harper Torchbooks, 1962, p. 1. Reprinted by permission.
2. Or to put it in the research jargon, actor A's power over actor B is "diiectly proportional to B's motivational investment in goals mediated by A, and inversely proportional to the availability of those to B outside of the A–B relation." R.M. Emerson, "Power-Dependence Relations," *American*

Sociological Review, **XLVII** (1962): 32, cited in Wally D. Jacobson, *Power and Interpersonal Relations*, Belmont, Calif.: Wadsworth, 1972, p. 2.

3. David Augsburger, *The Love-Fight*, Scottsdale, Pa.: Herald Press, 1973, pp. 52, 53 and 218, 219. Reprinted by permission.

4. David W. Johnson, *Reaching Out: Interpersonal Effectiveness and Self-Actualization* Englewood Cliffs: Prentice-Hall, 1973, pp. 210–211.

5. Augsburger, *op. cit.*, pp. 52–53. Reprinted by permission.

6. *Ibid.*, pp. 51–52.

7. Maurice S. Friedman, *Martin Buber: The Life of Dialogue*, New York: Harper Torchbooks, 1960, p. 90.

8. Martin Buber, "Education," in *Between Man and Man*, trans. Ronald Gregor Smith, New York: Macmillan, 1965, p. 96.

9. Friedman, *op. cit.*, p. 89. Reprinted by permission.

10. Buber, "Distance and Relation," in *The Knowledge of Man*, ed. Maurice S. Friedman, trans. Ronald Gregor Smith and Maurice S. Friedman, New York: Harper Torchbooks, 1965, p. 70.

11. Paraphrased from part of Friedman's translation of Buber's essay "Elements of the Interhuman," in *The Knowledge of Man, op. cit.*, pp. 79–80.

12. George R. Bach and Peter Wyden, *The Intimate Enemy: How to Fight Fair in Love and Marriage*, New York: Avon Books, 1968, p. 19.

13. *Ibid.*, p. 80.

14. *Ibid.*, p. 81.

15. Buber, "Elements of the Interhuman," in *The Knowledge of Man, op. cit.*, p. 82.

16. Buber, "Distance and Relation," *op. cit.*, p. 69.

17. David W. Johnson, "Effects of the Order of Expressing Warmth and Anger on the Actor and the Listener," *Journal of Counseling Psychology*, **XVIII** (1971): 571–578.

18. Johnson, "The Use of Role Reversal and Intergroup Competition," *Journal of Personality and Social Psychology*, **VII** (1967): 135–141.

19. Johnson, "Effects of Warmth of Interaction, Accuracy of Understanding, and the Proposal of Compromises on Listeners' Behavior," *Journal of Counseling Psychology*, **XVII** (1971): 207–216.

20. Buber, *Between Man and Man, op. cit.*, p. 6.

21. *Ibid.*

22. Exercise adapted from David W. Johnson, *Reaching Out: Interpersonal Effectiveness and Self-Actualization*, Englewood Cliffs, N.J.: Prentice-Hall, 1973, pp. 206–207.

ADDITIONAL RESOURCES

If you're interested in looking at communication and conflict form a trans-actional analysis perspective, read Thomas A. Harris *I'm OK—You're OK* (New York: Harper & Row, 1967). Several of the students in our classes who were willing to learn the vocabulary of transactional analysis have told us that Harris's book helped them to understand their behavior in conflict situations.

David Johnson's book *Reaching Out: Interpersonal Effectiveness and Self-Actualization* (Englewood Cliffs, N.J.: Prentice-Hall, 1973) is worth reading for two reasons. First, Johnson makes some suggestions for handling conflict that we don't include in this chapter. Second, he provides several activities that'll help you to experience some of the things we've been talking about.

We don't agree with Dr. Eric Berne that most people are always playing "games" with one another, but we think his book *Games People Play* (New York: Grove Press, 1967) is worth reading—if you haven't already read it. Berne provides many examples of conflict situations, and his analyses of those situations can help you to develop an understanding of why conflict occurs.

Much of what we say in this book has been influenced by the writings of Martin Buber. We've recommended Buber's works in other chapters, but we'd like to re-emphasize the contribution that he can make to your understanding of interpersonal communication. If you're interested in reading only *some* of what Buber has written, see his essay "Elements of the Interhuman" in *The Knowledge of Man*, ed. Maurice S. Friedman (New York: Harper & Row, 1965), pp. 72–88; or the collection of short excerpts from his writing called *The Way of Response: Martin Buber*, ed. N. N. Glatzer (New York: Schocken Books, 1966), Chapters 2, 4, and 5.

If you're willing to spend more time with him, you might enjoy Aubrey Hodes' biography *Martin Buber: An Intimate Portrait* (New York: The Viking Press, 1971); Maurice S. Friedman's comprehensive commentary *Martin Buber: The Life of Dialogue* (New York: Harper Torchbooks, 1960); Buber's *I and Thou*, trans. Walter Kaufman (New York: Charles Scribner's Sons, 1970) and *Between Man and Man*, trans. Ronald Gregor Smith (New York: Macmillan, 1965).

George Bach and Peter Wyden's book *The Intimate Enemy: How to Fight Fair in Love and Marriage* (New York: Avon Books, 1968) is also worth looking at. We think they could have said what they say in less space, but there are some good suggestions in the book, suggestions that grow from practical experience with "warring spouses."

For some practical suggestions about handling conflict in groups, committees, business meetings, etc., see Irving J. Lee's *How to Talk with People* (New York: Harper & Row, 1952).

9

Overcoming the Barriers of Context

INTRODUCTION

Throughout this book we've emphasized that each of our communication experiences tends to have one of two possible qualities: we tend to treat people primarily as objects or primarily as persons. We've said that for us, the word "interpersonal" names not just any communication between people, but communication of a certain quality. That quality emerges when the persons communicating are willing and able both to be aware of others as humans instead of objects and to reveal or share something of their own humanness. In this chapter we're suggesting that the quality of human communication we've been talking about— interpersonalness—can happen in a variety of different settings or contexts. In other words, because we're humans, we are choosers, and that means that no context dictates completely for us how or what we will communicate. Because of our choice-making capabilities, we're able to promote interpersonal-quality communication just about whenever we're really willing to. In some contexts, however, it's much more difficult than in others.

For purposes of clarification, human communication contexts are usually generalized into four categories: (1) public; (2) group; (3) mass media; and (4) sociopersonal. Of course, not all contexts fit neatly into one of these four categories; it's usually a matter of degree. Sometimes, for example, when members of an organized group communicate as if they were each giving speeches, the context is as much public as group.

Or, when a person is giving what we'd ordinarily call a public speech but the audience is small, the atmosphere is comfortable, the person's approach is personal and spontaneous, and there are immediate exchanges of verbal comments between speaker and listeners, it might be more accurate to call that situation group or sociopersonal.

In this chapter we'll focus specifically on how you can promote interpersonal-quality communication in the public-speaking and small-group contexts. We're not dealing with mass media—television, radio, magazines, books, etc.—because we're not convinced yet that inter-personal communication is possible in those settings. When mechanical or electronic transmissions is used, the participants aren't face to face, there's no opportunity for immediate exchange of ideas, and the author, announcer, or actor's perceptual awareness of the audience focuses on stereotypes, statistics, and other objectifying characteristics rather than on the audience as persons. In that context it's difficult for the communication to be anything but objectifying. We've tried to communicate as persons in this book, but as you know, you've had little or no chance to respond to us, and until you do, we can't be aware of *your* humanness. In short, the media context allows one person to reveal his or her humanness, and there may be the chance for delayed interpersonal communication, but as yet we haven't developed adequate methods of suggesting how that can happen.

We're also not dealing specifically with sociopersonal contexts in this chapter, primarily because we've been discussing them throughout the book. Sociopersonal contexts are, as the photograph on p. 287 suggests, those situations in which you talk face to face with someone in relatively informal and unstructured environments. They include "by chance" meetings, social conversations, and in general any of those times when the opportunity exists for immediate and spontaneous exchanges of ideas, with very few rules about who talks when, about what, for how long, and so on.

But we haven't dealt directly in previous chapters with those occasions when you're standing up in front of an audience, giving a speech, and those times when you're participating in a meeting of an organized, small group. Even though these two contexts overlap, we think that each is distinct enough to deserve separate consideration. Each evokes a relatively identifiable set of perceptual expectations, social and structural norms, and other such conventions or rules, all of which exert a significant impact on the communication that takes place. We'd like to see you develop your ability to respond in those settings, that is, to promote interpersonal communication when you're giving a speech or meeting with an organized group. To do this, we think you'll need to understand the barriers that exist within each of those two settings and what you can do about them.

PROMOTING INTERPERSONAL COMMUNICATION IN A PUBLIC SETTING

COPYRIGHT 1972/DISTRIBUTED BY UNIVERSAL PRESS SYNDICATE.

As the cartoon suggests, communication in the public-speaking context often involves objectifying—by both speakers and listeners. Consequently, the public setting is one of the most difficult ones in which to promote interpersonal communication. There are several reasons for this. First, both speaker and listeners usually bring certain expectations to the public context, and these expectations sometimes discourage sharing and being aware. For example, people usually assume that this type of context is a formal one and that only one person (the speaker) is supposed to talk while the other persons (the listeners) are expected to sit and listen. When one person is the primary source of verbal cues, it drastically reduces the possibilities for *mutual* sharing and being aware. In addition, public speakers—especially inexperienced ones—frequently believe that there's a prescribed role to conform to or imitate; in trying to fill that role, they objectify themselves and therefore communicate *im*personally. Finally, when the audience is large, it's almost impossible to treat each person as a unique individual; so generalizations are made, stereotypes are formed, and the listener is objectified, too. But even though every public-speaking setting has structure and rules unlike those found in informal, personal situations, there are ways to promote interpersonal communications in public contexts. Our suggestions will be for you to: (1) look at the ways you tend to define the public-speaking context as impersonal; and then (2) work to redefine the context; (3) be aware of how you typically define yourself when you're giving a speech; then, if necessary (4) change that definition; and finally (5) try to develop an informed definition of your listeners.

Defining the Context

We tend to define public-speaking contexts as:

Separating and formal.   We've talked before about how the physical environment affects human communication. The physical context of a public-speaking situation is deliberately set up to maintain a separation between speaker and audience and to reduce the opportunity for the give-and-take of conversation—both between speaker and listeners and among listeners. In the typical public setting, for example, the speaker stands behind a lectern, desk, or table, and the audience sits in rows facing the speaker. Everything physically possible is done to focus attention exclusively on the person giving the speech. This tends to set audience and speaker apart, as if each were a separate entity. The context need not be set up that way, but it usually is.

Depending on the specific setup, for example, the personal space between speaker and audience can be anywhere from 10 to 40 feet or more. This spatial distance can have a tremendous impact on the relationship between the speaker and the persons in the audience. A personal space of over five feet isn't typically associated with a warm, personal conversation. Ordinarily, you stand that far away from someone because it's physically impossible to stand closer or—and here's the important point—because you don't *want* to get close physically or psychologically. To the extent that wide personal space between persons is interpreted to mean formal, structured, businesslike relationships, the space usually encountered in a public setting works against interpersonal communicating.

Linear and one-way.   The person who either assumes or behaves as if public speaking is linear and one-way communication assumes that the audience doesn't participate in the event. If that person were to diagram his or her communicating, it would probably look something like this:

An inexperienced speaker using this model as a guide enters the public-speaking situation with a packaged message (the speech) and delivers it as if it were a static chunk of previously constructed information that's being poured into the heads of a passively receptive audience. In other words, the model assumes that the speaker communicates and the audience doesn't. Since the speaker is the only communicator, the most important thing in this context is the prepared speech—nothing else really matters; nothing else is happening; audience analysis has already been done; concern is only with the message cues being sent out. Audience feedback is the farthest thing from the speaker's mind. With this model as a guide, the speaker thinks, "Why be aware? There's nothing to be aware of."

Work to redefine public-speaking contexts as:

Personal.   Even before you plan your speech, one of the important things for you to do is to define the public-speaking context as a personal event rather than as a completely impersonal one. You'll obviously be confronted with some unavoidable structure. The audience, for example, will bring with them certain expectations about the formality of the event. They won't expect your talk to be completely off the cuff. They'll expect you to have some things to say that you've thought about in advance. They'll also expect you to do most or all of the talking. But those expectations aren't irrevocable. It's been our experience that listeners usually respond positively when we make an effort to remove some of the structure and formality from the public context.

For example, one of the ways I (Gary) have learned to deal with personal space is by gaining psychological control over it. I work to define my relationship with the other persons rather than let the personal space define the relationship for me. To do that, I've had to unlearn some things. I no longer assume that distances of five feet or more automatically mean formal, businesslike relationships. Also, I don't accept the idea that it's impossible to talk with an audience conversationally when they're 30 or 40 feet away. If you can unlearn some of your stereotypes about personal space and redefine it so that even at wide distances you can see the members of your audience as persons, and if you can recognize that even at wide distances, conversational-spontaneous communication can still happen, you're much more likely to promote person-to-person communicating in a public setting.

When I (John) was living in Los Angeles, I watched and listened to the Episcopal priest Malcolm Boyd redefine a public-speaking situation in the ways we're talking about here. He spoke in a church during a Sunday service, but he managed to create a personal, conversational atmosphere even in that setting. One of the persons reviewing this book* experienced Malcolm Boyd doing the same kind of thing:

> For me a fantastic experience was listening to Malcom Boyd speak to 2500 people. He sat on a high stool on the platform and talked as if only five or six people were present. But I felt as if I were one of those five or six! A couple hundred people left during the first 15

---

*Joe Munshaw of Southern Illinois University at Edwardsville.

minutes, most of them disgusted because they expected to hear a "speech." But those who stayed felt elated, as if they had been in a dialogue with Boyd.

Interdependent.   Being aware of the audience's humanness is also an important dimension of defining public speaking as a personal event. To develop your ability and willingness to be aware, recognize that the individuals in an audience *do* participate in the public-speaking context, that is, try to get away from the linear, one-way viewpoint. Members of an audience select, organize, and go beyond the verbal and nonverbal cues you make available, and they are continually making nonverbal cues available to you. Even though you may decide not to be fully and consciously aware of those cues, they exist. In Chapter 2 we said that two persons who are perceptually aware of each other are interdependent. That is, what one person says and does affects the other person, and vice versa—they influence each other simultaneously. In the public setting, the things you say and do affect your listeners, and the way they behave affects you. Rather than thinking about public speaking as linear and one-way, it makes more sense to view it as an event in which both speaker and listeners are active, interdependent participants. A speaker doesn't exist apart from the audience; an audience doesn't exist apart from the speaker. Both participate. Both communicate. Be aware that your listeners are communicating with you. Make an attempt to understand what the people are "saying."

Not rule-bound.   You can also encourage interpersonal-quality communication in the public setting by breaking out of the imposed formal structure. As speaker, you have a distinct advantage in redefining the speaking context. Unless you drastically violate audience expectations, you can get by with making a variety of choices. If you say, "It's okay to be informal," its usually more acceptable than if an audience member were to say, "Hey, let's be more informal." Not all public-speaking events lend themselves to complete informality, but sometimes you'll want to break the "rules" which say, for example, "Focus must always be on the speaker" or "Audience members must not interact verbally." In other words, you may want to change the nature of the context to allow persons in the audience to interact with one another and with you as you talk with them.

There can be several advantages to breaking some of these rules. In the first place, you'll have a much better idea of what your listeners are thinking, and consequently you'll have a better chance to clear up misunderstandings. In addition, because of the ambiguity of nonverbal cues, it's generally much easier to interpret, synthesize, and respond to verbal feedback from an audience member. Also, immediate verbal interaction between speaker and audience increases the potential for mutual sharing and being aware.

There are also some possible disadvantages. Sometimes, verbal interaction between speaker and listeners strays from the central theme. Also, audience participation takes time, and you may not finish everything you wanted to say in your talk. Or, a member of the audience may promote an argument or may not want to pursue a topic that doesn't interest the other listeners. Therefore, whether or not you encourage your listeners to participate verbally depends on several things: number of persons present, your goals as a speaker, the expectations of the audience, the nature of the event, etc. You won't always want to give part of your time to your listeners, but you should think of it as a strong option.

An opportunity.   We've observed that people in our classes frequently define the public setting as a liability, an undesirable hurdle they have to get over. We get such comments as: "How can I speak in front of that many persons for 15 or 20 minutes? What do I talk about for that long?" or "I don't know anything about important topics; I don't have anything to say that would take even five minutes." Because they view public speaking as a liability, the speech becomes forced, formal, and impersonal.

It's true that as a speaker, you'll be expected to do most of the talking for 10, 15, or maybe 20 minutes. But instead of defining that as a liability, try seeing it as an opportunity. Having most or all of the available time in a human communication context can be an advantage to you. In a conversation, for example, you seldom get more than one or two minutes at any given time to express your views. Such short time segments don't always allow you to fully explain yourself. A public context, on the other hand, almost guarantees that you'll be given enough time and attention to explain your views, qualify your position, and respond to objections people might be thinking about. Unlike a conversation, you won't have to feel embarrassed or self-centered about using the time for yourself. If you thought about it just for a minute, we think you could name several issues you really *care* about—all of us feel strongly about some things. A public-speaking context is the perfect place for you to share your thoughts and feelings about an idea you really believe in, an event that excites you, an organization that you strongly dislike, a political figure you intensely admire, or whatever. In other words, when you have something you want to say and when you want time to say it without frequent interruptions or without worrying that you're dominating the conversation, public speaking gives you more of an opportunity than the sociopersonal context does. But you must have something you want to say, and this means that you need to get in touch with the topics, ideas, etc., you care about and to realize that much of what you care about *is* appropriate for public speaking.

Care.   Actually, that's one of the most important suggestions we can make. It's almost impossible to promote interpersonal communication in a public setting unless you *care* about what you're saying. But your caring has to be genuine. Speaker and audience expectations, spatial distance, and formal structure can all make the public setting unusual and threatening. It just doesn't make good sense for you to create additional problems for yourself by trying to pretend that you care about your topic when in fact you really don't give a damn. On the other hand, when you do genuinely care, it's relatively easy both to share some of your own humanness and to be aware of the humanness of your listeners. We don't mean that you should try to make every talk a heartrending, impassioned plea. But you should be willing to admit that you *do* care about things—issues, ideas, organizations, interests—and those things often make excellent speech topics.

Recently, someone in one of my (Gary) speech classes couldn't think of anything to talk about and didn't want to give a speech because, as he said, "Public speaking is an irrelevant activity for me." I suggested that he talk about that. He did, and his speech provoked someone else into giving a speech she called "Public Speaking and Decision Making: A Positive Point of View." When the two discovered that they could talk on an issue they felt personally attached to, they both used the public-speaking setting as an opportunity to express their views; neither felt that the time allotted was enough, and each had much more to say than would fit into the five or ten minutes of the assignment. You, too, will have a much better speaking experience if you'll get in touch with the things you care about and then adapt those topics to the public setting.

Individual Application: Topics You Care About

We're sure that there are issues, ideas, organizations, and interests that you *do* care about. The important thing is to get in touch with some of them and to realize that they can make excellent topics for communication in a public-speaking context. The intent of this activity is to help you do that.

1. Think back to the most interesting conversations you've had in the past week or so.

   a) What were the topics?
   b) Which statements did you strongly agree with (if any)?
   c) Which statements did you strongly disagree with?
   d) Did anything happen in those conversations that might suggest an issue or idea you care about?

2. Sometimes, you can discover topics you care about by analyzing what you do with your time. For example, maybe you read a lot. If so, an analysis might go something like this:

   What books do you read the most? Textbooks? Why? Because they're required? Because you want to get high grades? Which textbook, if any, do you enjoy reading? Does that say something about your interests? For instance, if you enjoy reading a textbook about mass communication, that might suggest that you'd care about such topics as "the effects of television violence on children" or "the boredom of modern radio" or "does television distort our views of reality?" Do you tend to avoid reading textbooks as much as possible? Why? Is there something about the way texts are written that turns you off? Do you feel strongly that textbooks could be written differently? How so?

   You might list here some other books you spend time reading:

   _____

   _____

   In what other ways do you spend a lot of your time? Try analyzing those choices to see if you can come up with topics, ideas, issues, etc., that are important to you.

3. Sometimes, knowing what attracts your attention gives you an idea of things you care about.

   a) When you read a newspaper, what's the first thing you read? Comics? Why? Could you build a speech around a comic strip? Sports? Why? Is there something in athletics you really care about? Editorials? Front page? Stories or articles about crime? Sex?

b) What kind of movies are you usually attracted to? Does that put you in touch with anything that's personally relevant and important to you?

c) What other activities attract your attention? Political events? Music festivals? Concerts? Artistic events? Sports events?

4. Each of us has a value system, which is to say some things are more important to us than others. Here's a list of issues, objects, behaviors, etc. Add to the list if you like. Then put a "1" beside those that you definitely care about, a "2" beside those that you care about a little, a "3" beside those that you feel relatively uninterested in, and a "4" beside those that you definitely don't care about.

_____pornography	_____rock music
_____gambling	_____folk music
_____freedom of speech	_____classical music
_____censorship	_____socializing
_____grading	_____dieting
_____religion	_____reading the Bible
_____parent-child	_____writing
relationships	_____playing sports
_____labor unions	_____meditating
_____ television	_____attending classes
_____poetry	_____achieving sexual
_____painting	freedom
_____farming	_____stock market
making money	_____photography
_____drama—theater	_____antiques
_____movies	_____inflation
_____foreign aid	_____family
_____taxes	_____insurance
_____sexism	_____encounter groups
_____medical quacks	_____divorce
_____dreams	_____vocational education
_____inferiority complexes	_____prisons
_____social work	_____racism
_____nursing	_____ageism
_____sex education	others:
_____child abuse	_____ _____
_____communes	_____ _____
_____marriage	_____ _____

Defining Your Self as Public Speaker

Stereotyped self-definition.   I (Gary) have always been curious to know why people change so much when they get up to give a speech. When I converse with a person in an informal context and sense the spontaneity, conversational language, and human sharing, and then watch that same person give a "speech," I'm amazed at his or her sudden change to rigid, formal, unnatural communicative behaviors. As John and I talked about this and as we observed and listened to the persons in our classes and public-speaking workshops, we discovered that many students had developed role definitions of how a public speaker *should* behave. Whenever they'd get up to give a speech, they'd try to play that role. It was as if public speaking were a stage play, with the speaker as one of the actors.

The image or definition you construct of yourself as a public speaker can promote object-to-object communicating and work against your willingness and ability to share aspects of your humanness. You may sometimes think, for example, that there's a public speaker "personality" you're expected to project. You might have been thinking, "I'm supposed to be formal and deliver the speech in a perfectly continuous, flowing manner" or "I'm in charge and I'm expected to use a certain type of language—mostly formal English" or "I'm not supposed to be too personal." If you tend to define the public speaker in these ways, you're trying to imitate an artificial model rather than to project your own human qualities. You're trying to behave like someone else would in this same role, someone you've seen in the pulpit, on stage, at a banquet, in the classroom, on television, at a political rally, etc. Instead of getting in touch with your own humanness and sharing it, you're trying to figure out ways of playing the role properly. You'll usually find the role uncomfortable, unnatural, and noninterpersonal.

You'll not only feel unnatural filling the role, but also you'll often be unfairly critical of yourself. Usually, this self-criticism is based on the contrast between how you think public speakers should behave and how you see yourself actually behaving. One of the mythical definitions of the successful public speaker, for example, is that he or she is never afraid, never experiences anxiety. If you define the successful speaker that way, when you get up to speak and notice that your hands are sweaty and cold, your knees feel weak, and your stomach is churning, you're likely to believe that something is wrong with you. You think to yourself, "I'm scared and nervous. Successful speakers aren't supposed to be nervous; they're always calm. I'm probably going to blow this whole damn thing." Not only are you worrying about your fears, but you're also rejecting yourself for being afraid. It's as if "good" speakers don't have stage fright, and since you have it, you must be "bad." We'll have more to say about stage fright later; for now, we'd just like to help you see how a stereotyped definition of yourself as public speaker çan contribute to your uneasiness.

Work to redefine your self as speaker

A talker not a writer.   Your definition of self as speaker in a public context should be very much like your definition of self as speaker in a conversation. You'll feel more natural and do a better job of public speaking if you think of your speech as an *extended conversation*. As we said before, in a conversation you usually talk in blocks of only a minute or two; in a public speech the time may be extended to 5 or even 15 minutes. But this doesn't mean that all your communication behaviors should change drastically. For example, when you define the context and your self as "formal" and "impersonal," you usually tend to behave physically in unnaturally stiff and proper ways and to overarticulate or overprecisely pronounce words. A stiff, pedantic delivery usually sounds mechanical, and the audience will probably interpret it as unnatural and insincere. But if you define yourself as personal and conversational, your delivery will tend to flow more naturally and spontaneously.

    In addition, when you're conversing you use words that are *yours*; unless the situation is threatening to you, you talk naturally and spontaneously. The same should be true when you're giving a speech. The major difference between the languages of public speaking and informal conversation is that in the conversation you get by with more slang, colloquialisms, and nonstandard English. Many audiences would be turned off if a speaker said something like, "I ain't gonna talk about no stuff like that." But they'd probably also be turned off by "My intentions involve eschewing the abstract components" or "I do not intend to articulate on such matters." A more natural way to say it might be, "I don't plan to talk about. . . ." Our point is this: when you're preparing and giving a speech, keep the listeners and context in mind—use language appropriate to the situation, but also keep yourself in mind—use personal, conversational language, *your* language. Eliminate the ambiguties, the words that are much too formal for you and the situation, and the jargon words that only your friends might understand; talk mostly like you normally do in a conversation.

Individual Application: Using Spoken Language

It's important to remember that your *written* language may be different from your *spoken* language and that public speaking is *speaking*. Public speakers sometimes get the idea that a speech should be written and delivered just as they'd read aloud a formally written term paper. But listeners are usually interested in hearing you talk in a way that does not sound like verbatim recitation. To get an idea of the differences between your oral and written languages, try the following:

> Compose a short paragraph in formal written English—as if you were doing it for a term paper. Pick a topic you can write a little about— "Freedom of Speech," "Censorship," "Advertising," etc.

> Then write a paraphrase of that paragraph in the words you'd probably use in a conversation. It would help to have a tape recorder so you can record your paraphrase and then transcribe it; but if you don't, say your paraphrase out loud and write what you say. For example, suppose that your topic were "Attitudes and Behavior":

Formal written language

Attitudes, then, represent an individual's predisposition to behave toward some object (person, idea, event, etc.) in a particular context. The cognitive aspect of an attitude refers to what the individual believes, with varying degrees of confidence, about the various elements of the attitude object. One's likes or dislikes, pleasant or unpleasant feelings toward an object, etc., manifest the affective aspect of attitudes.

Relatively informal spoken language

So, we assume your attitudes influence your behavior. I'd like you to understand that an attitude includes two things—beliefs and feelings. Let's deal with these one at a time. A belief is something you think is true. Maybe you believe violence on TV is harmful to children. Maybe you believe our government has too much control over us. Maybe you believe a college degree will increase your chances of getting a job. There are hundreds of possibilities. The point is, your beliefs are a part of your attitudes. So, if we wanted to know something about your attitude toward "hitchhiking," we'd have to know what you believe ¡bout it—it's dangerous, it increases crime, but it's a cheap way to travel, or whatever. But those beliefs are only a part of your attitude toward hitch-hiking. We'd also have to know how you feel about it—do you like it? Dislike it? Enjoy it? And so on. Note that you may *believe* hitchhiking is dangerous, but at the same time you may also *like* it. . . .

Notice the differences between the written and the spoken language:

Spoken language is more redundant.
Spoken language includes more contractions than does written language.
Speakers are generally more direct with their audience than are writers.
Speakers include more personal pronouns than do writers.
Spoken language is made up of shorter sentences than is written language.
Spoken language includes more questions.
Etc.

Keep those in mind when you write your spoken paragraph.

Topic:_____

Term-paper style:

Spoken language:

Remember: We are *not* suggesting that you write out your speech word for word. The purpose of this exercise is to get you in touch with the differences between what you sound like when you're writing and talking and to encourage you to *talk with* your listeners, not to *recite* formal writing *at* them.

Prepared.   Not only is it important for you to define yourself in the public–speaking situation as a talker or converser instead of a writer, but it's also crucial for you to define yourself as genuinely prepared, as ready to talk. We're convinced that you'll *be* ready if you take the following five steps: (1) decide early what you want to accomplish; (2) become friends with your ideas; (3) give your talk a clear sense of wholeness; (4) prepare useful notes; and (5) say your talk before you give it.

Almost everybody suffers from at least a little procrastination. I (John) tend to put off answering personal letters—and I'm finding that it's a heckuva good way to alienate friends. When I was going to school, I sometimes put off studying for exams, writing papers, keeping up with required reading, and preparing a talk. You might do some of the same things. Somewhere along the way, though, it finally got through to me that I was often doing something a lot like hitting myself over the head with a brick. Procrastinating, I finally realized, was just making those things hard on myself; since then, I've developed a little more of the willingness and ability to "get ready early." Now, it's espeically important for me to prepare for a talk I have to give by deciding early what I want to accomplish in the speech. I've found that it really helps to decide at *least* several days before the talk—and preferably a week or more: (1) what my general topic is going to be, e.g., interpersonal communication in family situations, humanism in teaching, Martin Buber's philosophy of dialogue, or whatever; and (2) what my specific purpose is, e.g., to help people understand where I'm coming from on a topic, to suggest acceptance of a point of view I hold, to urge a specific action, or whatever.

That kind of thinking leads me to make a *statement* of my topic and purpose well before the time for the talk. It isn't enough just to think about it. I need to write it down, something like, "I want to help these people understand that a college class can be both rigorous and humane" or "I want to encourage the other teachers in my department to support the proposal for a new course that I'm offering." When I take that first step, I'm on the way to developing that confident, comfortable feeling that I really *am* ready when the time for the talk comes.

Making those decisions early also gives me time to become friends with my ideas, and I suspect that it could work the same way for you. If you know well in advance what your specific purpose is and at least roughly what you want to say about it, you can take the time to think through your ideas enough to get familiar with them. You can take spare moments—walking across campus, driving down the freeway, etc.—to run through your thoughts until they become like old friends—comfortable and neighborly. That also really helps when the time for the talk comes.

(As I write this, I (Gary) am experiencing what John is talking about. I'm preparing a public lecture on "Conflict in the Home," and one of the specific issues will be "vulnerability and belt lines." I've been thinking about this issue for several weeks—talking with friends about it, devising and going through individual activities, thinking about it in the shower, on the bus to school, etc. I've even found it illustrated in several television shows. Right now, the ideas are almost a part of me. I like the concept of vulnerability and belt lines; I've adapted it to my way of thinking, and I'm comfortable talking about it with just about anybody.)

A third part of the preparation process, one that happens along with the others, is organizing your thoughts. Here, we're talking about the kind of planning we discussed in Chapter 7 under the heading "Giving What You Say a Sense of Wholeness." We don't want to repeat everything we said there, except to stress the idea that especially in a public-speaking situation, it's crucial that your listeners get a clear sense of how your talk hangs together, i.e., why you start where you do, how the second thing you talk about is linked to the first and third ideas, and so on. The clearer a concept you have of the "whole" of your ideas, the more likely listeners are to organize their reactions around the same type of structure or sense of wholeness. Or, as we said in Chapter 7, humans *do* tend to see things and people in wholes made up of parts that are somehow related to one another. Therefore, communication that has a clear sense of wholeness is almost always easier to comprehend clearly than communication that doesn't. (It might be a good idea at this point to reinforce your memory of the specifics we talked about by reviewing Chapter 7. Most of the material there relates pretty directly to the public-speaking context.)

It might seem picky or irrelevant to include the suggestion "prepare useful notes for your talk." But we must say something about it, because we've seen too often what bad notes can do. We've seen potentially interpersonal communication become stilted and stiff because the speaker got lost in too-long notes or confused by obscure symbols and complicated arrows. We've also agonized with the speaker who is reduced to frantic searching and awkward mumbling by notes that looked okay when they were written, but that became unreadable in the increased pressure of the speaking situation. Again, try not to create problems for yourself! Unless you have a lectern or speaker's stand to put sheets of paper on, use cards. Use colors, indentations, numbers, and spaces to indicate key ideas, quotations, etc. Remember that the more you write, the greater the temptation will be to read at your listeners instead of talking with them. In short, create notes that help you stay hooked up with the persons you're talking with instead of getting in between you and them.

Finally, give yourself the benefit of hearing yourself talk *before* you go into the actual speaking situation. We are not saying that you should memorize your talk—*definitely not*. But we do believe that it is important for you to say your speech before you give it, to talk through your ideas in the order you've put them, at least two or three times before you face your listeners. You'd be amazed how few beginning speakers actually do this and how much it can help you feel confident enough to share yourself and be aware of others in the public-speaking context.

The important thing about this whole process of redefining your self as a speaker is that you shouldn't kid yourself. It's relatively easy to do that, to say, "Sure I'm ready, I've been thinking about this for over an hour" or "No sweat, I'll just ad lib for a couple of minutes, tell a few jokes, and it'll be fine." But unless you're experienced enough to do that kind of thing well, the deception will almost always backfire. You *know* when you're prepared and when you're not. If you want to feel comfortable in the speaking situation and to do an effective job of sharing your ideas, avoid shortcuts. Don't kid yourself. *Really* get ready.

Defining Listeners

We tend to define listeners as:

A collection. When your audience is large and unfamiliar to you, it's difficult, if not impossible, to relate to each person as a unique individual. Handling your relationship with a collection of listeners is easier, because, in a sense, you are dealing with only one unit. Sometimes, in a classroom speech or in a speech to an organization or group you belong to, you know the persons in the audience well enough to be able to see some individual personalities; but more often than not, you probably treat them as a whole. This happens partly because you have so much to think about while you're talking. Keeping 10 or 20 minutes of speech content straight seems to demand so much of your attention that you can't think about the multitude of separate personalities in front of you.

Faceless. Sometimes, it's difficult to define members of an audience as persons because not much of their humanness is made available to you during your talk. There's not much body movement, no verbal cues, and almost no facial muscle movement. Also, you're so far away from some of your listeners that it's difficult for you to pick up whatever nonverbal cues might be there. Part of the problem is that many listeners assume that they *shouldn't* respond overtly or explicitly. They assume, for example, that "The speaker has the floor and so it's improper to interrupt, move around, shift, make sounds, or express myself in any obvious way. It might be embarrassing to the speaker if I make my responses too obvious." In addition to these definitional assumptions, since members of an audience don't always know one another, their communicative behavior is influenced by the notion that "Most of the other people here are strangers to me." Whatever the cause, the result is that a group of listeners can look like a faceless, inert blob.

Too complex to respond to.   On the other hand, we sometimes define an audience as too complex to respond to because there's too much information available.* Most of your communicating takes place in informal contexts; only a few people are involved, and the personal space is from one to five feet. Consequently, you get used to being aware of the verbal and nonverbal cues of only a few persons at a relatively close distance. But in the public-speaking setting, you have to keep in touch with a great many people all at once from a relatively long distance away; most persons are *not* used to that kind of communicating. When you're speaking in front of 30 or more people, for example, you're usually standing about 10 feet away from the front row and about 20 feet away from the back row. At one time two persons in the back row might be nodding affirmatively while two people in the front row are looking at you with almost emotionless faces, one individual in the middle is shifting back and forth nervously, and one person is smiling and another is yawning. Trying to assimilate feedback from just those seven persons—let alone all 30—can be overwhelming. It's easy to experience information overload, because you're not practiced at being aware of and synthesizing so many cues from so many different persons. Because there are so many things to be aware of and because it's so difficult to process that much information, you may avoid as much of it as you can, that is, you may decide that the best way to deal with the overload is to ignore responses from the audience. Then, you'll behave

---

*Many of the ideas for this section were generated in a conversation with Ken Morgan, a graduate student in our department.

as if communication were linear and one-way, and when this happens, person-to-person communicating is impossible.

A threat.   Your definition of your listeners also usually includes your predictions of how the listeners will respond to you as a speaker. If you predict that the audience will be accepting, for example, you're likely to communicate comfortably and to feel free to share aspects of your humanness with them. Unfortunately, however, speakers sometimes build images of their audiences based on negative fantasies. Sometimes, the inexperienced speaker regards listeners as "a group of critics just waiting for me to make a mistake." In extreme cases, a speaker may define the audience as "a bunch of rejectors ready to pounce at every opportunity." These definitions aren't always explicit or conscious. But nervousness and impersonalness are frequently evoked because of a strong fear of listeners, a fear based on the speaker's definition of them. In other words, when you define the audience as a threat, you're much more likely to hold back your humanness—your genuine, present self— for fear of rejection, and the result is likely to be object-to-object communication.

Work to redefine your listeners as:

Individuals—as much as possible.   Whenever you're talking with a large audience, some objectification of the persons is inevitable. You'll have to make some generalizations. Keep in mind, however, that they *are* persons and not "listening machines." They have attitudes, values, beliefs, and feelings that affect their responses to you. It'll be easier to keep this in mind if your definition of your listeners is *well informed.*

The questions you can ask before your talk are almost unlimited. For example, you might want to ask: "Who decided I should speak? Why was I chosen? How much does this group know about me? What are their attitudes toward me? What expectations does the group have? What's the purpose of the meeting? What are their attitudes toward my topic? What speakers have they had in the past? How have they re-sponded to those speakers? How much do they know about the topic? Will there be a business meeting before I speak? Any other speakers before me? If so, what will they talk about?" Answers to these questions can come from a variety of sources. Talk with whomever you can, e.g., the person who asked you to speak, the person who introduces you, members of your audience, etc. If you're talking to an organization, find out as much about the group as you can from the officers, the members, or any literature they've distributed. What are the goals of the organization? Values? Past accomplishments? Occupations of the members? And so on. You'll also help yourself by knowing something about the educational level of your audience, economic status, ages, etc.

You'll never know all you need to, but the effort to answer questions about your listeners before your talk can help you in several ways. First, when you know something about the people, you won't be talking to a collection of total strangers, and this can relieve some of your anxieties. The uncertainty of talking with strangers—not knowing who they are, what they might do, how they'll respond, what they expect—sometimes makes public speaking a threatening situation because you don't really know what to say, how to say it, and what the consequences will be. Audience analysis won't solve all of your problems, but communicating is almost always easier and more comfortable when we have some idea of what to expect from the other persons involved. Also, with an informed definition of your listeners, it'll be much easier for you to adapt to them. One audience may know absolutely nothing about your topic, another may be well informed about it; one group of listeners may have a great sense of humor, whereas another group may take the topic very seriously—no jokes allowed. Finally, perhaps the strongest reason for obtaining information about your audience centers on a point we made earlier; public speaking is a process in which both speaker and audience participate. They can reach a high level of understanding only when both speaker and listeners put themselves into the psychological shoes of the other. Since listeners do very little or not talking during the speech, a speaker must find out where they're coming from before and, as much as possible, during the talk and must let them know where he or she is coming from, so that effective mutual adaptation can happen.

A valuable source of information.   The cues your listeners make available while you're talking don't have to be overwhelming. On the contrary, by paying some attention to your listeners' nonverbal behaviors while you talk, you'll have access to information about how they're responding to what you're saying. That is, your awareness during the speech lets you know something about their immediate human responses—feelings, understandings, or misunderstandings, moods, interests, etc. Seldom is an audience completely immobile. Through silence, grimaces, smiles, laughter, shifting, head movements, etc., people in the audience express themselves as persons, as individuals. As we said earlier, you'll sometimes assume that the audience is too complex to respond to, that it's too difficult to synthesize so many different cues coming from so many different persons. But you can do several things to help yourself.

First, recognize that you can't assimilate everything. None of us is equipped or prepared to absorb all the nonverbal cues that listeners make available. As we explained in Chapter 3, our sensory limitations prevent that. But recognize that you can assimilate *some* things. You *can* take advantage of your ability to selectively perceive some cues and avoid others. So, instead of letting information overload you, pay attention to as many of the responses as you can while still maintaining control over yourself and your message content. As you get more and more experienced at public speaking, your ability to absorb and then adapt to information from an audience will increase. You'll probably find that the more aware of your listeners you become, the more automatically you tend to respond to them. But until you get to the point where you're able to synthesize many nonverbal cues, work to synthesize just a few. For your first talk, that may mean you'll see only a few responses. But as you continue to give speeches, try to increase your awareness to the extent that the sample of responses you're able to assimilate is a fairly good representation of how most of your listeners are responding.

Our second suggestion is that as you select responses, be careful how you interpret them. Some things about a conversation generalize well to public speaking—conversational language and voice, natural movements, personal examples, and so on. But not feedback. In conversational contexts you're likely to receive immediate verbal feedback, facial expressions, and subtle eye and body movements; most of the time, silence is the exception rather than the rule. But in public speaking the rules are different. Silence is the norm; that's the way most listeners believe they're supposed to behave. If you interpret silence in a public-speaking situation the same way you do in a conversation, it might have a negative impact on you. In other words, keep in mind that silence doesn't automatically mean disinterest or boredom; before you infer that your audience is bored, you should get more information than "they're awfully quiet." The same kind of careful interpretation should be used for other audience cues, too. Fidgeting or yawning might indicate more about the room temperature, time of day, past activities, or furniture comfort than it does about your talk.

Our final suggestion is that you try to respond to your listeners interpersonally. We've been talking about being aware of, synthesizing, and interpreting feedback. Now, we're saying that how you treat the persons in an audience will determine in large part how much information about their responses they'll make available to you. Most audiences respond honestly and openly when: (1) they believe that the speaker *wants* them to respond openly; (2) they sense that the speaker *feels comfortable* when they respond; (3) the speaker *acknowledges* some responses from listeners; and (4) the speaker responds back interpersonally, that is, accepts or partly accepts and tries to understand his or her listeners. Through your tone of voice, choice of words, eye contact, etc., you can be confirming, understanding, and nonintimidating. For example, if, after you say something controversial, you notice several people grimace and shake their heads negatively, you might say something like, "I know that bothers some of you; I can understand that. But let me go on for a moment before you tune me out." Or, as one reviewer* of this chapter suggested, you can respond to fidgeting or yawning by shifting gears. "Is it too hot in here?" or "Shall I open a window?" can be ways of showing your concern.

Supportive, not threatening.   As we said earlier, fear sometimes prevents a speaker from sharing aspects of her or his humanness and from being aware of aspects of the audience's humanness. For example, a speaker who is afraid often focuses his or her eyes on the lectern, the floor, out the window, or on the speech notes. There may be short spurts of eye contact with listeners, but there's very little awareness. Sometimes, an inexperienced speaker will give a 15-minute talk and afterwards won't even be able to remember what happened. Uncontrolled stage fright, in other words, can work against your being aware of the human qualities expressed by the audience during your talk. So what can you do about your fears?

The first thing to realize is that with very few exceptions, audiences are *not* out to get speakers. Generally, people are intrigued by other people. Consequently, your listeners are interested in you as a person, are almost always at least mildly interested in your topic, and are often even in agreement with your point of view. To verify that, check your

---

*Mike Hanna from Northern Illinois University.

own listening behavior. Do you poise ready to pounce on speakers you hear? Do you listen primarily for their mistakes and spend most of your time looking for any awkward movements or nervous fidgeting? Or, do you find yourself at least neutral and often interested and supportive when listening to a speaker? Sometimes, for one reason or another, we listen hypercritically. But most of the time we're willing to consider and even to accept what a speaker says. Consequently, it's more accurate to define your listeners as supportive than as threatening. Usually, they want you to succeed.

At the same time, the public speaking situation is unusual enough for most of us that we will always experience some anxiety. So, the second thing to remember is that feeling nervous before, during, and even after a speech is a *natural part of your humanness*. Since it is, it's important to learn to *work with* anxiety; you can't expect to eliminate it completely. I (Gary) teach one class of 230 students. I lecture to that class about three days a week every school term. Each time I walk into the classroom, I experience some anxiety. It's not excessive stage fright, but I'm always somewhat nervous. I don't expect to get rid of that feeling, and I wouldn't want to; it keeps me "up," tuned in to myself and to the class. Similarly, you'll probably always experience some anxiety when giving a talk. Rather than rejecting yourself for being nervous, try accepting it; it'll have much less power over you.

Individual Activity: Working with Your Speech Anxiety

Take some time now to find out what it really means to accept stage fright as a natural part of some human experiences.

1. First, think back to experiences when you actually performed well under pressure:

    a) Taking an important exam?
    b) Participating in an important athletic event?
    c) Asking someone for a date?
    d) Talking to an instructor about missing the last week of class?
    e) _____
    f) _____
    g) _____

Now, try to explain why you think you were able to perform as well as you did, even though you were nervous:

Your explanations_____

_____

_____

(Example: "I was nervous during the statistics exam—nervous as hell. But I did well. I think it was primarily because of two things. I had the material down pat. There was very little I didn't know. Also, I didn't pay any attention to my nervousness at the time. I didn't think much about it until after the exam.")

2. Below are two factual examples of persons who learned that even though they couldn't get rid of pressure or anxiety, they could gain psychological control over it. The situations are not public-speaking contexts, but they do suggest some things that might be useful to you as you learn to control your anxieties. We'll describe the situations as they were explained to us; *you write the advice you would have given the persons*. Then look at what they actually did—written upside down.

Example 1

A professional golfer confided that she hated to play in Pro–Am tournaments. She said, "The amateurs have no code of ethics; while I'm trying to make a putt of two feet, an amateur says, 'Be careful; that's a pressure putt; easy to miss.' That shakes me up. I miss those putts half the time."

What would you suggest the pro say, think, or do?

Here's what she taught herself to *think*:

"You're right! It's a hell of a putt. But that's what this game is all about. You have to learn to putt under pressure and while feeling nervous. It's not a matter of eliminating the pressure; if I wanted to do that, I'd get out of pro golf. It's a matter of learning that to hit a good golf shot, you do it in spite of feeling nervous."

Example 2

A laboratory technician said, "I'm about to go crazy! Every time I sit down to do some lab work, my boss stares over my shoulder and says things like,

'That's not the way to do that; you're making too many errors; we can't put up with sloppy work.' Not only does she constantly criticize me, she does it in front of everybody else. It makes me nervous, and I can't do my work right. I've tried everything. I've talked to my boss's boss—that didn't do any good. I can't quit; there's nowhere to go. How can I handle this situation without quitting?"

What would you suggest the lab technician do?

Here's what this person did to *help herself*:

"I found part of the solution when I realized that my boss had psychological power over me; I was letting her bother me. I defined her as a threat, and I defined the criticism as fact rather than as perception. I did two things that helped me. I redefined the situation as one in which a person learns to work under a state of anxiety; instead of worrying about making mistakes because of my nervousness and trying to get rid of the nervousness, I taught myself to work with accuracy, even though I was nervous. Also, I'd say to myself, 'The boss is right. We can't afford to have sloppy work.' It was a strange thing. I couldn't get rid of the cause of my anxieties or of the anxieties themselves, but I could and did gain control. I think the answer is in how you define the situation, how you define the criticism and yourself."

It's also easier to deal with your fears when you remember that the audience knows much less about your internal anxieties than you do. You can feel your heart beat faster, the cold sweat on your hands, your dry mouth, and the adrenalin flowing. But the audience can't. Consequently, speakers often exaggerate the extent to which their anxieties show. If you infer that your listeners can see inside you and can recognize all of your physiological anxieties, it'll bother you much more than if you realize that an audience is usually aware only of the most obvious kinds of overt behaviors that reflect fear. One of the best ways to verify this is to watch yourself giving a speech on video tape. Most of the persons in our classes are amazed when they see how little of their uneasiness is recognizable; they usually discover that they've greatly overexaggerated what the audience can see.

Finally, as we've already suggested, there's no substitution for genuine preparation. If you conscientiously work through the five steps we discussed above—(1) decide early what you want to accomplish, (2) become friends with your ideas, (3) give your talk a clear sense of wholeness, (4) prepare useful notes, and (5) say your talk before you give it—you'll almost always find yourself a lot more confident than you thought you would be.

In Summary:
(so far)

Public speaking is one of the most difficult contexts in which to promote interpersonal-quality communication. But it is possible. The first step is to recognize the barriers, i.e., the ways we tend to define the context, the speaker, and the listeners. Problems are created because:

We tend to define the context as:
  separating and formal
  linear and one-way

We also tend to define a speaker as:
  filler of a prescribed role
  formal and impersonal.

And we tend to define listeners as:
  a collection
  faceless
  too complex to respond to
  threatening.

Overcoming these barriers requires you to redefine the context, your self as speaker, and your listeners. We're suggesting that you:

Redefine the context as:
  personal
    · persons can meet even across wide personal space
    what's happening is not linear and one-way
    when appropriate, it helps to break out of the imposed formal
    structure.
  an opportunity to share something you care about.

You can also redefine your self as speaker as:
  a talker not a writer
  prepared.

And you can redefine your listeners as:
   individuals—as much as possible
   a valuable source of information during your talk
     recognize that you can't assimilate everything
     increase your ability to be aware of some things
     be careful about misinterpreting
     respond interpersonally to your listeners
   supportive, not threatening
     Listeners are interested in you as a person, are interested in your topic, and are sometimes even in agreement with your point of view.
     Feeling anxious is a natural part of your humanness.
     Listeners know less about your internal anxieties than you do; don't exaggerate what the audience can see.

PROMOTING INTERPERSONAL COMMUNICATION IN SMALL GROUPS

We live in a world oriented toward group activity. Some estimates place the number of groups at four or five billion,[1] and you can probably think of at least half a dozen groups that you belong to. Three class members doing a project together, a five-person awards committee in a sorority, a small couples' club at church, the seven sales directors of a pharmaceutical company, and a college pep staff or rally squad are all examples of small groups. Psychologists Dorwin Cartwright and Alvin Zander emphasize the pervasiveness of groups when they say:

> If it were possible for the overworked hypothetical man from Mars to take a fresh view of the people of Earth, he would probably be impressed by the amount of time they spend doing things together in groups. . . .He would observe that the education and social-ization of children tend to occur in . . . groups in churches, schools, or other social institutions. He would see that much of the work of the world is carried out by people who perform their activities in close interdependence within relatively enduring associations. . . . Finally, he might be puzzled why so many people spend so much time in little groups talking, planning, and being "in conference." Surely he would conclude that if he wanted to understand much about what is happening in Earth he would have to examine rather carefully the ways in which groups form, function, and dissolve.[2]

What Is a Group?

In just about every book on group communication, you'll find a differ-ent definition of what a group is. But rather than categorizing the term "group" in a single definition, we'd like to identify the nature of a group by comparing and contrasting the group-communication setting with informal conversation.

Size. In this portion of the chapter, our primary concern will be small groups, which generally consist of three to ten members. When ten persons are conversing socially and informally, they'll almost always break up into smaller units of two to five. But an organized group will usually meet as one unit. So, as a group increases in size, fewer people get a chance to express themselves to the group; there's less time to exchange feedback to clear up misunderstandings; fewer people com-municate with one another at a personal level; the chairperson—when there is one—may exercise more direct control over the group; and communication between the chairperson and members becomes more impersonal. In addition, large groups frequently must turn their meetings into public-speaking settings, where few immediate exchanges take place.[3]

Perception of belonging.   In contrast to informal conversation, group members usually are aware of their membership in the group. With that awareness comes a sense of the obligations and responsibilities connected with membership. In other words, group members are usually willing to conform to certain habits, patterns of interaction, and so on. For example, since people don't necessarily have a sense of group identity in an informal conversation, they feel freer to move in and out without disrupting the unity. In a group, however, "moving out" may be seen as disruptive and damaging to the group's unity.

Membership also carries with it some rights and privileges. If you are *not* considered a member of a group, you aren't likely to communicate within that group, except by special invitation. On the other hand, if you are a member, you have certain rights to participate in the interaction and the group activities. With few exceptions, groups have "insiders" and "outsiders," and those who are inside communicate and behave with a sense of identity with the group. Conversations may also have insiders and outsiders, but the boundaries aren't so restrictive, and participants don't usually communicate with a sense of group identity.

Permanence.   Few informal conversations continue for months or years. People get together to talk informally, with no set agenda and no expectation that one conversation will be related to another. The participants in a conversation, in fact, usually have few expectations about whether or not they'll get together again and if they do, when it will be. To the extent that persons conversing do develop patterns of meeting, a group may be forming. Contrast the sporadic nature of conversations with the relative permanence of groups. Groups tend to connect one meeting with another by using similar agendas, themes, activities, etc. One of the things that keeps groups together is a focus on specific common interests and goals, and members expect that there will be some continuity from one meeting to the next in the discussions about those interests or goals. In other words, groups are much more permanent than are informal "get-togethers," and group members develop expectations about future meetings, expectations which influence their communicative behavior during each session.

Homogeneity.   "Members of an enduring group," Cartwright and
Zander say, "are likely to display a striking homogeneity of beliefs, attitudes, values, and behavior."[4] For example, "the members of an
adolescent gang are readily identified by their distinctive style of dress.
Work groups engaged in some specialized task develop a jargon that
seems esoteric to outsiders. . . . Even among dedicated nonconformists
one finds a . . . similarity of hair styles."[5] Groups, because they endure
over a period of time, have greater potential than do informal conversations to develop similarities in beliefs, attitudes, values, and behavior.
Groups sometimes form because the members are already homogeneous
or similar; at other times, however, homogeneity is not great when a
group first begins, but develops as a result of interaction, group
pressure, and other factors. Although there are always limits to the
homogeneity of a group, members who deviate from important values
shared by the group will be the objects of varying amounts of pressure
to conform; if they continue to rebel, the group may reject them.
Contrast that with a conversation; the participants may talk about a
topic of common interest, but they don't feel a strong pressure to share
common attitudes, beliefs, values, etc. Conversations aren't enduring
enough to promote homogeneity when it doesn't exist in the first place.
Groups, however, do sometimes endure for long periods of time, and
the resulting homogeneity increases interpersonal attraction among
members, which in turn contributes to the group's cohesiveness. Members of an enduring group almost always care about the extent to which
they share similar values, goals, or interests, and because they do care,
they'll use pressure when necessary to insure some homogeneity.

Nonverbal.   As we said in Chapter 2, nonverbal communication helps
us to express our emotions, to interpret the emotions of others, and to
define our relationships with other persons; in addition, the credibility
of the verbal cues we receive is in part determined by our interpretation
of the accompanying nonverbal cues. The nonverbal cues that are available in an informal conversation sometimes seem similar to those available in a small group. For example:

Informal conversation	*Small group*
Close personal space possible (six inches to four feet)	Close personal space possible (six inches to four feet)
Touch possible	Touch possible

Aroma cues possible	Aroma cues possible
Subtle facial, eye, and body movements are recognizable	Subtle facial, eye, and body movements are recognizable
Physical arrangement of persons—may sit or stand in a circle, rectangle, square, etc.	Physical arrangement of persons—usually sit, but may be in a circle, rectangle, square, etc.

But that doesn't mean people use or interpret these cues the same way in both situations. Although some kinds of nonverbal cues are similar in both settings, groups often develop norms of behavior and role definitions that prescribe how persons within the group may or may not communicate nonverbally. In other words, even though the nonverbal cues in conversation and small-group settings are potentially similar, nonverbal communication in a conversation is usually much more spontaneous than it is in a group. When you're in a conversation, for example, you'll usually have the freedom to choose who to talk to and how close or far you want to sit from that person. In a formal small group, the assigned seating arrangement may dictate not only who you sit next to, but also the spatial distance between you and the other person. Of course, you'll feel some obligation in conversations at times to sit next to and talk with persons you don't really care to talk with. But even in those situations, you'll still have more freedom of movement— you can shift your chair, move to the floor, or after a while move to talk with another person. During a school board meeting, on the other hand, it would seem disruptive for a member to suddenly move his or her chair away from its original position at the table, place it next to a friend, sit down, and start chatting.

Structure.   If you had never seen a group operate, you might think that five persons meeting as a group wouldn't be much different from five people talking in an informal conversation. In both instances, you'd note that there are a few individuals who are face to face and in close proximity to one another. Both settings would seem to provide opportunities for frequent and spontaneous exchanges of ideas, immediate feedback for clarification and understanding, i.e., perception checking, and discussion of a variety of topics. On the surface, those observations might make some sense. But if you'd look closer, you would find some distinct differences. You'd discover that the conversation contained some structured conventions or norms about language usage, touching behavior, spatial distance, etc.; you might also discover perceived status differential between the persons talking. But generally, informal conversation is relatively unstructured and permits frequent and spontaneous interaction. Topics change rapidly; there's no specific agenda; all persons included in the conversation feel relatively free to talk or to be silent; and the discussion follows no strict, predictable pattern.

A close look at the small group reveals a different kind of interaction. For example, some members, because of their earned or assigned position, have more power than do others; that is, they are perceived to have some control over the destiny of other members. A class discussion in which a faculty member is part of the group and has control over grades illustrates one kind of power differential, because students in the discussion probably will feel some pressure to conform to the instructor's expectations. As we've already mentioned, groups also often develop specific and strong norms or rules to guide members' behavior. To be accepted and/or successful within a group, a member must learn, accept, and behave according to certain prescribed conventions or rules. Groups permit deviation from norms, but the amount of deviation allowed depends in part on how important the norm is to the group and who the deviant is. Norms can include such things as *procedure:* What agenda will we follow? What topic will we focus on? How will we go about solving the problems? What parliamentary rules will we follow? Must we address the chairperson before speaking?; *dress:* what is seen as appropriate by this sorority, fraternity, Masonic, or Knights of Columbus group, etc; *language usage, participation:* Are we free to interrupt speakers? Do we all have equal time to talk? May we express opinions, or do we have to stick to "facts"? When norms become important to a group, pressure is exerted on members to conform to these norms; people who refuse to conform are usually punished in one way or another.

In addition to the norm structure within a group, "many groups create specialized positions, each with its own set of responsibilities and procedures, and members assigned to these roles are expected to act in the manner prescribed for each role. . . ."[6] A person who is seen as "leader," for example, is expected to fulfill certain expectations about how leaders are supposed to perform. When the leader doesn't perform as expected, the group may take action to exert pressure on her or him. A role, in other words, is a part played in the script; it's evaluated in terms of how accurately and how well it's played. Roles impose struc-

ture on individuals within the groups and very often dictate the negotiation of selves. That is, the definitions of self and of other may be prescribed by the roles assigned. Even a set of bylaws can sometimes determine how group members define and respond to one another. Bylaws,
for example, might define the "officers" as superior in rank and stipulate
that all members must "respond to officers with respect and dignity."

In sum, we can say that groups almost always develop and impose
structure on their members. The amount of structure and the intensity of
pressure vary from group to group. A sensitivity group, for example,
might have less structure and less pressure to conform than would a
military group, but *both* will develop predictable patterns of organization.

In this part of the chapter we want to focus on how to promote
interpersonal-quality communication in the small-group setting. We
believe that each of the characteristics of a small group affects your ability to do that—size, perception of belonging, permanence, homogeneity, nonverbal cues, and structure. Some of these characteristics of
groups *facilitate* interpersonal communication, e.g., perception of belonging. When people feel a sense of cohesiveness or closeness to one
another, they're likely to be willing to share some of their present selves
of others. Permanence also helps, because interpersonal communication
is always easier when you have the time to do it.

But some other characteristics of groups *work against* interpersonal
communication, and we believe that role structure is the worst offender.
Increased size may impose time limitations on group communication,
lessen the possibilities for immediate exchanges, and prevent verbal
interaction between certain members, but it never commands you to
define and treat others as objects. Similarly, the structure of communication flow, i.e., who talks to whom and through which available
channels, affects the potential for interpersonal contacts; however, like
size, this structure never predetermines for you the definition and treatment of the persons you interact with. Norms of procedure, participation, and dress also affect interaction, but do not prescribe the negotiation of selves. In short, none of those factors creates objectification, in
the way that the norms of role structure often do; only role structure can
effectively prescribe that a group member be defined and treated as a
nonperson. As we'll describe later, shared responsiblities are important to group process, but sometimes responsiblities become role-

definitions that actually *obligate* members to communicate in object-to-object ways. That's what our concern is about.

Individual Application: Your Group Inventory

You do much of your communicating in small groups. Think, for example, about yourself historically. You may have belonged to such groups as: preschool, neighborhood "gang," youth athletic teams, Indian Guides, Cub Scouts, Campfire, Boy/Girl Scouts, high school athletic club, booster club, student council, friendship cliques, etc.

Now try to get in touch with your current group memberships. List a few of the groups you belong to, and then try to identify the norms, homogeneity, and group pressures.

1. Group: (Gary and John) Board of Elders, Presbyterian Church

   Examples of norms of dress, language, etc.: Coat and tie preferred but not required at meetings; no profanity; structured agenda.

   What attitudes, values, beliefs, etc., do your group members share in common? Christian teachings; commitment to participate actively in church administration; importance of regular, meaningful worship; prayer.

   How does your group exert pressure on members to conform to group norms? Minor norm violations enforced by expressions of concern from other elders or from pastor; subtle forms of nonverbal disconfirmation and/or rejection. Extreme deviation from norms would probably result in a letter requesting my resignation.

2. Group: _____

   Examples of norms: _____

   _____

   Shared attitudes, values, beliefs, etc.: _____

   _____

   Methods of group pressure: _____

   _____

Roles

As you'd probably guess, group-communication researchers borrowed the term *role* from the theatre,[7] where it designates the part or character defined by the script and delimits the ways a person behaves in relation to the other characters. Groups frequently provide written or unwritten scripts which include roles and which prescribe how various members should behave when filling those roles. Sometimes, these clearly defined roles help the group function by preventing confusion. As communicologist Dean Barnlund puts it, "life without reasonable determinism would be impossible, for without it there would be no means of regulating human activity. It is apparent that [people] must learn to command to obey, to compete and to cooperate, to speak and to listen."[8] What Barnlund says makes sense, especially when you consider the chaos that might result if group members didn't cooperate and fulfill certain responsibilities. In a small-group setting, roles can decrease your uncertainty about how you are supposed to behave or about what the group is doing. Since confusion and frustration often work against group success, the assignment and acceptance of responsibilities can promote psychological comfort within the group. In other words, a well-coordinated structure of responsibilities can help a group to develop a system for working together, and when that happens, the group is much more likely to do a better job at accomplishing its task.

When responsibilities are clearly defined and each person in the group knows what other members are doing, identification of what the group is doing right and wrong becomes much easier. Even when members fulfill expected behaviors, groups do not always achieve the level of expected success. But when you have a clear idea of member responsibilities, you can more easily determine why your objective wasn't achieved. The group may find, for example, that one or two group members overestimated their competence or interest in a given assignment, that several members changed in significant ways so that their assigned roles were no longer appropriate for them, that members' definitions or images of one another had changed so that the person responsible for mediating conflict could no longer fulfill that responsibility effectively, or that roles need to be reassigned. In brief, clearly defined and acceptable responsibilities can be useful to groups in several different ways.

But roles often define more than just job responsibilities. Sometimes, group members set up roles as communication facades, or "fronts," and sometimes they develop objectifying expectations of other members. Sometimes, in other words, roles make it almost impossible for communication to occur between *persons*. We're convinced, in short, that: (1) fulfilling the responsibilities attached to a role in a group *can* be useful to the group's functioning, but (2) groups sometimes make the mistake of using roles to objectify members, so (3) it's sometimes better for you to violate role expectations and to allow others to violate your expectations if you want to promote interpersonal communication within your group.

Persons and roles.   Promoting person-to-person communication in a group is not easy. Most groups want to maintain comfortable inter-member relationships, but they also want to get things accomplished, and this usually requires members to accept certain assigned responsibilities. The problem, then, is how group members can be aware of the humanness of others and share aspects of their own humanness while filling role responsibilities. We think that an important answer to the question is for group members to be aware of the ways in which role definitions, role expectations, group demands, and group pressures objectify persons by failing to take into account the unique, changing, emotional, and choice-making nature of all humans.

Labels.   In interpersonal communicating, it's important not to put people in categories. As we said in Chapter 6, a person might behave in ways that are "bigoted" and "clumsy," but the same person also behaves in ways that are "supportive" and "thoughtful." So, it's not accurate to assume that he or she is only one set of behaviors. Unfortunately, some researchers study groups concentrate almost exclusively on labeling roles and role behaviors. Many group-communication scholars, for example, emphasize that a group is continually performing two different functions—accomplishing its task and maintaining relationships among group members. That emphasis sometimes leads to lists of "group-task roles" and "group-maintenance roles." For example, one book points out that when the group is working on its task of defining and solving a content problem, the following roles may be played by leaders or members.

1. Initiator-contributor—suggests new ideas, definitions of the problem, how problem might be solved, etc.

2. Information seeker—requests facts, data, clarification, etc.

3. Information giver—relates personal experiences to the group problem, offers "authoritative" information

4. Elaborator—offers examples, illustrations, a rational for suggestions made by another, tries to figure out the consequences of adopting various suggestions.

5. Orienter—summarizes what has occurred, raises questions, etc.

6. Procedural technician—"expedites group movement by doing things for the group—performing routine tasks, e.g., distributing materials, or manipulating objects for the group, e.g., rearranging the seating, etc."[9]

These authors also list such roles as opinion seeker, opinion giver, coordinator, evaluator-critic, energizer, and recorder.

In addition, they list several roles that apply to group maintenance and intermember relationships:

1. Encourager—offers acceptance, understanding, praise; communicates warmth and solidarity.

2. Harmonizer—mediates conflict, tries to relieve tension, etc.

3. Gatekeeper and expediter—tries to open communication channels by encouraging or facilitating the participation of others.[10]

Classification of roles can help us to understand how some groups operate. But one of the disadvantages of giving labels to roles is that the labels are often used to define the whole person rather than just the expected role-behaviors. A "discussion leader," for example, may be defined by group members only in terms of leadership qualities rather than his or her human qualities. Instead of classifying a person as an "information giver," it's better to talk about information-giving behaviors. Instead of labeling someone an "encourager," it's better to talk about the fact that the person sometimes behaves in a way that encourages other group members, and so on. It's better because it helps you to recognize that the person is capable of more than one set of behaviors, and you're much less likely to "lock" the person into a single category of expected behaviors. In short, an individual is much more than a set of expected behaviors, and sometimes role labels prevent us from realizing that.

Violating role expectations.   Too often, group members assume that if everybody would only completely fulfill their role expectations, things would get done, and the group would be productive and happy. Sometimes, that's true; more often than not, however, rigid role-playing can definitely work against interpersonal communicating. That's why we're encouraged when group-communication scholars suggest that playing a role perfectly isn't always good and that violating role expectations isn't always bad. Clifford Swensen, for example, is talking about violating minor role expectations when he says that

> this phenomenon may be observed in the judgment the public makes of public figures. Those figures who meet all social norms are often considered bland or stuffy, while those who violate relatively unimportant norms are seen as more "human" and as having a more clearly definable personality. . . .[11]

To verify his belief that "violating minor role norms may not necessarily be a bad thing,"[12] Swensen cites research which "found that in playing a role, people who completely met role expectations were judged *not* to have revealed themselves, while people who did violate expectations were seen as revealing more of themselves."[13]

Like Swensen, we believe that you don't share much of your personness when you meet all role expectations completely. But when you try to put into practice what we're suggesting, you may find yourself in somewhat of a dilemma. To promote interpersonal communication, you need to share aspects of your humanness, and to share your humanness you sometimes have to violate role expectations—you sometimes have to get out from under the restrictions imposed by a label. But just about any time you deviate from group norms, you'll experience pressure from other group members to "get back in line"; that's especially true if you violate important role norms.[14] What's the answer? How can you promote interpersonal communication without damaging your membership in the group? We think that the answer is: (1) for the *group* to develop the ability to *metacommunicate*, (2) for each member to recognize the need to *earn* his or her right to step out of role, and (3) to work to *encourage other's* humanness.

Metacommunicating—communicating about your communication—is one of the most useful skills a group can develop. First, effective metacommunicating can help the group accomplish its task. Such task-related comments as "I don't think we've ever decided exactly what we're supposed to be doing in this meeting—can we clarify that?" or "Why don't we see if we can list a number of alternative solutions before zeroing in on just one" can often increase the group's ability to accomplish its content goal. In addition, metacommunicating can help build cohesiveness or a sense of belonging to the group. When you feel that the need exists, it's often helpful to say something like, "I've noticed that we don't seem to be doing a very good job of listening to one another" or "I think some of us feel that all the work is being done by only two persons in this group—can we talk about that?"

As the group develops its ability to metacommunicate, members find it easier to violate role expectations. For example, if you feel that the group is giving its chairperson too much power, you might want to violate some expectations that go with the role of "good follower." That situation could really create hostility, unless at some point you explained why you felt it was all right to do what you were doing. The chairperson in this situation might also want to reduce the leader-follower status differential in the group and might be waiting for the chance to metacommunicate about the group's overrigid structure. In short, one way for the group to facilitate the violation of minor role expectations is to develop the willingness and ability to communicate about its own communicating.

As an individual group member, you can work in two ways toward sharing your humanness by violating role demands without alienating yourself from the group: (1) recognize the need to *earn* your right to step out of your role, and (2) *encourage others'* humanness, too. You can earn your right to violate role expectations by building a bank account of what some group researchers call "idiosyncracy credits."

Idiosyncracy credits are plus points you can earn by helping the group—by either helping it accomplish its task or enabling it to work smoothly and cohesively. As one book explains, idiosyncracy credits allow a member

> to depart from the prescribed role behaviors to some extent. For instance, a member who has earned his right to group leadership through his previous contributions to the group will be allowed to

transgress against a standard as long as his behavior is not harmful to the group. He may be forgiven if he loses his cool every so often, because the group members realize the strain he's under in bearing the role of leader.[15]

If you've demonstrated to the group your concern for them and your willingness to work with them, you can violate some role expectations without negatively affecting either the group's functioning or your own position in it. How can you recognize the idiosyncracy credits you've built up in your group? The best source of information is the other group members. Through metacommunicating, group members can share perceptions about how much each person has contributed to the group's functioning and maintenance. Exchanging perceptions is important because a given member may perceive that he or she has built up a large number of credits, while others in the group may perceive that this person hasn't done much of anything for the group. When you get in touch with the size of your own idiosyncracy-credit account, you can determine how free you are to violate minor norms or what you need to develop your freedom to do that.

Responding to role violations.   The second way out of your dilemma is to encourage others to communicate as persons instead of just as role fillers. We agree that for groups to accomplish tasks and solve problems, members will have to share responsibilities. But when sharing responsibilities means imposing inflexible and objectifying obligations on members and somehow punishing them when they don't live up to those obligations, we disagree. On the surface, you might feel the same way. But we'd like you to take a closer look at your own communicating in group settings to see if you're aware of all the ways you sometimes impose your expectations on other persons. That's important, because many times people think that they're promoting interpersonal communication when in reality they're helping prevent it.

How do you, for example, respond when someone doesn't fulfill your expectations? Do you feel like doing something to punish that person? Do you tend to reject his or her violation of your expectations, or do you tend to accept it? Do you tend to intimidate or to disconfirm the other person? Or, do you still confirm him or her? To put it another way, when you think back to the last time you were upset or angry with someone, was it because he or she didn't fulfill your expectations?

It's important to remember that not all expectations have to become obligations, i.e., just because a group expects certain behavior, that specific behavior doesn't have to be demanded. For example, Mary and Fran are friends. Mary sees friendship as a role, she believes that there are certain behaviors a friend is obligated to perform. Her friends, she thinks, should always be on time, should never ignore her in a conversation, should always laugh at her jokes, and should drop what they're doing and pay attention to her whenever she calls. When Fran doesn't perform these behaviors, Mary gets upset or angry. She communicates nonverbally and verbally that her feelings are hurt, and in the process she usually evokes some type of guilt feeling in Fran. Mary behaves, in short, almost as if she partly "owns" Fran—as if Fran weren't a unique, changing, conscious, emotional, choosing *person*. That's what we mean by expectations that turn into obligations.

We don't believe that a genuinely interpersonal relationship can be described in terms of fulfilling obligated behaviors. Similarly, a group cannot promote interpersonal communicating when it obligates members under threat of punishment. Genuine interpersonal communication allows mutual freedom of choice. In groups, expectations work best when they're nonobjectifying, i.e., when they allow individual freedom without threat of intimidation, disconfirmation, or rejection. It's not good for group members to be completely unpredictable. But it's also wrong to be rigidly tied to dictated behaviors.

In short, when you're communicating in a group, you can encourage others to break out of rigid role behavior by being aware of their humanness. You do that by not obligating or commanding a person to behave in certain ways; you recognize his or her unique, changing, and choosing nature. When you do that, you realize that although expectations are developed, individuals may choose to do something other than what is predicted—and for good reasons.

In addition, when you're unhappy that someone hasn't met your expectations, it helps to limit your evaluations to his or her behavior. Try to stick to "You didn't do the things I expected you to" rather than "You never get done on time" or "You always do a terrible job," both of which evaluate actions as if they were a natural, inherent aspect of the person. It might help you to think of it this way: when an actor does a poor job of playing a role, you might consider him to be, in that instance, a "poor *actor*." But you wouldn't necessarily infer that one poor performance makes him a "poor actor," much less a "poor *person*." In the same way, when a group member doesn't play a prescribed role very well, it isn't fair to evaluate the *person* negatively. If your comments are critical, keep them aimed at the "acting job" instead of at the person.

Finally, in your group meetings use the suggestions we've talked about in previous chapters. Many of those suggestions apply to small, face-to-face groups as well as to informal conversations. Here's a brief summary of how some of those chapters might relate to promoting interpersonal communication in your groups.

In Summary:
(so far)

Chapter 1, "Objects and Persons"

At least two ideas from this chapter can help in your group communicating. Remembering the differences between humans and objects will help groups to realize when they're assigning objectifying roles and when they're seeing and treating members as humans. Also remember that interpersonal communicating within groups is a *mutual* thing; it's dependent on all the members involved. Each member can promote person-to-person communicating, but he or she cannot make it happen alone.

Chapter 5, "Sharing Some of Your Self"

Sharing your humanness—historical *and* present selves—will help get you out of the objectifying role labels, especially when those labels tend to "lock" you into a category of behaviors.

Chapter 6, "Being Aware of the Other"

Interpersonal listening skills are especially important when you're evaluating role violations. Try to use a win/win mental set, confirming behaviors, and perception checks. Try to postpone specific evaluations and to limit negative evaluations. Own your evaluations, keep your evaluations tentative, and actively solicit responses from the others.

Chapter 7, "Interpersonal Clarity"

When responsibilities are clearly defined, well understood, and accepted, a group will function more cohesively, and less conflict between expected behaviors and actual behaviors will occur.

Chapter 8, "Handling Conflict Interpersonally"

Use the suggestions in the previous chapter to keep the inevitable disagreements that emerge in your group from becoming person-destroying arguments.

CONCLUDING THOUGHTS

Both the cohesiveness that almost always develops in a group and the regularity with which most groups meet can help group members communicate in person-to-person ways. But, like the public-speaking setting, the groups setting also presents some special challenges to members who want to promote interpersonal-quality communication. Role structure is, we think, the most significant of those challenges. Although fulfilling the responsibilities attached to a role in a group can be useful to the group's functioning, groups often make the mistake of using roles to objectify group members. Therefore, it's sometimes better to violate role expectations and to allow others to do the same if you want to facilitate interpersonal communication in your group. You can transcend your own role behavior without being bounced out of the group if you remember to combine your idiosyncratic behavior with words and actions that demonstrate your commitment to and support of the group.

You can also encourage others to behave like persons by not letting expectations become obligations, by evaluating behavior instead of persons, and by incorporating other skills we've talked about in previous chapters.

EXERCISES

Individual Application: Expectations and Obligations

Here's a way to find out if your expectations sometimes turn into obligations: Write down the names of your classroom instructors. Pick one of those instructors and write down the expectations you have of that person. For example:

1. I expect his or her lectures to be:

    smooth

    organized

    interesting

    _____

    _____

    _____

2. When the lecture isn't what I expect, I usually respond in this way:

I figure that's the way college life is; profs can't perform well all the time.

I get the urge to go in and tell him/her a thing or two.

I get the urge to drop the course.

---

3. I expect an instructor to be available to students:

whenever the student needs help

whenever it's convenient for the prof

---

4. When an instructor isn't available, I usually respond in this way:

Now do the same thing with a friend's (classmate's, spouse's, relative's, etc.) name. When you've finished, carefully look over each response and write down whether you think you're responding interpersonally or whether you're obligating those persons.

Individual Application: Labels

Pick one of the groups you belong to and list the labels attached to each of the roles members play in that group. The important question here is; Does the group attach labels to roles? If they do, are the labels "locking" members into categories of behaviors? How? What could the group do about it?

Individual Application: Interpersonal Responses to Violations of Expectations

In each of the situations below, we've written a person-oriented criticism that might occur within a group when a member violates role expectations. We've also included situations involving parents, children, employers, employees, etc. Your job is to write a response that would be more interpersonal, i.e., one that recognizes expectations, focuses on behavior, recognizes humanness of the other, etc., than the ones we provide. For example:

Situation: group project in a speech class:

Comments aimed at the person	*Interpersonal responses*
"You did a crappy job, Jim. Get with it. Don't you care about this group? You're being inconsiderate."	"We didn't like the outline you handed in for the project, Jim. We expected a thorough, complete sentence outline, and you turned in a very brief, sketchy outline. Maybe you could give us an idea of where we go from here."

Situation: parent talking to child who just spilled an entire casserole on the floor.

"Damn it! Can't you do anything right? You weren't being careful like I told you to! Why are you so clumsy?

Situation: employer criticizing employee who just walked into his/her office unexpectedly.

"I'm a little tired of your interruptions. I've asked you never to impose yourself on me like that. You're always being informal when I require formality."

Situation: woman talking to her male companion, who refuses to dance.

"You're square. Just because those kids are out there, you're embarrassed. What are we supposed to do, sit here and talk about nothing? Some companion you are."

Group Application: Metacommunication

Like other skills, communicating about your communication is not very effective when it is imposed artificially. But self-conscious, artificial meta-communicating can be an important step toward comfortable, spontaneous metacommunicating.

Establish groups of five, and give each group a specific problem to solve or a task to accomplish. For example, one group might develop a position on a hot political or social issue or respond to a campus crisis, another might design a suggested format for the final exam in this class or for student participation in class evaluation, etc.

A sixth person should be assigned to remind the group about metacommunication, and each group should be given a specific amount of time to reach its goal.

While the groups are deliberating, they must abide strictly by the following rule: *during the first 20 minutes of discussion, every seventh comment made must be metacommunicative.* That is, every seventh contribution must be a communication about the group's communicating at that moment.

The sixth person's responsibility is to help the group remember the rule by counting contributions and signalling each time a metacommunicative comment is required. After approximately 20 minutes, the sixth person should indicate that the rule is lifted. After another 20 minutes or so, the rule should be re-applied for approximately 15 minutes.

When the group has accomplished its task, it should prepare a brief oral statement about the effect metacommunicating had on the group's deliberation and should share that statement with the other groups.

Group Application: Group Teaching

Here's a practical, but lengthy, exercise. Break your class up into eight groups. Assign each small group a chapter of this book (Chapters 1–8). Their task is to present an in-class demonstration of how that chapter applies to small-group communication. You might use media (slides, audio tapes, etc.), skits, panel discussion, games, etc. For example, you could write a script for a radio drama, get some other students to play the parts, record it, and then play it back to the class and discuss it.

NOTES

1. Ronald E. Applbaum, Edward M. Bodaken, Kenneth K. Sereno, and Karl W.E. Anatol, *The Process of Group Communication*, Chicago: Science Research Associates, 1974, p. 5.

2. *Group Dynamics: Research and Theory*, ed. Dorwin Cartwright and Alvin Zander, New York: Harper & Row, 1968, p. 3. Reprinted by permission.

3. Many of these characteristics are discussed in Cartwright and Zander, *ibid.*, p. 499.

4. *Ibid.*, p. 139.

5. *Ibid.*

6. *Ibid.*, p. 147.

7. See Roger Brown, *Social Psychology*, New York: The Free Press, 1965, p. 152.

8. Dean Barnlund, *Interpersonal Communication: Survey and Studies*, Boston: Houghton Mifflin, 1968, p. 170.

9. Kenneth Benne and Paul Sheats, "Functional Roles of Group Members, "*Small Group Communication: A Reader*, ed. Robert S. Cathcart and Larry A. Samovar, Dubuque, Iowa: Wm. C. Brown, 1974, pp. 179–188.

10. *Ibid.*

11. Clifford Swensen, *Introduction to Interpersonal Relations*,Glenview, Ill.: Scott, Foresman, 1973, p. 388.

12. *Ibid.*

13. *Ibid.* You might want to read the empirical study Swensen is referring to: E. Jones, K. Davis, and K. Gergen, "Role Playing Variations and Their Informational Value for Person Perception," *Journal of Abnormal and Social Psychology*, **LXIII** (1961): 302–310.

14. See especially Stanley Schachter, "Deviation, Rejection, and Communication," *Journal of Abnormal and Social Psychology*, XLVI (April 1951); 190-207.

15. Applbaum, Bodaken, Sereno, and Anatol, *op. cit.*, p. 152.

ADDITIONAL RESOURCES

Although we've talked about how to communicate interpersonally in public and small-group settings, we haven't covered many specific public-speaking skills, and we haven't dealt with many of the complexities of small groups. We're especially hopeful that we can suggest some things here for you to read that will broaden your perspective and increase your communicating skills. Your instructor knows your needs better than we do, and you'll probably want to consult with her or him about this list or about other possible sources.

Public Speaking

There are literally dozens of textbooks on public speaking. Some have been around for years and treat their subject in fairly traditional ways. Others are more innovative and nontraditional. Almost all of them have something to offer, but we would especially recommend the following:

1. Wil Linugel and David Berg's book *A Time to Speak Or How to Prepare and Present a Speech* (Belmont, Calif.: Wadsworth, 1970) is one of the best short, to-the-point, contemporary treatments. They cover much of the topic in five main chapters: "Be Relevant," "Be Clear," "Be Interesting," "Be Believable," and "Let's Put It Together."

2. Thomas H. Olbricht's book *Informative Speaking* (Glenview, Ill.: Scott, Foresman, 1968) is one of the few texts on public speaking that sets its subject in its historial framework, establishes a clear but simple audience-centered philosophical position, *and* offers practical advice on audience analysis, organization, language, clarifying, and reinforcing your ideas. It's a short book—just over 100 pages—but a good one.

3. In his book *Speech Communication and Human Interaction* (Glenview, Ill.: Scott, Foresman, 1972), Thomas Scheidel considers the two-person conversation as a basic paradigm of all speech communication. He suggests that "the differences between the converser, the discussant, and the public speaker are merely matters of degree" (p. 47). You'll find some useful suggestions for public speaking in Scheidel's book, including such concepts as organization, development of ideas, delivery, etc.

4. William D. Brooks covers many different topics in his book *Speech Communication* (Dubuque, Iowa: Wm. C. Brown, 1974), but in Part III he focuses specifically on public communication. He talks briefly about the credibility of the public speaker, explains various aspects of delivery, organization, idea development, and language, and offers a thorough treatment of audience analysis.

Group Communication

If you're interested in reading only a chapter or so, but still want to get a broader perspective of what's involved in small-group communication, read Chapter 13, "Interacting with Others: Face to Face in a Small Group," in John Keltner's book *Interpersonal Speech-Communication: Elements and Structures* (Belmont, Calif.: Wadsworth, 1970), pp. 286–317.

If you're interested in reading an entire book about small groups, one that is easy to read and that covers norms, roles, nonverbal communication, cohesiveness, leadership, etc., we recommend a recent one by Ronald E. Applbaum, Edward M. Bodaken, Kenneth K. Sereno, and Karl W. E. Anatol, *The Process of Group Communication* (Chicago: Science Research Associates, 1974). These authors use empirical research to supplement their discussions, but their writing is relatively free of scientific jargon terms.

Another recently published book that's worth reading is Lawrence B. Rosenfeld's *Human Interaction in the Small Group Setting* (Columbus, Ohio: Charles E. Merrill, 1973). It's also informed by behavioral research, covers a wide variety of topics, and will give you an interesting perspective on group communication. Rosenfeld is one of the scholars in our discipline who believes that group communication involves much more than just task accomplishment and problem solving. He's also done some empirical research and is thoroughly familiar with small-group research literature.

Robert Cathcart and Larry Samovar have collected a series of articles for their book *Small Group Communication: A Reader* (Dubuque, Iowa: Wm. C. Brown, 1974). Each article focuses on some aspect of group behavior or on a topic that's directly applicable to group communication. In Cathcart and Samovar's book you'll find articles that deal with leadership, roles, encounter groups, principles of communication, group processes, and so on. The book offers a wide variety of readings.

At a more advanced level, there's a book by Dorwin Cartwright and Alvin Zander, *Group Dynamics: Research and Theory* (New York: Harper & Row, 1968), that's highly respected in the area of group communication. It's difficult to read, but it contains a wealth of rigorous empirical studies; also, the introductions by Cartwright and Zander to each section help you to synthesize the material. You may not want to get into this book until you've had some background in the theory and research of groups.

If you're interested in learning more about role theory, we'd suggest three books. First, the Cartwright and Zander book mentioned above will help. Second, Clifford Swensen's *Introduction to Interpersonal Relations* (Glenview, Ill.: Scott, Foresman, 1973) deals comprehensively with role theory on pp. 373-415. Swensen relates roles to more than the small-group setting; for example, one of his topics is "Roles and Marriage," and another is "Roles and Psychotherapy."

Dean Barnlund also writes about roles in his book *Interpersonal Communication: Survey and Studies* (Boston: Houghton Mifflin, 1968). My (Gary) first exposure to roles and social structure came from Barnlund's introduction to "The Social Context of Communication" on pp. 151–173.

We'd like to end this book with a story instead of a summary. The story is from a children's book called *The Velveteen Rabbit*, a tale of the adventures of some special stuffed animals.* It's a happy—if poignant—story, one that might at first sound naive or even trival. But if you believe that the eyes of children often see much more clearly than yours or ours do, you might find in this story—as we do—a beautifully simple and clear statement of much of what this book is all about. We aren't asking you to analyze the story, just enjoy it, and its meaning will unfold.

> . . . The Skin Horse had lived longer in the nusery than any of the others. He was so old that his brown coat was bald in patches and showed the seams underneath, and most of the hairs in his tail had been pulled out to string bead necklaces. He was wise, for he had seen a long succession of mechanical toys arrive to boast and swagger, and by-and-by break their mainsprings and pass away, and he knew that they were only toys, and would never turn into anything else. For nursery magic is very strange and wonderful, and only those playthings that are old and wise and experienced like the Skin Horse understand all about it.
>
> "What is REAL?" asked the Rabbit one day, when they were lying side by side near the nursery fender, before Nana came to tidy the room. "Does it mean having things that buzz inside you and a stick-out handle?"
>
> "Real isn't how you are made," said the Skin Horse. "It's a thing that happens to you. When a child loves you for a long, long time, not just to play with, but REALLY loves you, then you become Real."
>
> "Does it hurt?" asked the Rabbit.
>
> "Sometimes," said the Skin Horse, for he was always truthful. "When you are Real you don't mind being hurt."
>
> "Does it happen all at once, like being wound up," he asked, "or bit by bit?"
>
> "It doesn't happen all at once," said the Skin Horse. "You become.

The Velveteen Rabbit by Margery Williams. Reprinted by permission of Doubleday & Co., Inc.

It takes a long time. That's why it doesn't often happen to people who break easily, or have sharp edges, or who have to be carefully kept. Generally, by the time you are Real, most of your hair has been loved off, and your eyes drop out and you get loose in the joints and very shabby. But these things don't matter at all, because once you are Real you can't be ugly, except to people who don't understand."

"I suppose you are Real?" said the Rabbit. And then he wished he had not said it, for he thought the Skin Horse might be sensitive. But the Skin Horse only smiled.

"The Boy's Uncle made me Real," he said. "That was a great many years ago; but once you are Real you can't become unreal again. It lasts for always."

The Rabbit sighed. He thought it would be a long time before this magic called Real happened to him. He longed to become Real, to know what it felt like; and yet the idea of growing shabby and losing his eyes and whiskers was rather sad. He wished he could become it without these uncomfortable things happening to him.

Index